The Girl Who Invented Dusty Springfield

The Girl Who Invented Dusty Springfield

The Story of Mary O'Brien

Donella Campbell

Einstein Publishing

In memory of Paula Maria Conroy.
A dedicated Dusty fan.

Preface

Deciding to take on this project I could not foresee the many people I would meet, places I would visit, events I would discover and diverse topics I would learn of in the process of uncovering Mary O'Brien's young life.

My journey has taken me to Dublin and Tralee in Ireland, to New York, to High Wycombe, to Brighton, to London and to Canterbury. I have visited the National Archives in Kew; The BBC Written Archives Centre in Reading; The Keep in Brighton; the New York Public Library; the National Library of Ireland and the General Register Office in Dublin; the National Library of Scotland, and the Bishopsgate Institute in London, as well as Glasgow University Library, the Mitchell Library, Glasgow, and local libraries in Tralee, High Wycombe, Ealing and Glasgow.

The Bucks Free Press generously printed an article about Dusty Springfield on their Nostalgia page along with an appeal for information about the O'Brien family during their stay in High Wycombe. Former friends and neighbours made contact, some had known Mary and others were able to give me a picture of life in Sands at the time.

Through Friends Reunited I have found girls who shared memories of Mary and of St Anne's Convent in Ealing. Ancestry, Find My Past, Family Search, Irish Genealogy, the Society of Genealogists are among the genealogy sites which have enabled me to access public records and to trace Mary and her family's progress through the years, to verify dates and times and places. More information has been found in Census Data, the 1939 Register, and Electoral rolls.

I have searched newspapers and entertainment magazines with mention of Mary or one of the groups she was a member of – these publications contain interviews given by her, articles written about her and others written by her. I have investigated the clubs she played in, on her own, with her brother Dion, and with the Springfields.

I have carried out extensive research on her career with the Lana Sisters and with the Springfields, finding information about the theatres they played in and the artists who shared the bill with them, as well as on their TV and radio appearances. I have interviewed friends she talked to about her musical passions and influences and with whom shared tales of her childhood. In short, I have endeavoured to make this story as authentic and true to the life she lived as is possible.

Donella Campbell 2023

Introduction

Dusty Springfield was already 24 years old when she launched her solo career in 1963. Older by some years than the other girls seeking fame in the pop world; Cilla Black was 20, Marianne Faithfull 17, Sandie Shaw 16 and Lulu 15. There was good reason for this, by the time her solo career began, Dusty had served a long apprenticeship during which she had learned her craft. Petula Clark was the only pop singer older than she was. After more than two years with the Lana Sisters and three and half years with her brother in the Springfields, Dusty was a leading talent in popular music. She was a seasoned professional who had invested many hours in developing her artistry, her voice and her stagecraft.

When I decided to write this story, I was faced with a problem. The problem of talking about one person who, for most of her life, had two names. Baptised Mary O'Brien she was known by that name for all of her young life. Later, as she grew and developed in show business her name evolved. So that by the time she was ready to begin her solo career, she had already adopted the name Dusty Springfield. The girl is Mary Isabel Catherine O'Brien. At first, she collaborated with her brother, Dionysius Patrick O'Brien. They performed together in West End clubs and later, successfully as the Springfields. Dion O'Brien changed his name then and became Tom Springfield, but outside of show business, Mary was always Mary. She lived her life with this paradox of being the private person (Mary) and the public persona (Dusty). Confronting the question of which name to use in this book, for me the answer is simple: the girl is Mary O'Brien, and this is HER story.

Little is known of Mary O'Brien, the person hidden by the wigs and make up, the guise of Dusty Springfield. Even less has been discovered about the girl before she achieved stardom in the Sixties. Her childhood and her growing up, her first steps in entertainment and her introduction to showbusiness are passed over in a few pages by the biographies that have been written of her.

This book is an attempt to redress that balance. Only Mary O'Brien knows the true story of her early years, it would only be possible to learn it from her. But given her love of invention, she might not have told us the truth anyway. This is my take on the life of Mary O'Brien, based on the facts I have discovered; of the time, the places, the people and the events in her world. It tells of the girl as she began her life in High Wycombe, went from shy show off in her convent school in Ealing to confident performer about to take the stage as a solo singer. It examines the social and historical context of the 40s, 50s and 60s and is grounded in the popular culture of the times. It ends in October 1963, just as the Springfields are about to appear on stage at the London Palladium in their final live performance.

The story is rooted in the information that I have discovered about Mary's life and this forms the basis of the book. One scene depicts a real event that took place when Mary was five and living in Sands (High Wycombe). It is a memory given to me by a man who also lived in Sands, in 1944. Another scene portrays Mary's audition with Iris and Lynne before she joined the Lana Sisters. I hope, by using these scenes, and others like them, to create a sense of the time and place.

DC 2023

Contents

Prologue

The small child went hurtling along the path, heading for the wide-open gate of the park and towards the roar of passing cars on the main road beyond. 'Mary! Stop! Stop!' Her mother came running behind, desperate to catch up with her and save her from danger. Mary kept on running, 'Stop her,' pleaded Kay O'Brien. An approaching stranger rugby-tackled the child and brought her to a halt. 'Thank you,' said her mother panting wildly. She bent down to the child, took her by the shoulders and scolded her. 'You mustn't run away from Mummy like that. You know that, don't you?' Mary nodded and gave a petulant shrug.

Her mother was at her wits end. This child was so full of energy and almost out of control, constantly getting into scrapes. As a baby she fell from her pram and hit her head on the pavement; another time she climbed up on the kitchen table, only to come crashing down onto the hard floor. She had no fear, no sense of danger. It drove her mother to distraction. From the time Mary had learned to walk she had exhausted her mother, who constantly feared for her safety. Kay O'Brien couldn't understand, it had been so easy with her brother, Dion. She wondered at the difference with this child. Of course, she had been so much younger when the boy was born, but he was calm and biddable, unlike his sister who demanded so much of her attention. But then Mary was just two years old. As she grew, she was every bit as impulsive and energetic, but now Kay was able to teach her some sense of safety, and to lessen the most dangerous of her activities.

All Mary wanted was to be loved, to be happy, and to be noticed; she craved attention. When she didn't get it she felt ignored, particularly by her parents. In truth, she demanded and gained a great deal of their attention. But it was never enough. At first, she would sing along to her favourite songs – she could hold a tune even before she was able to pronounce the words. By the time she was five it was clear that there was something special about this girl. She loved to dance and show off, and it seemed clear she was going to be an entertainer. She was a mimic and a goon, and her spot-on impersonations kept everyone in stitches. In 1965 she reflected:

> *My brother says that anyone could tell when I was a kid that I was going to do something with my life. I had this determination, this 'look-I-am-here' air about me even then.*[2]

She was going to be famous; even before she understood what it meant, she knew it. It was a sense that grew within her. With this great need to be noticed she knew she wanted fame and fortune, but she had no idea how she could achieve it. As a child she was consumed by the glittering artifice of Hollywood musicals, peopled by blonde goddesses such as Betty Grable and June Haver. She learned that the key to achieving her aim would be to act and sing and dance. From then on, her longing for fame was interwoven with the sparkling allure of those musicals and the whole idea of America, a place that she saw as a land of hope and opportunity. Her movie magazines showed the glossy world of witty, bright, glamorous and beautiful stars. In her dreams she became a part of that world.

That was her dream, but when she looked in the mirror she saw the reality, and doubts began to creep in. Her confidence was shaken. How could she, this disaster area, the worst kid you ever saw in your life, ever hope to be a star? Was she good enough? Would she be 'found out', exposed as an impostor? And what if people knew she was gay? What of her career hopes then? Her bright and breezy exterior, her exuberance and fun-loving personality, hid a deeply questioning nature, and lack of confidence in her own abilities.

But that was then. Now she was on the brink of that fame she so desperately craved. This was to be her last live appearance with her brother's group, the Springfields. She had achieved her ambition of going to America, touring there and recording several songs for an LP.

What follows is the story of Mary O'Brien and how she became Dusty Springfield.

---

2 Dusty Springfield, 'Fame Has a Flipside Too', Woman's Own 1965, in Dusty Springfield Bulletin No. 65 July 2008.

The Story of Mary O'Brien

A lot of my life has no real clarity. But I look at old TV clips and I remember the circumstances very clearly. Was I happy or not happy? If I don't identify with the person, it's because I invented her in the first place. She was an invention, but my own invention. I was my own Svengali.

Irishness is a state of mind rather than a geographic thing. I'm not English. My name is O'Brien and I'm glad it is. I've got nothing against the English and I'm glad I was born here. But I'm glad my mother came from Kerry and I'm glad my name is Mary Isabel Catherine Bernadette O'Brien and I can weep at Riverdance on TV, and it makes me laugh. [3]

— The Dusty Springfield Interview, *Mojo*, July 1995

---

3 Paul du Noyer (July 1995) 'The Dusty Springfield Interview', *Mojo* .

Part 1: Life in the Chilterns:

1939 - 1951

Beginnings

Mary O'Brien came into the world a few months before the start of the Second World War, the second child of Kay and Gerard O'Brien. She was born on 16 April 1939, in the Caerthillian Nursing Home in Hampstead, and baptised Mary Isabel Catherine O'Brien. Kay and Gerard brought their baby daughter from the nursing home to their splendid new home in Maida Vale that they had moved to just over a year before. Mary was unlikely to have any memory of that gorgeous flat at 97 Lauderdale Mansions. Not long after, and before the war began, the family left there to continue their life in Sands Village, High Wycombe.

At first sight, Mary's childhood might seem ordinary and uneventful. Hers was a solid, conservative middle-class Catholic family. But this complex creature was formed from the many strands of her ancestors. She combined talent, ambition and rebelliousness, along with an independent streak that embodied all things emotional and sexual. In addition, the image she developed; her visual trademark, guaranteed her fame during her life and beyond. The person she became, was created from a multitude of social and religious influences, not least the musical loves of her father and mother and the deep understanding of music she cultivated for herself. And, not forgetting, her fierce ambition and drive to be famous.

That summer of 1939, Kay went out in the afternoons; with Mary in her pram and her young son, Dion, clinging to the handlebars, walked down by the canal. Sometimes she went to Browning's Pool, where the Regent's and Grand Union canals meet. She would find a spot where they could sit in the cool shade of the trees, look across to the island with its willows and wildfowl and eat their picnic lunch. Here they could watch the canal ponies on the towpath pulling their barges filled with cargoes of coal and grain and fish. They were intrigued by the sight of

1

the narrow boats slipping quietly through the streets along their ribbon of water. Generations of Londoners have had their imaginations stirred by seeing the canal boats floating by.

Mary's Parents

Although Mary's parents both came from comfortable middle-class families, the contrast in their childhoods and early lives could not have been more marked. Her mother, Kathleen (Kay) Ryle was born in Dublin and lived in Tralee up to the age of 16. Mary's father, Gerard Anthony Joseph O'Brien, was born in India in the days of the British Raj. He was ten when he travelled to England to be enrolled in a boarding school.

Mary's mother, Kay O'Brien, was baptised Catherine Anne Ryle. The 1911 census lists her as Kathleen, and that is how she was known by her family.[4] When Kay was born in 1900, her father, Maurice P. Ryle, was acting editor of the *Irish Daily Independent*, in Dublin, and she was one more member of the expanding Irish Catholic family that his wife, Bridget Myles, was kept busy caring for. (In interviews many years later, Mary espoused the romantic notion that her great grandparents had been members of a travelling Gilbert and Sullivan company. The truth was much more prosaic. Both sets of Irish great grandparents came from farming stock.)

Kay's father Maurice, brought his family back to Tralee in 1902, where they settled into an eight-bedroomed Victorian terraced house. 19 Garryruth in Ballymullen was in a row of attractive middle-class houses. The house was big, but could only just contain the family of 14. This included Kay's brothers Denis and Jack, her sister Agnes and seven more siblings. In addition, there were two nannies, Josephine and Ellen.

Committed to the ideal of Home Rule, Maurice had decided to publish his own Catholic and Nationalist newspapers. He would use them to promote the rights of his fellow Irishmen, and fight for self-government. The first edition of his weekly *Kerry People* was printed on Saturday 27 September 1902; its sister paper, the twice-weekly *Kerry Evening Star*, came out a few days later. Maurice knew that many of his fellow Irishmen, particularly if they were Catholic, did not have the same opportunities he had been given. He believed that the lack of national

---

4 Census of Ireland 1911, Residents of a house 19 in Garryruth.

self-determination was holding his country back. He was an ardent social reformer; through the pages of his newspaper, he supported the common man in Ireland. He pursued this passion and campaigned for Home Rule for Ireland, and for the improvement of working and living conditions of Irish men and women, throughout his life.

Maurice was a perfectionist, and passionate in pursuit of his goals, with a highly charged approach to life. His crusading spirit was passed down to his descendants, with many members of his family striving for excellence in the same way. In her drive towards stardom, Mary exemplified Maurice's spirit of perfectionism and his high-octane approach to life.

Kay's mother, Bridget, was a talented pianist who also played the organ at St John's Church in Tralee. She loved to play the piano, and on St Patrick's Day she would rise early to play Irish country airs for her family. The Ryle family was known for their very gentle and kind temperament, and Bridget demonstrated this kindness in a practical way. Kay's younger brother Colm, who was close to his mother, told his son Muiris of the time she took his shoes from him for the day, and gave them to a traveller child who was making his First Communion.[5]

Growing up, Kay was a dreamer; she was a regular at the Theatre Royal, where she saw opera and drama productions. Then, in 1913, James T Jameson brought his shows to town. There had been nothing like it in Tralee before. The performances presented by Jameson in his travelling film and variety shows were electrifying. This was when Kay's ambition to be a performer was conceived. To sing, to dance, to act – up there onstage, with the lights and the music and the cheering audience – that was her dream. She was always seen as something of a bohemian, by her family. As a young girl she longed to leave Tralee to seek fame and fortune in London, and the First World War gave her that opportunity. Companies were stripped of their clerks, shopworkers, etc., as young men were conscripted or volunteered to fight in the Great War. These roles had to be filled, and young women from all parts of the nation flooded into London to take up these posts. Kathleen was one of them; she learned that banks in the city were offering employment to suitably qualified young women, and she sent off her application. Her brother

---

5 Muiris Ryle, Dusty's cousin, in personal correspondence with the author, 2016.

Colm remembered seeing her leaping on the bed with joy, when the letter arrived telling her that she had been accepted. So it was that, in 1916, in the midst of this 'war to end all wars', she escaped the bitter effects of the Easter Rising and travelled to London with her sister Agnes. This was her chance to realise her dreams.[6]

~

Mary's father, Gerard Anthony Joseph O'Brien, was born in Nagpur, Bengal, in 1904, the son of Joseph and Frances. His father was Deputy Comptroller of the Post Office in Nagpur.

Gerard's early years were spent living amid the heat and the smells and the noise and the dust of India — in Nagpur, Calcutta or wherever his father was posted to work — with his parents and two sisters, Maude and Isabel. In common with all colonial homes of the era, the O'Brien's would expect to have a multitude of servants. A constant presence in Gerard's life from the time he was born, was his ayah. Her task was to care for him and soothe him to sleep with stories and lullabies.

All British mothers had ayahs, or nannies, to help look after their children:

From the children's point of view, ayahs were gentler than most nannies. In adulthood, men and women still kept a memory of a much-loved ayah, usually a small plump woman with gleaming, oiled hair, dressed in a white sari, who had sung to them, comforted them, and told them wonderful Indian stories.[7]

When Gerard was five, his sisters disappeared from his life, sent to boarding school in Belgium, where they were educated for the next five years. Now he was the only child at home, loved and cherished by his parents. Then, in 1914, Joseph took up the post of Secretary to the Council in Simla, the Viceroy's summer capital. The time had now come for Gerard to continue his schooling in Britain. His parents truly believed that the best education for him was to be had in the home country. They duly arranged passage for him and his mother on a steam ship to England:

---

6 Muiris Ryle, Dusty's cousin, in personal correspondence with the author, 2016

7 Margaret MacMillan (1988) *Women of the Raj*, London. p. 137.

Any parents who could possibly manage it sent their children away to boarding schools by the time they were seven years old, partly after the example of the middle classes at Home, but also because fears about the effects of India on the children took ever more elaborate forms. Children brought up in India were felt to be somehow of inferior quality, a belief that affected the marriage prospects of girls and the careers of boys.[8]

After a rough three-week sea crossing, the ship docked in London. Noise and clamour engulfed the docks there. London was a huge city, noisy and smelly, but very not at all like Calcutta, the city he had grown up in. It was a warm spring day when they arrived, a far cry from the fierce heat he was used to in India. From the port, Gerard and his mother took a cab to the railway station and caught a train to Edinburgh where he met his mother's cousins. Later, they travelled on to Elgin, where his sister had been born all those years before; here he was introduced to more aunts and cousins.

The day soon came when Frances began preparations for Gerard's start at school. He was enrolled as a boarder at Mount St Mary's College, in Derbyshire, and on 29 September 1915, Gerard and his mother arrived at Eckington Station, one mile from the school.[9] It was a rude awakening for Gerard. No longer nestled in the bosom of his family, indulged by his father, loved by his mother and spoiled by his ayah, he was to bed down in a huge, cold and draughty dormitory, surrounded by hordes of boys he knew nothing of. Pastoral care, health and well-being for all of the boys was in the hands of Matron and the headmaster's wife.

We can only imagine the speechless anguish caused by the parting from his mother; almost too much for Frances to bear. She had no way of knowing when she would see her son again. Soon Gerard would come to realise that it would be almost impossible for him to go home, even in the long summer holidays. A return passage by sea that used up six weeks of the holiday would be too difficult and very costly; it could not

---

8 Margaret MacMillan (1988) *Women of the Raj*, London. p. 139.

9 Mount St Mary's School Archive

be undertaken easily. This great distance to India meant he spent most of his time at the school until he was old enough to leave.

The separation was hard on everyone emotionally. For the children being sent away, it was the greatest shock of their early lives. It was one from which some of them never really recovered; is it surprising that they found it difficult to trust anyone again?[10]

In common with all of the boys at the school, during this period Gerard was starved of the love and warmth all children need. It is undeniable that he will have suffered a great deal of emotional damage during this time of enforced separation from his parents. He was deeply traumatised by it, and struggled to form close personal relationships ever afterwards. Inevitably this also impacted on his children.

The census in June 1921 lists 16-year-old Gerard at 15 St Andrew's Square, Surbiton. His mother Isabella is shown as a visitor at the same address. It can only be assumed that she came to England in order to spend some time with Gerard during his holiday from school that summer. It is only by chance that they are both recorded in this census. It was originally planned for April 24 that year but was delayed for two months in the wake of the Black Friday strike by railwaymen, coal miners and transport workers.

When Gerard's father retired from the Indian Civil Service in 1926, he and his wife set up home in an area of London known as Little India. Gerard went to live with them until their move to Marlow, in Buckinghamshire, where Joseph died in 1933. In 1927 Gerard passed the entrance exams for the Inland Revenue, and took up a post as Junior Assistant Inspector of Taxes and Ministry of Health Junior Assistant Auditor.[11]

~

Gerard and Kay meet

Kay took up her post in the bank, but still determined to follow her dream of a career on the stage, she found a place with a dance company. She left her job and began to travel with the troupe. But the constant

---

10 Margaret MacMillan (1988) *Women of the Raj*, London. p. 140.

11 London Gazette 1927. Civil Service Evidence of Age

grind of travel and performances, the seedy digs, the back biting of her fellow dancers, and the exhaustion took the sheen from her hopes. She gave up her thoughts of being an entertainer, and went back to the safety of a steady job and comfortable digs shared with her sister, Agnes.[12]

As a sop to her stage ambitions, Kay joined an amateur dramatic society. Gerard, who was known as OB, joined the same society. They both loved music and performing, and drawn together by their shared passions, they were married on 19 December 1931, in St Mary's Roman Catholic Church, Hendon. They made their home at 104 Sumatra Road, Hampstead, and Mary's brother, Dionysius (Dion), was born a little over two years later, on 2 July 1934. Mary was born five years later after their move to Lauderdale Mansions.

Kay and OB cherished their life in London. They each had their favourite pastimes. One of Kay's passions was the cinema – the Picture House at Maida Vale was a favourite place for her. Or, for visits to the city, the tube at Maida Vale station was just a few minutes' walk away. From there it was just two stops to Paddington, or one or two more into the centre of London and the department stores on Oxford Street, Regent Street and Piccadilly. OB loved music, mostly classical. The free invitation concerts at the BBC Studios, just round the corner, were a great boon for him. He could attend performances by the BBC Symphony Orchestra led by Sir Adrian Boult. And then there was Lord's Cricket Ground nearby.

During the Blitz all the beautiful shops loved by Kay: Harrods, John Lewis, Selfridges, Bourne & Hollingsworth and Peter Robinson, were destroyed by the bombs. When they learned that bombs had exploded close to their old flat in Lauderdale Road, it must have caused them a great deal of distress. Sands may have been dull and unexciting but at least they were safe there!

Sands

The 1939 register, compiled by the Government in September of that year, records the O'Brien family as living at 2 Hylton Road, Sands. This

---

12 The Electoral Roll for 1930 lists Kathleen, along with Agnes Theresa and her husband Phillip Netley, at 84 Clifden Road, Twickenham. Prior to his marriage in 1931 Gerard's home was in a house in Hendon.

.e time before London was decimated by German bombs during .z. Mary's father was employed as an income tax manager at the and it's possible his company made the decision to move out to safer rural setting. [13] He was short-sighted, and this could be the son he wasn't called up to fight. For most of the first 12 years of her e, Sands was home for Mary and her family.[14] Their house was an ordinary two-up, two-down semi, a world away from their mansion flat in London.

FIGURE 1.1. 2 HYLTON ROAD, SANDS (AUTHOR)

---

13 1939 England and Wales Register

14 London, England, Electoral Registers, 1832–1965

Sands village spreads itself across the side of the Chiltern hills, just outside High Wycombe. During the Second World War this small community had everything the residents could need. Sands Primary School on the main road through the village was close to the O'Brien's home.

The village had one telephone box, outside the Post Office, next door to Mines the newsagents. Langston's, the bakers in Mill End Road was across from Wakefield's fish and chip shop, then nearby was a milkman's depot, a butcher's shop, and an iron monger. The Park in Mill End Road, between two branches of the river Wye, was always full of kids. There were grass tennis courts and swings, provided by the Council with a little hut that sold ice lollies; the park keeper kept an eye on all the children. In the summer went paddling in the river. [15]

Horses and carts were still a common sight; there was the coalman, hauling bags of coal on his shoulders, and the grinder, who came offering to sharpen knives – their horses stood patiently waiting chomping from the bag of oats that hung over their noses. Then there was the rag-and-bone man who came on his round with his shout of 'Any old iron'. His horse was festooned with balloons that he handed out to the children in return for the odds and ends they brought him. He collected old clothes, junk and broken metal things.

Kay joined the Sands Women's Institute and their jam making exploits. They organised blackberry-picking parties that lasted for most of the day. In their old clothes and carrying their sandwiches the women and children took the footpath to Newmer Common then spread out into the old sand pits and Whittington Park to fill their baskets with berries. At the end of the day, they caught a bus back into Sands.

For Mary those early years were peaceful and unspoiled. The war raged across Europe and bombs ravaged the major cities in the country, but very little of it impacted her life in Sands. Mary's mother and father claimed they didn't like living in High Wycombe – Kay felt stifled by the village atmosphere, and was always concerned about the prying eyes of the village gossips. The distance from London was counted in more than just miles; Sands was another world. The place, the people, the house,

---

15 Alan Smith, 'Dusty Goes Back to Own Childhood', *New Musical Express*, 15 July 1966.

all were contrary to the life they had known before. They longed to go back to the busy metropolis, and insisted they were leaving soon. But although Kay said she was a restless soul who needed always to be on the move, the O'Brien's' stay in Sands extended for six years beyond the end of the war. Dusty recalled:

My mother was so set on the idea that we wouldn't be stuck in Buckinghamshire that she deliberately refused to unpack a case and it remained there packed up for eleven years.[16]

~

Happening

One day, when Mary was five and at home with her mother in Sands, there was an incident that can only have left a lasting impact on her.

Witnesses tell of the noise – a terrifying drone that soaked through the neighbourhood, getting louder by degrees; the sound was alien and terrifying. In the distance a black mass was visible in the sky; gradually it separated itself and revealed a multitude of planes. In Sands school, once the teachers were assured that these planes were on their side , the kids came spilling out of the building and into the playground. They all stood there, mouths open, staring up at the sky, as hundreds of aircraft towing gliders, and squadron upon squadron of planes, flew over the rooftops, all heading east. The seemingly endless waves of aircraft were an awesome sight.[17]

For days before this spectacle the whole of Sands had been overrun with soldiers in kilts and khaki uniforms. They were camping in the woods near to the houses, and there had been groups of these men in little huddles around the village. Soldiers queuing outside Wakefield's fish and chip shop, rifles stacked against the wall, became a familiar sight. Then, as suddenly as they had arrived, they were gone, and a day later the planes came. They didn't know it then, but this was a sign that the D-Day invasions had started. Planes flew from Buckinghamshire airfields for night raids over Germany, and on D-Day, June 6 1944.[18]

---

16 Dusty Springfield, 'Fame has a Flipside too', *Woman's Own* 1965, in Dusty Springfield Bulletin No. 65, July 2008.

17 Ken Wakefield, interview with author, 2016.

18 https://heritageportal.buckinghamshire.gov.uk/theme/tbc567.

Mary as a Girl

Mary would later describe her childhood as being somewhat unconventional. Day to day may have seemed quite ordinary, but life in the O'Brien household was never dull. Kay was a fiery person; she sparked with pent-up energy. Home could sometimes be like being in a Marx Brothers movie; for example, when Kay was involved in a mundane job, she might suddenly pick up some food and fling it at the wall. It was insane and exhilarating, and quite often the whole family joined in. That was the somewhat crazy and bohemian approach Kay took to life. [19]

Mary's father couldn't have been more different from her mother. Quiet and introspective, he moved slowly and deliberately, like a great ponderous bear. If Mary sometimes got on the wrong side of him, he would be gruff with her and might even give her a slap across the legs, but he mostly kept to himself.

Mary's craving for attention combined with Kay's volatile temperament sometimes led to unhappy confrontations between mother and daughter. Given their personalities, these clashes were inevitable, and it's likely Mary was unhappy as a result. On the other hand, there were lots of good times. She went to the movies with her mother, learned about music from her father, listened to her favourite comedy programmes on the radio, and spent time with her friends or sitting quietly in her room reading and daydreaming; her life was a combination of all these things.

In reality, Mary's relationship with her mother and father was no better or worse than that of her contemporaries. She came to realise that she had tested their patience, and she was grateful for everything they had taught her when she was growing up. That included a good set of values and clear appreciation of right from wrong! [20]

And then there was Dion, her big brother. She adored him. As they grew up, they had some serious fallouts, but she always looked up to him. Jealousy between siblings is a given, and Mary and Dion were no

19 Dusty Springfield, 'Fame Has a Flipside Too', *Woman's Own* 1965, in Dusty Springfield Bulletin No. 65, July 2008.

20 Veronica Groocock, 'I've Found that 99% of People are Insincere' *Record Mirror*, 3 September 1966.

exception. She was a sensitive child – she could and did construe things that had nothing to do with her as being her fault. It seemed to her that Dion could 'get away with it', while she was always in trouble. She formed the belief that her parents saw him as the clever one, and gave him all their praise. 'Dion seemed able to sail through all his exams without swotting at all, while I had to work really hard to get anywhere.'[21] Of course, Irish mothers had a particular relationship with their sons compared with their daughters. There was no way Mary could fight against this 'Mammy Syndrome'. Even if she didn't have a name for it, she knew it was there.

Even Dion's illnesses were more glamorous than hers. She would get colds while Dion caught glandular fever, so that she 'envied him like mad'.[22] Brother and sister competed for their parents' attention, but in fact, they were a mutual support system. In the evenings they would sit talking quietly about what they were going to be when they grew up. Dion loved to make music; while still at school he started his own Latin American band.[23] At one performance he played piano and sang, surrounded by 15 percussionists. He told her his ambition was to have his own band, and Mary said she wanted was to be a blues singer, even though she had no real idea what that meant.[24]

Later, looking back on her life, Mary said that:

up to the age of seven or eight I was quite pretty with nice frocks, but when I had measles it all went wrong and I got fat and horrible. I was a podgy little girl with hideous wire-rimmed National Health spectacles.'[25]

One of the not-so-great times for Mary was hair-washing night. Her fiery red hair fell almost to her waist. Combing and brushing it every day was a chore, and wash nights were the worst. There was no conditioner then, and her hair was a mass of tangles when it was wet. Getting them out was a long, slow and painful process that she dreaded. Kay would work at the tangles with the comb, tugging at Mary's scalp as she tried to untie the knots. When the pain got too bad, Mary would scream aloud

21 Dusty Springfield, 'Fame Has a Flipside Too', *Woman's Own* 1965, in Dusty Springfield Bulletin No. 65, July 2008.

22 Dusty Springfield, 'Fame Has a Flipside Too', *Woman's Own* 1965, in Dusty Springfield Bulletin No. 65, July 2008.

23 'The Natives were Friendly', *Record Mirror*, 26 August 1961.

24 Dusty Springfield, 'Fame Has a Flipside Too', *Woman's Own* 1965, in Dusty Springfield Bulletin No. 65, July 2008.

25 Alan Smith, 'Dusty Goes Back to Own Childhood', *New Musical Express*, 15 July 1966.

as tears sprang to her eyes. At the end of this exercise her mother would twist her hair in rags to form ringlets. There were no hairdryers in those days, so she would sit in front of the fire, reading or listening to music on the radio, waiting for it to dry. The rags stayed in overnight to keep the ringlets in place. Later, the tears came when her hair was bleached to turn her into a blonde.[26]

~

First School

Mary started at the nursery in Mill End Road, where she met Doreen. They were firm friends all through their time in primary school. Doreen's mum, Iris Bond, and Kay O'Brien liked to find a corner where they could sit and have a cup of tea and a good old natter, setting the world to rights.[27] This is also where Mary discovered tambourines; the teacher picked up a strange kind of drum with rattly bits on it, she tapped it with her hands so that it jingled and made everyone laugh and want to sing.

When the family arrived in Sands, Dion was enrolled at Sands County Primary. The school was visible from their front windows. Mary Dawson, a pupil at the time, remembers a podgy and bespectacled Dion O'Brien in her class, and his mother bringing his sister to the school Open Day.[28] Mary started there when she was five, at a time when the school was still suffering the effects of the war. Class sizes were huge because of the large number of evacuees in the area. [29] A school report from her time at the school, shows she was a good student, placing third in a class of thirty-three. [30]

Once Mary started school Kay O'Brien went back to work, which meant she wasn't always around when school came out at the end of the day. Instead, Doreen's mum met the girls and took them home to her house, where she gave them a snack, and took care of them while they played together until Kay arrived to take Mary home.[31]

---

26 Dusty Springfield, 'Fame Has a Flipside Too', *Woman's Own* 1965, in Dusty Springfield Bulletin No. 65, July 2008.

27 Richard Bond, brother of Doreen Bond, email to author 2016.

28 Mary Dawson, pupil at Sands County Primary, email to author 2016.

29 Sands County Primary School Report 1947.

30 Paul Howes (2013) 'Looking Good Isn't Always Easy'.

31 Bucks Free Press article about Doreen Bond, childhood friend of Dusty

FIGURE 1.2 SANDS COUNTY PRIMARY (BUCKS FREE PRESS)

Sands County Primary School, built around 1903, was extended, and the main school building altered in 1940. This small school had five classrooms and a hall with a little room for the headmaster and staff with cloakroom and stockroom. Although the building had been upgraded it was still freezing in the winter. The big old-fashioned stoves were meant to give heat but didn't seem to help a lot. Winters were very cold and steam could be seen coming from wet clothing that was hung on the stove railings in the classroom. The little bottles of milk given to the children at break froze in the cold and were put in front of the stove to thaw out, but that meant that the milk was either tepid or scalding hot when it was time to drink it. Either way it was awful! The wooden huts at the top of the playground were smelly and cold, with woodwork that was splintered and decaying; basically, the buildings were falling apart. It was a steep climb up there, which was bad enough, but when it rained it became muddy and slippery and the children struggled to get to the top. It was even worse in the snow and ice. The girls and boys had separate playgrounds, and the girls were confined to the top section, where they skipped with a long rope that two of them twirled for their mates to show off their skills. They did handstands against the wall, and played games such as 'What's the time Mr Wolf?'. The boys played football and tag in the bottom section, and in winter made an icy slide on the playground surface.

When Mary started school, she learned to read, using the 'Old Lob' books as the first readers. They featured Old Lob the farmer and his horse Dobbin. Once she could read, she immersed herself in books and that was it, she would be lost to the world for hours at a time. She learned her colours, the various kinds of weather, and the alphabet. The children sang a lot at Sands Primary, both hymns and the usual songs, such as 'Frères Jacques' and 'Greensleeves', accompanied by pupils enthusiastically banging various percussion instruments. Mary adored those times; the attention seeker in her always wanted to be noticed. Her voice was peculiar and special and she knew it. People noticed when she sang, and so when the teacher asked if anyone would like to sing, her hand shot up, and she was in her element, standing up in front of the class to sing her songs.[32] The school choir performed in High Wycombe's Town Hall each year, along with the other primary schools from the town.

~

Wartime Life

The whole of Mary's young life was governed by the war. In her early years she saw the many sights and sounds of wartime, such as the Home Guard marching in the village square. There was the nightly ritual of closing the blackout blinds at every window and checking there were no gaps before any lights were turned on. Not even the tiniest light could be visible to the German planes flying overhead. Air Raid Wardens patrolling to enforce the blackout, would shout *Put that light out!* or *Cover that window!*, and every pane of glass was criss-crossed with brown tape in case the glass was shattered in a bomb blast. 'The pitch-black nights and the lack of street signs meant that finding directions was almost impossible.' [33]

Mary's mother taught her about rationing and how it affected their lives, as she juggled the household supplies. Evacuees, pale faced, lost-

32 Dusty Springfield, 'Fame Has a Flipside Too', *Woman's Own* 1965, in Dusty Springfield Bulletin No. 65, July 2008.

33 Ottakar's High Wycombe, Roger Cole, History Press, 2001

looking children, swelled the numbers in school, and Doreen's mum took in one from London. This life was normality for Mary.

The keening wail of the air raid sirens - this sound that wound up then faded away, over and over again - warned of the approach of German bombers. At just two years of age, Mary felt the fear from her parents as they scurried into the air raid shelter. They stayed there all night, or until the all clear was sounded and they were sure it was safe to leave. No doubt it was an adventure for Mary; her family were lucky to never emerge from the shelter to find their home destroyed by bombs. In the school grounds was a shelter where the kids could be safe if there was an air raid. Inside it was very damp smelling; big jars of sweets sat on a shelf high up on the wall.[34] But since no bombs landed anywhere near to Sands, the sweets weren't needed. High Wycombe never felt the real terror of bombs during the war. Sometimes the crump of distant explosions could be heard in far-off London, or an orange glow could be seen in the night sky from fires at the docks. But at that distance it looked more like a fireworks display.

Everyone had to carry a gas mask around with them during the war; the square box slung over their shoulders. The children took their masks to school every day; they had regular gas drills, but when they discovered they could make 'rude' noises by blowing out through the rubber, they'd all fall about laughing! After that they couldn't take the drills seriously. There was even a special gas mask for babies, a great contraption of metal and canvas that mothers put their babies into, and then had to pump with air to ensure they didn't suffocate.

As the war was coming to an end, great efforts were put into developing the housing stock; everywhere there was some kind of building or road works going on. Most of the dads worked in the furniture trade. Doreen's dad was a French Polisher. There were workshops dotted about the place in Sands. Walking past they could see the men working in there, they heard the screeching of power tools; caught the smell of resin from the newly cut wood, and saw woodchips spilling out onto the pavement. Most of the kids in Sands came from

---

34 Mary Dawson, pupil at Sands County Primary

ordinary families; their clothes were hand me downs from brothers and sisters or cousins. [35]

Life in Sands was idyllic. When she was very small Mary mostly played with Doreen, but as she got older, she longed to join in with Dion and his friends. When they disappeared at the weekends, Mary was desperate to go with them because their games were exciting, especially Tracking. One of the boys would go ahead and lay a trail along the path behind the houses, which went up through the woods and into the fields. The rest of the boys, with Mary tagging along at the end, had to work out the clues and find the treasure at the end of the hunt. Mary always got lost and was last to find the leader; she cried bitterly when the others got ahead of her.[36] Dion's friends gave Mary the nickname Dusty because she loved to play football in the streets with them.[37] She was a tomboy who ran wild and played rough-and-tumble games with friends. [38] But many times, she would sit alone in her room, lost in a fantasy, dreaming about the big wide world and wondering what would become of her when she grew up.

Music in the Family

Mary's cousin Angela shared her memories of Mary's father, OB. She described him as 'a gentle, witty man with great musical gifts but no yearning to perform.'[39] In an interview broadcast on BBC Radio 2 in 2000, *Remembering Dusty Springfield*, Mary said:

My father taught me about classical music. In fact, that is all I listened to until I was about 13. It was only then I discovered first jazz and then pop music. A good burst of Mozart can restore one's faith in the entire world and then light burst of Vivaldi because it is so incredibly sparkling. And then if you really want to get down there and be depressed you've always got good old sobbing Tchaikovsky, it's incredible, just fantastic, that hits me right in the middle.

---

35 Paul Davies, Memories of Sands, email to author 2016.

36 Dusty Springfield, 'Fame Has a Flipside Too', *Woman's Own* 1965, in Dusty Springfield Bulletin No. 65, July 2008.

37 Dusty Springfield: Once Upon a Time 1964–1969: Ryan's Roost Interview.

38 Tony Bromley, 'Mary was a Tomboy', *New Musical Express*, 2 July 1965.

39 Angela Hunter, email to author 2016.

OB taught Dion and Mary an appreciation of classical music: the great classical composers: Beethoven, Bach, Vivaldi, Tchaikovsky and Mozart. He taught them how to listen to the music: to the rhythm, the cadence, the structures. He told them to pay attention and focus on the music. And he demonstrated that their brains were amazing pattern-finding machines; soon they discovered that they could start creating a blueprint for understanding the music.

Mary was introduced to the prolific compositions of Vivaldi: 'The Four Seasons', 'The Gloria', 'The Violin Concerto in A minor', etc. Like Mary Vivaldi had flaming red hair, he was known locally as 'il Prete Rosso,' or 'the Red Priest.' Later in life she talked about appreciating 'light bursts of Vivaldi, because it's so incredibly sparkling'. The great Russian composer Tchaikovsky was another favourite; he created a personal but unmistakably Russian style. The principles that governed melody, harmony and other fundamentals of Russian music differed completely from those that governed Western European music. Speaking to the *Village Voice* in 1995, Dusty explained how Tchaikovsky's music made her feel.

> *It was Enya, actually, or Tchaikovsky, which would really do it any day — overlooking the canals with the rain falling into them, my head between the speakers, just letting it out.' She laughs at the memory. 'I don't suggest that people do that with my records, but it's certainly a good thing to do with Tchaikovsky.'* [40]

OB taught them about Haydn too, that he was among the creators of the fundamental genres of classical music, and that his influence on later composers was immense. That led to discussions of Ludwig van Beethoven, Haydn's most celebrated pupil. OB revered Beethoven above all other composers, believing that his musical form cast a huge shadow over the music of subsequent composers, such as Schubert, Mendelssohn and Brahms. He encouraged his children to explore. If they liked something, they should find out what else was like it, what came before it, who inspired it, who the composers' friends were — anything that would bring it to life.

---

[40] Stacey D'Erasmo, 'Beginning with Dusty', The Village Voice, 29 August 1995.

OB used to gently tap out the notation from a piece of music on the back of Mary's hand and ask her to guess the piece from the rhythm of his fingers. Sometimes he would play a piece on the piano and ask Mary and Dion to name the composer.[41] He played his best-loved records on the gramophone, and music on the radio was a constant presence. Mary's love of music and the benefits of her father's teaching stayed with her; he taught her how to listen to music, how to understand its form and how to appreciate it. That appreciation and understanding informed the whole of her life in music.

~

Russell Chamberlen

It is not quite certain when Russell Chamberlen appeared in Mary and Dion's life, it seemed that he had always been there. He was five years or so older than Dion. In 1939 he had been evacuated to Sands, where he lived at 11 Hylton Road with his mother and brother.

OB had met Russell at the bus stop on his way to work one morning. That is how their friendship began. They had a shared love of shortwave radio – they were 'radio hams'. Russell quickly became a regular visitor to their house, and Mary got used to seeing him and her dad in a huddle in front of a great bank of instruments on the dining room table. But OB's enthusiasm went beyond just listening to transmissions on his radio. He took great pains in building his receiver, which meant there was always a collection of tools, wiring, sockets, switches, tubes, bulbs and lamps on the table.[42] He passed on his expertise to Russell, and they used to fiddle with the dials, fine-tuning until they found a channel where they could listen to the distant exchanges. Mary would recall the screeching sounds of this searching years later when, hidden under her bed clothes, she tried to find Radio Luxembourg on her transistor radio.

Russell also shared OB's passion for music. First learning the violin at four, he quickly abandoned it in favour of the piano and learned to play by ear. He was a brilliant pianist, and listening to the radio for hours heard all his musical heroes – Denis Wilson, Bill McGuffy, Carol Gibbons, Kay Cavendish, and more, who performed on popular radio shows at

41 Dusty Springfield, Full Circle, Universal Pictures (UK) Ltd, 1994

42 Dusty Springfield, Full Circle, Universal Pictures (UK) Ltd, 1994

that time. He came to Sands in 1939, with his mother and brother. He often visited the O'Brien house, listening to the radio receiver, playing the piano and talking about music with OB. Russell taught Dion his first chords on the guitar, and encouraged him as he got to grips with the instrument. Dion was a gifted musician, who also learned to play the piano by ear, quickly becoming proficient. As Dion improved on the guitar he and Russell began to jam together, playing and singing their favourite pieces.

~

Voice

Mary was born with a talent: her voice was her gift and she knew how to use it. She had been singing her entire life and some of her earliest memories were of her mother sitting her on a stool at the age of four or five, where she would sing her version of her favourite songs for their neighbours. She could quickly memorise the words to a song – whether it was on the radio or sung by her mother, she instantly knew them. It was natural and effortless, and as she got older, she began to sing with Dion and Russell. [43] She knew her voice had an unusual sound, and she could hold a tune and belt out a song.

Kay liked to share stories about her life back home in Tralee. She told Mary about her grandmother, Bridget Ryle, who died when Mary was only three. Kay told her how Bridget played traditional Irish tunes on the piano at home, and hymns on the organ at St John's Church in Tralee.[44] Mary also learned about traditional Irish music and songs from Kay, who told of watching musicians play the bodhrán, fiddles, pipes and horns at fairs and when the circus came to Tralee. Kay also told her children about attending a recital given by the great tenor, Count John McCormack, in Tralee. Mary was to discover a song he recorded, 'My Lagan Love', which she performed on her TV programme many years later.

~

---

43 Russell Chamberlen, interview with author, January 2016.

44 Muiris Ryle, Dusty's cousin, email to author 2016.

Drama Group

Kay O'Brien was a bundle of nervous energy who talked non-stop and chain-smoked fancy oval Du Maurier cigarettes; she was always seen with one in her hand. [45] One outlet for her effervescent personality was the local drama group which she joined along with her friends Iris Bond and Mrs Stevens. This was something that helped to satisfy her need for attention. We can imagine the feverish atmosphere in the O'Brien house as the date of the next production drew near. For weeks ahead there would be the sound of lines being recited, and she disappeared to rehearsals two or three times a week until the day of the actual performance. The show itself was performed in the chapel in Chapel Lane.

~

Victory in Europe Day

On 8 May 1945, the Prime Minister, Winston Churchill, announced on the wireless that the German generals had surrendered to General Eisenhower, and that the war was over. He said, 'Advance Britannia, long live the cause of freedom. God Save The King.'

Mary may have struggled to remember that day in detail, but it was surely evident that her parents seemed lighter somehow. It was almost as if they had been holding themselves in for a very long time and now they could relax and breathe properly again. This was a time for celebrations. A party was planned by the Women's Institute (WI). Kay was a member of the Young Wives Club and also made jam and cakes for the WI. The WI ran market stalls to raise money for ambulances. Everyone helped with preparations for the big day, the parents donated food and the children were dressed in their finest. This was a big treat; it brought in everyone from the neighbourhood. Union Jacks and bunting were strung up between the lampposts and great long tables covered in white table cloths were arranged in the streets. There were sandwiches and pies, corned beef hash (Mary's favourite) and cakes piled up for the party. And there was music; someone dragged a piano

---

45 Russell Chamberlen, interview with author, January 2016.

out onto the street and banged away on it while they all joined in the singalong. Everyone was happy and relieved that the war was over. [46]

Sadly, that feeling of euphoria didn't last for long, they soon realised that rationing was to stay for a few years more.

~

Dion and Royal Grammar

The Royal Grammar School (RGS) in High Wycombe sits at the top of Amersham Hill about a mile from the railway station. When Dion was ten, he passed the Special Place Examination for the school. To get there he had to set off early and catch two buses. Mary was five at the time and began her school life at Sands County Primary.

RGS was a state school for boys that liked to pretend it was a private one, and it was well known for its incredible academic success. First established in the reign of Edward VI, in 1562, it was granted a Royal Charter by Queen Elizabeth I. The headmaster, Mr Tucker, seemed to represent the Empire, God, and Society. The tales of his handiness with the cane went before him; a boy didn't have to commit any great misdemeanour to earn a few whacks from him. In fact, most boys received a regular annual beating, whether they deserved it or not. Dion often arrived home from school with tales of Mr Tucker's latest bad-tempered tirade. The story of the rugby match between the staff and the Old Boys is one that became a part of school legend.[47] This was an important match and the entire school was required to attend. It had rained heavily that day and the players were slipping about badly on the field. Suddenly, Mr Tucker crashed down and landed with his face in a huge patch of mud, to wild cheering from the boys, who howled with delight and passed quite a few unkind comments. Mr Tucker didn't see the funny side of it, though, and the next day he caned the whole school.

RGS was a boys' schools which ran a Combined Cadet Force, and everyone at some time or other had to be part of it, starting off in the Army but later joining the Navy or the Royal Air Force, if you had a special interest. Dion will certainly have gone through the indignity and

---

46 Alan Smith, 'Dusty Goes Back to Own Childhood', *New Musical Express*, 15 July 1966.

47 L.J. Ashford and C.M. Haworth, The History of the Royal Grammar School, High Wycombe, 1562–1962.

discomfort of becoming a member. There was the humiliation of going to school on a Thursday with army serge next to his skin, itchy shirts, itchy Jackets, itchy trousers and foot-crushing boots, with stiff puttees halfway up his legs., which he had spent the previous evening blancoing, a deeply unpleasant experience for him. He then had to walk down Mill End Road; with girls he had known all his life. and who were already working in offices, teetering behind and sniggering.

If Mary was sometimes jealous of Dion's long holidays (he had seven and a half weeks in the summer and four weeks at Christmas and Easter) there would have been no envy of his long school day; he had to attend until half past four each day and every Saturday morning.

Dion had joined the school at the start of the new academic year in 1944. He is listed as a pupil at RGS, in the School Grey Book, between 1944 and 1950. After surviving the worst wrath of Mr Tucker, he got through school quite successfully, and passed the Oxford School Certificate not long before he left in the summer of 1950, just after his sixteenth birthday.

~

Movies with Mum

Kay O'Brien was just 12 years old when she discovered the cinema. Jameson had brought his travelling film and variety show to the Theatre Royal in Tralee and she saw every performance. The films that played then, were accompanied by the delicate strains of Miss Queenie D'Arcy's Orchestra. This combination of films and variety acts were a revelation to her. She was fascinated, besotted even, and she clung to the hope that one day she might be one of them: up there on the screen, the star, all eyes on her.

Almost 40 years later, when Kay went to the pictures, she took her daughter with her. The films were now in colour and a Hammond organ had replaced the orchestra. The films they saw were 'talkies'; the voices of the singers and actors blasted from speakers set in the walls, and the dancers moved to the rhythm of the music. This was an explosion of colour, sound and movement.

Even as a small child, as she sat watching the flickering images of her idols on the screen, Mary knew that was what she wanted to be. Just as her mother had, she yearned to be famous, to be noticed. Many years later, she reflected on the movies she saw as a child and the effect they had on her:

It was sheer glamour, and that really gaudy Technicolor, the Betty Grable red lips look, the slash of scarlet – it was absolutely marvellous. It was just the whole glitz of it, it was everything I wanted to be and would never be. I wanted to be in there with them doing it. I'm not a dancer and I don't know what it was about it, it was just sheer trashy glamour. I knew that even when I was four, I wanted trashy glamour, it's great [48]

Saturday afternoon at the cinema was a ritual for Mary and Kay. The bus into High Wycombe left from the Hour Glass pub in Sands. It took them all the way to the terminus at the railway station. They walked from there down the hill and along Castle Street to the Odeon. At the cinema, the usherette checked their tickets and pointed down the aisle with her torch to help them find their seats in the endless rows. They were confronted with a sea of heads; plumes of smoke curling up from their cigarettes. The inside of the cinema was ornate, designed in a Venetian atmospheric style, it had murals of mountainous countryside covering the walls and turrets painted in the foreground. The organ slowly appeared from the depths, sound swelling and filling the giant auditorium as it came. The organist sat at the console smiling and playing the songs Mary would come to know well, such as 'That's Entertainment', 'Singin' in the Rain', 'Chattanooga Choo Choo', and 'Tea for Two'. Even before the movie began, she had been transported into a magical world. Mary's first love was Judy Garland and, with her ability to learn a song and sing in tune, Mary quickly learned the words of the songs from The Wizard of Oz and made them part of her repertoire.

Mary and her mother would sit through the main film and then the trailers, followed by adverts and the news bulletin before the B movie was shown. After the interval, they stayed to watch the main feature all over again. This was Kay's time; she was off her feet for the afternoon and would wring everything from it that she could. When the movie was over, they came blinking back into the evening air, and wandered around the town window shopping. They would cut through the lane by

---

48 Brian Linehan, *City Lights*, Citytv, 1981.

Frogmoor to Murrays store where they browsed for a while. Then on to the bookstore on High Street, where Mary and Kay bought their favourite magazines. The High Street was always a mass of people, some hurrying about their business and others strolling, just like them. In those days High Wycombe was filled with a great mix of voices - the local Bucks accents, some Welsh and Cockney, distinctive American sounds and West Indian voices from Jamaica and Trinidad. The town was crowded with servicemen; RAF Bomber Command was based in High Wycombe, and the American Air Force had set up camp in Wycombe Abbey. These men were all smartly dressed, RAF airmen in their grey-blue battle dress, and the American airmen who seemed always to have the smartest uniforms and the prettiest girls on their arms. But she would also see men wearing brown overalls with a big round yellow patch on the back. These were Italian prisoners of war from the camp in Chairborough Road.

On their way out of town, Kay and Mary stopped to buy cakes from the bakers on the corner, then they caught the bus at the railway station; went back home to Sands in time for tea.

A few years later Mary saw 'Easter Parade'. Judy Garland starred in that film too, with Fred Astaire. The story of an eager young singer who longed to be famous and was given a lucky break was Judy's top-grossing film at MGM. Mary picked a couple of songs from the film – 'When that Midnight Choo Choo Leaves for Alabam' and 'I Love a Piano' – and another of Judy's songs, 'Pretty Baby' written by Irving Berlin, to learn and record. She used the techniques her father had taught her to understand how the songs were structured. She mimicked the performances in an attempt to produce the right sounds, and then, after lots of practice, she found she could sing them almost as well as Judy herself. With Dion on piano, she recorded the songs on her father's reel-to-reel tape recorder. The recordings have survived and are available on the 'Simply Dusty' CD.

~

Catholic Education

St Augustine's Convent

When she was eight or nine, Mary's parents decided it was time for her to receive a proper religious education, and enrolled her at St Augustine's Convent on the London Road. Now she caught a bus to school every morning. It drove down the twists and turns of the roads through Sands and finally went bowling down the hill into High Wycombe to her stop. She joined this rather ancient school, opposite a huge area of parkland known as the Rye. Pupils were taken there for PE and sports day and to play hockey. There were roundabouts on the Rye, slides and swings and an ice cream booth nearby; mothers took their young children there to play. No doubt Mary went there with Kay when she was very small.

This school was overrun with mice, rats, chickens and nuns. Mice would nibble at anything vaguely edible, so that anyone careless enough to leave their books out in the open would find them chewed the next day. Rats lurked in the cellars and terrified any child sent to fetch coal. Chickens were kept as part of the curriculum – pupils were taught about caring for animals – and they were given the job of collecting the eggs, which they ate for lunch. When the snow came, it brought the fun of snowball fights. On one occasion, when the teachers ordered the children inside one poor unfortunate was locked in the chicken run; a nun was sent out into the storm to rescue him.

Teaching at the school was under the care of the Order of the Daughters of Jesus. Nuns taught the children all the practical subjects – English, history, maths, geography, etc. – but, more importantly, they provided spiritual guidance. Mary was a very good student,[49] and later said of Sister Marie Louise, a nun who was her biggest influence there, 'Her face was so serene. I suppose it came from inner peace'.[50]

The school was quite small – with only three or four classrooms – and rather old. When it was very cold in the winter, trips to the loo out in the playground were a nightmare. The toilets themselves were ghastly – cold, dark and damp with peeling whitewashed walls and saturated

---

49 'Dusty – The Ultimate Interview 1993', in Dusty Springfield Bulletin No.50 November 2003.

50 Dusty Springfield, 'Fame Has a Flipside Too', *Woman's Own* 1965, in Dusty Springfield Bulletin No. 65, July 2008.

with the smell of urine and carbolic. It is easy to imagine that, as was the case with all small children, Mary was nervous about going there on her own, and would desperately try to hold on until break time. One strange feature was that both boys' and girls' toilets were provided with urinals.[51]

First Communion

To prepare for her First Communion, Mary had to go through the ritual of first confession. The following section describes how Mary is likely to have experienced this rite of passage:

The class was assembled in the vast and silent church; Mary overcome with nerves stood in the queue waiting for her turn. The only sound came from the squeak of the confessional door as it opened and closed when the next child was called into the dark unknown. Mary had no idea what to say, so she confessed to sometimes being naughty, and even a bit cheeky to her parents. The priest told her that she must show remorse for her sins and that her parents required her to respect them. Following her Act of Contrition – the set formula required by the penitent to show that they are truly sorry – he gave her a few prayers to say as a simple penance.

Getting ready for the day of their very First Communion was an exciting time for the kids; they had so much to take in. First, they had to learn how to bow to one another. In the classroom the nuns explained the importance of this act – to acknowledge the presence of Jesus in each of them, and to know that they were the living body of Christ. They practised bowing, as well as the act of receiving the host: they were told not to bite it, but just to let it melt on their tongues. The sisters made them recite portions of the Mass, and they rehearsed the hymns until they were word perfect. Mass was held once a week in the class, and on Sundays they went to church with their parents.

Mary and her mother went looking for the dress she would wear. They searched through the racks until they found one they liked. Kay took the dress and held it up to check the size; Mary was thrilled by the prospect.

---

51 David Gardiner pupil at St Augustine's Convent

Now all they had to do was get the veil from the Sister, and she would be ready for her First Communion.

On the morning of the Communion, she put on her lovely new dress, knee length white socks and her white shoes. She felt as a bride might on her wedding day, or the closest she could ever be to the Blessed Mother, or an angel. They drove to the church, where the other kids were waiting, boys dressed in their stiff new suits and girls in their dazzling white dresses.

The sounds of the organ gradually grew louder as the children lined up two by two. They began their slow progress down the centre aisle of the church, led by the Processional Cross. On either side of them the congregation of families and friends packed the pews. Faces rapt with concentration, the children battled to ensure the angel did not fall from their fingers that were pointed upwards in prayer. They sang the Processional Hymn as they moved towards the sanctuary. The first pair bowed to the altar, turned to face each other and bowed again, then sat down and waited until all of the children were seated.

Mary was about to receive the Eucharist for the very first time. She watched the pageant of priest and his helpers; she heard his murmurs as he performed the ritual of changing the bread and wine into the body and blood of Christ through the power of the Holy Spirit. The Mass in those days was entirely in Latin. She didn't properly understand what it was all about, nor did she remember the teachers ever providing the translation. But being an actor in that scene, one that she had seen played out so many times before, she began to feel very grown up, with a sense of being united with Jesus Christ.

Once the ceremony was over the children were all given a special Rosary and prayer book. Their fast from the night before had left them starving, and they thought of little other than the breakfast feast waiting for them back at the school.

~

Holidays in Bognor

There came a time, once the effects of the war had eased, the O'Brien family felt able to go away for their summer holidays. They would pile all of their gear into the car – suitcases full of holiday clothes, buckets and spades, swimming cossies and sun hats. They couldn't forget raincoats, rain hats and umbrellas. (You never could tell what the weather would be like!) They added all the paraphernalia they would need for a picnic and drove through the narrow, twisting country roads to Bognor Regis. It took most of the day and Mary was often sick in the car. But she was excited too; they were going to meet their cousins David and Angela, with their mother, Aunt Maude.[52]

FIGURE 1.3 MARY WITH HER BROTHER DION AND COUSIN ANGELA IN BOGNOR

In the morning, Mary and Angela went out to explore, to see whether the place had changed since the last time they were there. Just about every day was spent on the beach. Deck chairs were hired, and the grownups settled in with their books and newspapers. Mary's father rolled up his trousers to the knees and sported a knotted handkerchief on his head, while Kay and Maude set up the wind breaks and organised the picnics. The kids played games, dug in the sand, built sandcastles and buried each other up to their necks. The downside was they couldn't escape that icky feeling when their costumes were full of sand. The shore at Bognor is shallow – you can go a long way out and still be no more than knee deep. They had a lot of fun running down to the sea and

---

52 Email from Angela Hunter – Dusty's cousin

jumping and splashing in the water. Then, of course, modesty had to be protected when changing out of their swimming gear. Many strange contortions were gone through, holding a towel with one hand while struggling out of a wet costume with the other. Donkey rides cost 6d, but parents had to be badgered for the money. They went searching for crabs in the rock pools, and whiled away hours combing the beach for interesting shells and stones.

An ever-present line of coaches was parked along the sea front. They brought day trippers into the town, and people flooded the Esplanade and down onto the beach. Bognor was steeped in a lovely feeling of post-war happiness. The crowds were unbelievable, and the beach was swamped, so to get a good spot they had to plan to get there early. Otherwise, they would be left to camp close to the sea, or crammed up next to the sea wall. Although these summers were seemingly filled with endless hours of sunshine, there were times when it poured all day. The poor day trippers from London, along with their children, would have to spend the entire day camped in the shelter of the promenade.

On balmy summer evenings they would wander along to Hotham Park, where the Alamein Band performed. A lovely young man sang songs such as Gilbert and Sullivan's, 'Take a Pair of Sparkling Eyes', and 'A Wandering Minstrel', or 'The Flower Song' from Carmen. They played most of the old-time Victorian ballads that were still popular with people of a certain age, who attended the concerts. Mary might have imagined herself up there performing to the crowds, even though she couldn't think how she could ever make that happen.

The very long pier had a miniature railway that charged a penny for the trip to the end. It was a long way to the amusements and children's playground in the Pavilion.

Bognor wasn't always a Regis. That came about because King George V went there to convalesce in 1929, after a lung operation. He bestowed the name in gratitude to the town after his recovery.

~

St Bernard's Convent

The 11-plus exam, which tested whether pupils qualified for a place at grammar school, was Mary's next challenge. She got frustrated and confused when she saw Dion pass his exams without seeming to try. She, on the other hand, had to slog her guts out to achieve anything, and it took her two attempts to pass. She recalled:

I suppose the greatest disappointment of my childhood was failing the 11-plus (but I passed it the second time). I was so anxious to do well, to be top, and it shattered me that Dion seemed to be able to sail through all his exams without swotting at all, while I had to work really hard to get anywhere. Failing that exam broke my heart. [53]

Based in a huge old house on the London Road, St Bernard's was right next door to St Augustine's. Mary's move from one school to another caused her little trouble, and although the location didn't change, there was an alternative culture. St Bernard's was a fee-paying school, whereas St Augustine's was free. A little arched gate between the two schools, which would have given easy access, was always kept locked. The children attending these schools were never allowed to mix; they didn't even share sports day.

St Bernard's was run by the Daughters of Jesus, the same order of nuns in charge of St Augustine's, and the nuns were lovely. Headmistress, Sister Mary Gertrude, was also Mother Superior of the community. She had a very real understanding of children and maintained an interest in their growth and development. She knew them as individuals and was sympathetic and understanding with those who were sick, or suffering from any kind of disability. The pupils were encouraged by the nuns to care for the sick and underprivileged. A strong desire to please meant Mary learned quite a lot from them.

Mary had very few memories of the school, but she would recall the feeling of being squeezed in with her schoolmates. The classrooms, in general, were too small to cope with the number of girls in the form, and some rooms were so cramped they seriously restricted movement and activity, particularly those used by the younger children. The stairs and corridors were very narrow and the classrooms had hardly any space to store books etc. Some of the rooms still had old dual desks and there was a small library room on the top floor, with a good collection.

---

53 Dusty Springfield, 'Fame Has a Flipside Too', *Woman's Own* 1965, in Dusty Springfield Bulletin No. 65, July 2008.

Mary was taught a range of subjects, as well as religious instruction, there was English and history, geography, Latin, and mathematics. An Inspection Report praised the English teacher for her gifted teaching; Mary was fortunate to be at the school at this time. The girls couldn't exercise indoors as there wasn't enough space and nowhere to get washed or changed. When they wanted to play hockey and tennis, pupils had to walk up Marlow Hill to the playing fields on Daws Hill. They went to the local baths to swim from time to time, though that wasn't Mary's favourite pastime.

In the winter the classrooms were heated by a coal fire. The usual harsh sooty smell and fine coal dust seemed to get everywhere in the room. The girls were asked to put their chairs on the tables at the end of each day, then they said a prayer. It took quite a few years for Mary to realise that there was no religious significance in putting their chairs on the tables, rather, it was done to help the cleaners. She felt well and truly had!

There were the usual rituals amongst the girls at school. Each of them had an autograph book with squares drawn in the pages. This was passed round to all their friends and classmates, who each signed in one of the boxes. Figure 1.5 shows a page from Lavina Gee's autograph book. you can see Mary's message in the second row, third box from the right. Lavina was a bit older than Mary, and they travelled to school from Sands on the bus together. She remembers being invited to Mary's birthday party on one occasion.

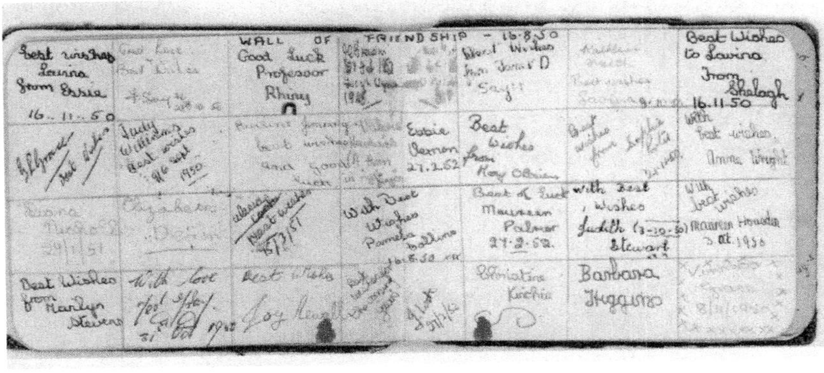

FIGURE 1.5 AUTOGRAPH 1951 (COURTESY OF LAVINA GEE)

Mary had been a pupil at St Bernard's for only a few months when her mother told her they were leaving High Wycombe. Kay finally had her wish – they were going back to London.

This was summer 1951. Mary was 12 and rapidly turning into a young lady, although she didn't see it that way herself. Three things were impacting on her life now: music, faith and sexuality. Her approaching life in Ealing would be where she would learn and develop in all three.

Part 2: The Girl on the Stairs

1951 - 1955

St Anne's Convent

LONDON BOROUGH OF
EALING LIBRARY SERVICES
Postcard Series L3

OLD NORTHFIELDS AND LITTLE EALING
Ealing Park c 1880
(now St. Anne's Convent School)

Produced by
Pamlin Prints
Croydon

FIGURE 2.1 ST ANNE'S CONVENT. REPRODUCED BY PERMISSION OF THE LONDON
BOROUGH OF EALING LIBRARIES (LOCAL HISTORY CENTRE)

The smell of beeswax polish was almost overpowering; it was a smell that would always remind Mary of that day. Mother and daughter had caught the bus from outside their flat in Kent Gardens and travelled down to St Anne's Convent in Little Ealing Lane. Mary had an interview with the headmistress, Sister Stanislaus.

From the bus stop the pair walked to the massive iron gates at the entrance to the school grounds. They entered through the little gate next to the gate house and passed the trees that hid the building from the road. Then they walked around the lawn and under the portico that led to the heavy wooden door of the ancient house, knocked and waited. The door was opened by a nun.

Mary's mother told her that they had an appointment with the headmistress. The door opened wider and they were invited into a large, panelled reception hallway with a beautiful marble staircase leading to the upper floors. The nun, wearing very soft slippers, walked noiselessly down the corridor in front of them. She pointed to a wooden bench where they perched nervously. They sat there in the dark quiet corridor, in the almost palpable silence of this grand, formal old house. Shortly, another nun came out of a nearby room. She extended a hand from under her robes and greeted them in a soft Irish accent.

A tiny lady in a full nun's habit, she introduced herself as Sister Stanislaus, the headmistress of St Anne's. She invited the pair into what Mary would soon discover was known as Sister Stanislaus's Parlour; its usual function was to receive visitors. This room was small and dark with large wooden furniture and hard, upright and uncomfortable chairs; the pungent smell of beeswax polish was strongest here. In front of the Sister was a table covered with a brown chenille tablecloth: a faint scent of incense came from the sacristy next door.

Kay O'Brien had heard about the school from friends and neighbours; they told her that the Sister was a brilliant leader of the school community. The Sister's air of quiet authority it calmed their nerves.

Sister Stanislaus began by asking Kay O'Brien about their family and why she had chosen St Anne's. Kay explained that they had recently moved to Ealing and when she learned about St Anne's reputation it seemed an obvious choice. She explained that this quiet suburb was convenient for her husband's commute into London, her son had completed his schooling in High Wycombe and Mary had just started her secondary education.

Next, Sister Stanislaus asked Mary about her subjects and grades at school. Mary's mumbled answer didn't quite satisfy the Sister. She asked about her favourite subjects. 'I love reading and composition and I quite like drawing,' said Mary. When she was asked about her interests, Mary came alive as she spoke about her love of music and singing.

The Sister suggested she might like to join the school choir; she spoke about the many fine performances they gave throughout the school year, in particular the great success they had had when they performed in the Ealing Music Festival at the Town Hall. Later, Mary would win her heat in a talent competition in an Ealing theatre but decide not to go on to the finals as she was chosen for the school choir.

They learned about the school and the system of school houses from Sister Stanislaus; 'St Anne's, St Michael's and St Jeanne Antide. She told them that a teacher is assigned the role of House Mistress and one of the senior girls is chosen as House Captain every year. Each pupil is allocated to one of the houses. They are given black marks for bad behaviour and for not wearing their school hat while travelling to and from school.

Two days after the interview a letter arrived, offering Mary a place at the school. It was settled; Mary would be a pupil at St Anne's Convent for the next five years. [54]

Kent Gardens

After their interview with Sister Stanislaus, Mary and her mother went home to their new flat in Castle Bar, an upmarket area of West Ealing. It had had a most illustrious resident in the Duke of Kent, the father of Queen Victoria, who had lived in Castle Hill Lodge. Houses from the ambitious mid-Victorian scheme of 1860 were built by Henry de Bruno Austin, the successor to Castle Hill Lodge,. He had planned a large estate of detached villas of which only 20 were built before he went bankrupt in 1872. There were a few ten-bedroomed villas in Cleveland Gardens, and Kent Gardens was lined with large semi-detached houses. These houses were converted into flats after the war and it was there the O'Brien's took up residence when they arrived in Ealing in the summer of 1951.

This huge, grey-stone building was a marked contrast to the semi they had just left in High Wycombe.[55] At the front, steps led up to the portico which was supported on either side by pairs of large, round, stone columns. Inside, their flat was vast and on a scale unlike anything Mary had known before. It had a huge living room, and their table seemed dwarfed in the enormous kitchen. Old and slightly worn, their furniture looked a bit lost and forlorn.

---

54 From a description given by Yvonne Messenger, former pupil of St Anne's Convent School for Girls

55 The O'Brien's moved into flat 4 in a large, semi-detached house at 2 Kent Gardens, West Ealing, in 1951.

School ethos

St Anne's was an energetic, lively school that encouraged all the usual sports of hockey, netball and tennis. There were annual school fetes and bazaars, dance displays and music concerts. It had a Legion Praesidium of Mary, junior and senior choirs, a music and dramatic society, had recently acquired a long wished for orchestra and its own Guide company and Brownie pack.

The school was run by the Sisters of Charity of St Jeanne Antide. Sister Stanislaus had been with the order since 1925 and was appointed headmistress in 1935. St Anne's, with all the hallmarks of a traditional Catholic convent school, was led by this remarkably open-minded and forward-looking nun. Under her direction, along with all the usual religious observances, pupils were offered summer breaks, including tours to Lourdes, holidays in France and pilgrimages to Rome. There were visits to Royal Greenwich and to the Lyon's factory. They went to the cinema, saw stage plays (often Shakespeare) and exhibitions and even visited the House of Commons. The school also presented the girls with geographical films that gave them a wider view of the world.

Speaking at the school prizegiving one year, Sister Stanislaus told parents that they should be just as ambitious for the future of their girls as their boys. She believed that it was worthwhile to continue girls' education and that this would equip them both for married life and for possible future careers. Her liberal views were reinforced when the girls were introduced to adventurous and emancipated young women who were not ready to conform to the conventions of the time.

One such was Beryl Miles, who visited the school in October 1952 to give a talk on her travels in Australia with Gordon Donkin. She joined his expedition to the Australian interior in search of Aboriginal cave paintings. The trip lasted six months and covered 8,000 miles. Beryl's vitality and zest for life was demonstrated in her description of the adventures she had on her trip with the Donkin Kimberley Expedition.

Old girls talk fondly of the headmistress. They say that she was strict but kind and fair, and she always had time to listen if a girl really felt the need to talk about something. She spoke softly with just a hint of an Irish accent. There was an aura about her, an air of quiet authority that meant she could keep order without raising her voice. One former pupil recalled:

> *She was kind to me personally. Once when she saw I was feeling stressed during some exam or other, she said, 'Don't worry, my dear,' and she fished in her pocket and gave me a holy picture for my consolation. The gesture was enough to make me feel a bit better.*[56]

However, Sister Stanislaus was absolutely uncompromising when it came to bad behaviour. Once, a girl was very rude to the nuns on playground duty at the time. Sister Stanislaus dealt with it calmly and with total resolve, saying 'Lack of respect is not tolerated.' It might be possible to get away with naughtiness but this was lack of respect. The culprit was expelled at once and the expulsion announced at assembly, with the misdemeanour described in great detail.

During Mary's five years at St Anne's, she experienced all the usual rites of passage of a young Catholic girl. And yet, there was something unusual about this school.

~

Starting School, 1951

Mary started at the school soon after her interview. It is well documented that she was very shy and self-conscious throughout her life. We can perhaps imagine the dread she felt facing the first day at her new school. The outgoing and gregarious personality that later emerged hid a deeply insecure person; she would have been terrified at the prospect of meeting this group of unknown classmates.

The stop for the number 97 bus was just outside Mary's flat. She boarded this bus and left it when it reached the Plough Inn across the road from the school. Sister Stanislaus met her outside the chapel and led her up to the classroom on the first floor. Miss Regamey, the class teacher, stood at the door waiting to greet her. As she looked into the room, she saw the girls sitting in straight rows, neat in their white shirts, ties and gymslips; their hair brushed and tied up in pig tails. The desks were the wooden kind with a lid that could be lifted up to keep books inside. Thirty pairs of eyes looked back at her, curious, expectant. A

---

56 Yvonne Messenger, former pupil of St Anne's Convent School for Girls: interview with author

blush started to crawl up through her chest and her face, her cheeks were on fire.

**FIGURE 2.2 CLASSROOM IN ST ANNE'S CONVENT
(FROM STEVECANN.CO.UK_FILES)**

The class teacher sat Mary next to a striking, willowy, sporty-looking girl with dark curly hair. This was Eileen O'Leary, who Mary would come to know well.

Eileen recalls Mary as being a short, well-built girl, covered in freckles, with her red hair cut short in a boyish style and wire-rimmed National Health spectacles perched on her nose. Her first impression was that Mary was shy and almost introverted. In fact, she later described her as 'not at all outgoing, and sometimes distant in many respects, nothing like her new persona of later years.'[57]

Until recently, Mary's red hair had fallen in ringlets down to her waist. but the daily ritual of brushing it to take out the tangles had become such a chore that she decided to have it cut off. Now, though, it was so short and shaved into a point at the back that it made her look boyish,

---

57 Eileen O'Leary, former pupil of St Anne's Convent School for Girls: email to author

and she felt even worse. Her new school uniform was huge on her as her mother, of course, had insisted on buying a size too big so she could grow into it, and the shapeless gymslip swamped her. The velour hat, with its wide band, was just awful, but Mary soon learned that, for fear of being seen by one of the nuns or a prefect, she had to keep it on within a mile or two of the school. After that, she could throw caution to the wind, pluck the hated hat from her head and stuff it into her schoolbag. Anyone caught without a hat earned several black marks for her house and had to write out 'I must wear my hat at all times' a few hundred times. It didn't stop her though, and whenever she had the chance, the hat came off.

Mary went for lunch. School dinners were given very mixed reviews by the girls at St Anne's. The food, thick lumpy gravy that congealed on the plate, mashed potatoes that still had hard lumps and vegetables boiled so hard that all the goodness had left them, was generally hated. Dinners were sometimes known as YMCA (yesterday's muck cooked again) or, in more polite terms, yesterday's menu cooked again. Some girls loved the puddings and if it was apricot tart, would have three or four helpings of them. They volunteered to do the washing up for the whole dining room just to get extra pudding. Two nuns, Sister Mary of Lourdes and Sister Ignatius, were responsible for the school meals.

The School

The school Mary found herself in was a 17th Century mansion which, after a series of eminent owners had been taken over by the Sisters of Charity of St. Jeanne Antide Thouret in 1903. The nuns fully utilised every scrap of space. The chemistry lab was tucked away at the top of a steep staircase. This gave access to the attic and onto the roof where the spectacular views encouraged almost every girl in the school to climb out there at some time even though it was strictly against the rules. On the ground floor along with the chapel and the gym, there was a small parlour where the Mother Superior entertained visitors. The first floor housed the library and most of the classrooms.

Under the building the cellars – used as air raid shelters during the war - were also out of bounds but curiosity drew generations of girls to explore them. There were stories of tunnels that ran under the buildings and legend had it that a tunnel led to the Plough Inn across the road and that Dick Turpin had used it to escape to London!

Outside there was a strange hexagonal little building that looked like a temple. It was known that Alexander Pope, who many years before had been a frequent visitor, used it as a retreat.

At the end of Mary's first day at school, she took all the books she'd been given, put them into her bag and escaped. On her way home she saw quite a few St Anne's girls on the bus. Two of them left the bus at her stop. Cecelia and Angela Trasler were sisters, after that they often travelled to school together.

Now whenever she arrived at school Mary first went to morning assembly. She lined up outside the gym with the other girls from her form, waiting to take their places. Prefects were there to ensure the girls went into assembly in an orderly fashion. The gym didn't have a stage then, so to address the pupils and be visible, the speaker had to stand on an upturned bench. Sister Stanislaus would sweep into the room in her flowing black robes and step up onto the bench to take the assembly. She conducted prayers for the day, and a hymn followed. Then came news of the school houses. Mary had been assigned to St Jeanne Antide's, whose recent performance had been quite bad, with many black marks.

A week after her start at the school, Mass was celebrated in the newly decorated chapel. This was an oasis of quiet and peace; with cherubs painted on the ceiling, and huge French windows along one side that looked out through the colonnade to the school playground beyond. It had been redecorated during the holidays. Bright fresh smells and clean lines made it very welcoming. It was the domain of Sister Giocondina, a tiny little and incredibly old nun who had been at the convent forever. She took care of the chapel and spent most of her life dusting and polishing. Sometimes, when she struggled to get into a corner to dust, she would go out into the playground and grab a couple of pupils to help her.

Mary could only watch and listen while the choir sang, hoping to be able to join them soon. Singing was her whole life and she thrilled to the sound of the voices. Miss Asquith, a brilliant teacher and pianist, had taken over full-time as the music mistress early in 1951. She also led the choir, and she instructed the girls in an extensive repertoire of both secular songs and religious works in Latin. They sang at Midnight Mass, on Easter Sunday and all the major feasts, and learned a wide range of pieces, some of them very technical, such as Bartok and Mendelssohn. She taught them phrasing and the rules that govern the way notes combine to create the harmonies.

St Anne's was at the heart of Little Ealing, and the choir was at its centre. The girls who joined could have a break from school work and study and were given the chance to learn about teamwork, cooperation and discipline, while still having fun. Rehearsals were intense, but the girls were there because they loved music and they loved performing, and they gave their time willingly, rehearsing whenever they could. This commitment to the choir was huge, but the returns from it were more than just the pleasure of performing. The choir was respected, not just in the school, but also in the community.

Mary joined the school after the summer holidays in 1951, she slowly started to get to know the other girls in her class. Kathleen Malone (Kate Davies) was one and, of course, Eileen O'Leary, who sat next to her. But, when she joined the choir, her confidence was boosted by the realisation that as a member, she was part of a group that worked together with a single aim. When the senior choir took part in the Catholic Schools' Concert held at the Royal Albert Hall, Mary was a member of the junior choir so wasn't able to join them. At that time, she sang Benediction on Friday afternoons with them and Mass on all the feasts of Our Lady. The choirs sang for the Alexian Brothers at Twyford Abbey, at robing ceremonies, at the school prizegiving and in performances at the annual music concert, when they sang secular songs. Mary sang third voice – contralto – with Eileen; she was brilliant at harmonising. The girls enjoyed singing together in harmony. When she learned of Mary's death, many years later, Eileen recalled their time in the choir:

It was early afternoon. Very suddenly, I experienced an enormous blast of cold air and in a flash, I was transported back to school [...] Mary was sitting on a radiator strumming her guitar [...] Then we were singing in the choir again, the daffodils and 'Panis Angelicus' came into my head. Then I was looking for her to go onto the netball court (I was co-games captain) and she was always trying to avoid this. [58]

Jean and Angela

Mary met Jean and Angela when she joined the choir. The three girls became fast friends – they shared a joy in music and a love of the absurd, and they developed a bond that would last all through their years at school together, and beyond. Mary realised that her friends' love of music matched hers, and they were soon making plans to perform together in school concerts.

A lot of interesting information about Angela's family can be found in Chris Patten's book, 'First Confessions'. Angela's father, Frank Patten, was a jazz musician so perhaps her interest in music was no surprise. Born in 1909, he had learned to play the violin, at school, but then was seduced by the allure of the drums instead. Rather than taking his place at Manchester University, he joined a dance band that played gigs on the Isle of Man in the summer and travelled round the country the rest of the year.

Angela's mother, Joan Angel, was a very beautiful woman who loved her nickname, Bella. Born in 1915 in Exeter, she took up amateur dramatics as a young woman and was given favourable mentions in national publications like *The Stage*. She was even offered a place in their troupe by a professional repertory company, the Malvern Players. As with Mary's mother and the acting career she dreamed of, her parents refused to allow it. Bella was engaged to the son of a well-off business man, but then she went to a dance where she met and fell in love with the Irish Catholic drummer, Angela's father. She then abandoned her parents' religious views and became a Roman Catholic.

Like Mary, Angela was born in 1939. Her father went to war as an RAF officer in the Middle East. Afterwards he began using his contacts in the music business to get a job with a publisher of popular sheet music in Tin Pan Alley. This was London's West End; Bella always called it 'in town'. Frank bought a new house in Greenford and moved the family to London.

---

58 Eileen O'Leary, former pupil of St Anne's Convent School for Girls: email to author

Angela used to walk her brother to school when he was small. It was just over a mile and took half an hour. They went down an alley opposite the house, beside the playing field of Greenford Grammar School. In summer the wire fence on one side was covered in poisonous black berries. Angela told her brother it was smeared on the tips of arrows to make them certain killers, Roman Emperors used it to murder their opponents. She would pretend to eat a few of its berries and then do a Sarah Bernhardt death scene in the alley, a regular piece of dramatic acting which never failed to terrify her nervous brother. Theirs was a happy childhood.

Angela's father used to take singers and their agents to some of the best restaurants in the West End, hoping they would perform the songs he was publishing. Guy Mitchell was a successful American pop singer in the 1950's; Mary performed with him when she joined the Lana Sisters many years later. Possibly the quality of the starters at L'Epicure persuaded the American singer to record 'She Wears Red Feathers (and a Hula Hula Skirt)'. The song went to number one in the UK singles chart in March 1953 and stayed there for four weeks.[59]

The little that is known about the third member of the group of friends, Jean MacDonald, and her background, has been gleaned from the pages of the school magazines. She was very clever, a pretty, petite girl who was enthusiastically involved in the many activities of the school.

~

The Convent

There were lots of nuns at the convent and they had a variety of responsibilities. Some taught in the secondary school, some in the kindergarten and junior school, some supervised in the playground, some produced meals, and there were others that the pupils saw little of who, were responsible for keeping their convent running.

Most of the nuns were lovely, like Sister Stanislaus, but some of them could be quite unkind. Not just strict, they could be harsh and sarcastic when they spoke to the girls. Many of them were from southern Ireland, where families were often large and parents expected at least one of

---

59 Christopher Patten (2017) *First Confessions*, London, pp. 29–30

their children to embrace the Church in some way. For these girls it meant that they were forced into convent life. The girls weren't caned, but other severe punishments were employed: once, a girl was ordered to polish a floor.

Nuns could normally be heard before they were seen, their rosary beads clattered together so that the girls knew when they were approaching. But there was one nun who would scoop up her beads and hold them tight to her body so that she could creep silently up to the girls, in the hope of catching them out in some misdemeanour. Another nun might suddenly appear on the bus on the way home from school; she was there to check that the girls were wearing their hats.

~

The Teachers

Miss Cheriton taught both geography and history. Geography could be a dull subject and must have seemed far removed from anything of interest to the young girls at St Anne's. But the geography mistress brought the subject alive, and Mary quickly realised geography meant learning about distant countries and discovering exciting and diverse cultures. When she thought of the possibility of travelling to these exotic places, the subject suddenly came alive.

Miss Cheriton was a small, neat lady encased in an immaculate tweed suit – the uniform for spinsters of that time. This energetic and bubbly teacher was universally liked by the girls, and she loved them in return. She would bounce into the classroom full of enthusiasm for the morning's activities. The sight of her must have been a shock for Mary. Miss Cheriton was deaf and her hearing aid was a bizarre contraption. She kept her hair in a short bob, and a band across her head took the hair off her forehead. At either side was a huge trumpet, probably made of horn, with a tube going right into her ears. This was astonishing and unlike anything Mary is likely to have seen before. Believing they could take advantage of her deafness, the girls would sometimes act up, and although they tried not to let her see it, she somehow knew what was happening. Even with her back to them at the blackboard, she would spin round and if she thought somebody was being really naughty, talking, whispering or not paying attention, she threw a piece of chalk at them – she was a good shot.

Miss Larkin was an Irish English teacher who while not unpleasant, spoke with a very strong Irish accent, with a very harsh tone to her voice. The class studied Jane Austen in English Literature. Describing her schooldays later Mary would recall:

> I liked history and geography and French and English grammar. I struggled through to GCE, but I got a hate on about English because the book they gave me to read was Mansfield Park, which I didn't like. I was too wrapped up in Budd Schulberg. [60]

Mary possibly regarded the conservatism of a book like Mansfield Park, with its 18th-century mores, as too restrained and genteel. She was fascinated by the more edgy writing of Budd Schulberg, particularly his caustic novel *What Makes Sammy Run?*. This novel was inspired by the life of his father, the early Hollywood mogul B. P. Schulberg. The rags-to-riches story details the rise and fall of Sammy Glick, a Jewish boy born in New York's Lower East Side, and portrays the dog-eat-dog world where Sammy grew up.

~

Games

St Anne's culture of games included hockey, netball and tennis, but Mary had little interest in such things. She joined neither the netball nor tennis teams, but with hockey she had no choice: everyone had to take part, and she was no exception. It was played in winter, when the weather was always grim; the girls all hated it, but they could only be excused if they were really ill. On Friday afternoons they were made to walk the mile and a half to Gunnersbury Park, where Mary recalls being made to run around the wintry field, fingers blue and stuck to her hockey stick, and hearing the whistle blowing and shouts of encouragement from the teacher. Hockey was muddy, painful and ice cold, but somehow, in spite of her dread of the sport, in 1953 Mary was persuaded to play for the school as part of the First XI. She can be seen in Figure 2.3 grinning in the team photo from the 1954 school magazine.

---

60 Alan Smith (15 July 1966) 'Dusty Goes Back to Own Childhood', *New Musical Express*.

FIGURE 2.3 MARY AS PART OF THE HOCKEY TEAM, FAR LEFT ON THE FRONT ROW
(ST ANNE'S SCHOOL MAGAZINE)

The St Anne's school magazine of 1954/55 reported of hockey:

Last spring, we were not very successful, partly due to the weather and to the distance of the fields from the school. When we did manage to have practices, they were good ones and we are very grateful to Mrs Bradshawe for her patience. Many of us were very sorry to hear when we came back to school in September that Sister Stanislaus had decided to discontinue hockey for this year. [61]

It is easy to believe that Mary was relieved to hear this news.

~

School Life

Mary's first full year at St Anne's began on 15 January 1952. While 1951 was a transformative year for Mary – leaving Sands, arriving in Ealing and starting at this school – 1952 would also be a year of massive

---

61 St Anne's school magazine, 1954.

upheaval, both for Mary and the country. The year was marked by the death of King George VI, on 3 February, and the start of a new Elizabethan Age. On 8 February 1952, Princess Elizabeth was formally proclaimed Queen at a ceremony in St James's Palace, London. Girls were given time off school to attend the King's funeral on 15 February.

Faith

Mary's entire life was now informed by her Catholic faith. With parents who were deeply devout Catholics, church discipline filled Mary's life, both at home and at school. It seemed that the local priest was an almost permanent fixture in Kent Gardens, and Mary would often arrive home to find him there, taking tea with her mother. The jolly atmosphere led her to wonder if Kay's cup contained nothing more than tea. [62]

Confirmation

When the time came for Mary's confirmation, her most immediate task was to choose a suitable name. This would be a patron saint who would be a friend in heaven, someone to model herself after and rely on for prayers. Assisted by her mother, and maybe the priest too, Mary chose the name Bernadette, as her birthday, 16 April, was the anniversary of the date St Bernadette of Lourdes died. It was an obvious choice as a confirmation name for Mary: her long list of saints' names now included Bernadette.

Bernadette Soubirous was 14 when she first saw apparitions of a young woman (the Virgin Mary) who asked for a chapel to be built at the grotto at Massabielle. Lourdes has become a famous place of pilgrimage for those seeking healing. On 8 December 1933, Pope Pius XI declared Bernadette Soubirous a Saint of the Catholic Church. Her feast day was fixed for 18 February, the day her Lady promised to make her happy, not in this life, but in the next.

At the ceremony Mary watched as her peers went through the process of confirmation. When it was her turn, she was shocked by the strength of the slap from the bishop. She felt the sting from his fingers on her face long after the smack that sealed her with the Holy Spirit and made her into 'Soldiers of Christ'. The slap was symbolic and intended to

---

62 Penny Valentine and Vicki Wickham (2000) *Dancing with Demons*, London, p. 22.

remind her that she might be required to suffer hardship, torture and even death in defence of the faith. She did wonder why it had to hurt quite so much, though.

Mary wore a white dress and veil for the ceremony and sat together with her fellow pupils at the front of the church. The process for each child was short, but the fact that many children in the parish were 'done' on the same day, made it a long morning in church.

After the ceremony, the children were each given a confirmation medal and took pride in their status as a Soldier of Christ. From then on, a favourite hymn was 'Faith of Our Fathers'. Mary's confirmation present from her parents was a book about St Bernadette. *The Song of Bernadette* by Franz Werfel tells the story of St Bernadette and her reported 18 visions of the Blessed Virgin Mary in Lourdes, between February and July 1858. Mary and her mother are sure to have seen the 1943 film, starring Jennifer Jones, on the life of St Bernadette.

Throughout her life Mary's favourite colours were violet and rose. It is interesting to note that in Catholic Churches these are the colours for the Advent candles, they correspond with the colours of the liturgical vestments for the Sundays of Advent.

Lent

Lent was the next event in the Catholic calendar. In 1952 it began with Ash Wednesday on 27 February. St Patrick's Day fell in the middle of this period of self-denial and atonement. The school celebrated with the traditional Irish v English netball matches. St Patrick's Day was light-hearted fun, with everyone in fancy dress. Mary, of course, played for Ireland. The Polish girls could choose which team to play for.

A few days later Father Agius came to the school to give a talk on Fátima. The whole school were assembled in the gym hall to listen as he told them the complex details of the apparitions and their significance. The following year, a dramatisation of these events was directed by him in the newly built school hall.

May Day Procession

Next came arrangements for the May Day procession. Sister Stanislaus announced the details at assembly. All the pupils in the school took part, from the babies in the nursery class to the girls in form VI, young women ready to make their way in the world. The girls dressed in their summer uniform, now wearing boaters.

This year the May Queen was Neelia Roberts. Dressed in white robes to signify the purity of her role she led the procession, eyes lowered, head bowed and hands clasped. A boy from the Prep class had been chosen to carry the crown of flowers and walked in front with it carefully balanced on a cushion. Two more boys had the task of supporting the May Queen's train. They moved off slowly and with great ceremony. Snaking through the grounds, the column made its way out through the main gate and onto the roads close by the school. All the while they sang 'Ave, Ave, Ave Maria...', their voices raised in praise of the Virgin Mary. Following the streets surrounding the school they came back into the school grounds through the rear gate.

They continued to praise the Lord with their liturgy as they made their way to the lawn in front of the school. The little ones sat on the grass with their legs crossed. The older girls, gathered under the portico and watched as the May Queen took the crown of flowers and stepped forward to place it on the statue of Our Lady.

FIGURE 2.4 GATHERED ON THE LAWN FOR MAY DAY
(FROM STEVECANN.CO.UK_FILES)

School Bazaar

The school bazaar and garden party took place on 12 July. The weather was dismal but, in spite of this, the fete was a success, with 1,400 visitors enjoying a varied selection of goods to buy, games to play, and competitions to enter. The Reverend Mother, who had flown in from Rome a few days before, bought something from every stall. Entertainment included a presentation of excerpts from Alice in Wonderland by some of the young children and a puppet show by one child's parents. A dance in the evening rounded off the day, which raised £350 to add to the St Anne's Building Fund.

Each year the school held a dancing and skipping display. This was such a big event in the school calendar that most years Ealing Town Hall was hired to accommodate it. Miss Lehman, the gym teacher, instructed the girls in dancing, and she prepared them well. The shows were always of a high standard. But this teacher wasn't very popular, she made no allowance for anyone who might make a mistake, and could be verbally abusive. Mary had no choice but to take part; every girl had to do her bit. The girls rehearsed for two days before the performance. Lined up for the skipping display, with long ropes and, arms akimbo, the girls danced and balanced to music in a very ladylike manner. Jumping into the spinning ropes and keeping in time with the music was fairly easy to do and it looked good. They were well taught and were very well synchronised. These were always great shows. As the Reverend Mother wasn't able to attend the Town Hall, a special display was performed in the playground for her and her assistant, Sister Jeanne Antide.

~

Rosary Rally, July 1952

In the summer of 1952, the Reverend Patrick Peyton spent 18 weeks in Britain conducting his Family Rosary Crusade. Huge crowds gathered to hear him speak at rallies held throughout the UK. The triumphant final Rosary Rally was held in Wembley Stadium. This included a mime of the Mysteries of the Rosary and a Living Rosary performed by children drawn from local schools and colleges.

The pupils from St Anne's had followed Father Peyton's progress on a map from the time he arrived in London, and Mary and her parents were among the 83,000 people in attendance at this final rally – the maximum number allowed in the stadium when women and children were present.

The band of the Irish Guards played for an hour, while the stadium filled. People arriving were met by street vendors peddling their souvenirs, merchandise and literature: the *Sunday Graphic* was on sale with a special Rosary Edition; the *Sunday Dispatch* printed a long article by Father Peyton; and *Picture Post* had photographs and text. The miming of the Rosary began promptly at three o'clock and continued for an hour and a half. This day was cold, unlike the warmth of the previous day, and the muslin-clad performers suffered the effects of the chilly wind. A spoken commentary from the works of Catholic authors was broadcast over the public-address system by a priest who announced the successive Mysteries. As this mime of the 15 Mysteries of the Rosary proceeded, the Living Rosary – comprising 2,000 performers, including 30 pupils from St Anne's – slowly materialised.

Earlier that year the pupils of St Anne's had heard the story of Fátima from Father Agius. They were told that the apparition of the Virgin Mary in Fátima had issued this warning: 'If Russia is not consecrated, it will spread its errors throughout the world.' Peyton often repeated this. Conscious of the political nature of his crusade, he once said in a radio broadcast, 'The Rosary is the offensive weapon that will destroy Communism — the great evil that seeks to destroy the faith.'

The politicisation of the Crusade went further, and by 1959 the CIA had started to secretly fund Father Peyton's Crusade as a weapon of devotion to fight Communism during the Cold War. They paid for advertising, promotion and events, with Brazil a particular focus of the strategy. 'I consider the Crusades in Latin America throughout the decade of the sixties as the most significant and the most effective,' Peyton said. However, his superiors were not pleased by the secret funding, and when the matter was brought to the attention of the Vatican, Pope Paul VI ordered Peyton to stop.

The summer holidays began a few days after the Rosary Rally, and the girls took off in many directions to enjoy the time with their families.

Winter Term, 1952

School started again on 17 September and Mary moved into the third form. The move to St Anne's had been hard for her, but she had developed close bonds with Jean and Angela; their shared love of music and singing had brought them together. She was more at ease now and beginning to enjoy herself. Mary always took her guitar with her to school, and the trio performed whenever they had the chance. They were keen to take part in the school concerts, in particular the Sister Stanislaus Feast Day Concert.

Former pupils remember Angela and Jean as pretty girls, and those who speak of Mary recall her engaging personality and ready grin. Whenever the three friends were seen together in the corridor, she was definitely the leader, the one that everyone noticed first. Yvonne Messenger, a former pupil, recalls:

> *We all remember Mary as an outgoing fun-loving girl, singing and playing her guitar whenever there was an opportunity, and there were opportunities at school. Anyone with talent to entertain was co-opted for the annual November 13 concert or end-of-term activities.* [63]

~

School Hall Opening – 6 June 1953

Sister Stanislaus was convinced of the benefits a new school hall would bring, she persuaded the school board of them. The whole school community was involved in the fund-raising activities. In January of coronation year, they put on a production of Rumpelstiltskin, adapted from Grimm's fairy tales, to help to raise the sums needed. The story was written and produced by Mr Windscheffel, the father of three pupils. Mary had a small part in this her first school production; she played a dwarf. Pupils made the scenery under the direction of Mrs Scott, the art mistress, and the sisters made the costumes. Miss Lehman taught dance to the girls and Mr Parfrey set the songs to music at the piano.

All the pupils, Mary included, found ways to earn small amounts of money to add to the Building Fund. They went carol singing or did odd jobs in the neighbourhood. All of the contributions, small and large, were added to the pot until finally, there was enough money to finance the building of the school hall. During Mary's time at the school, it was

---

63 Yvonne Messenger, former pupil of St Anne's School: interview with author

always in need of repair and upgrading; regular requests went out to the parents to help top up the building fund.

Preparations for the official opening began. Eleven months earlier the site had been a desolate waste. Thanks to the efforts of the architect, Colonel Dixon-Spain, and Sister Stanislaus, the hall had been erected in double-quick time. St Anne's would now be able to put on all its shows in its own hall, with seats for 400, a proper stage, fronted with walnut, and acoustically conditioned walls. The two dressing rooms were each fitted with a hand basin and constant supply of hot and cold water. In the extension, the cloakrooms were provided with similar fittings.

The opening was marked by the celebration of High Mass, presided over by His Eminence Cardinal Griffin; Mary was a member of the choir. The hall had been dressed with flowers; their scent mingled with the distinctive smell of new paint.

All the pupils and many of the parents attended on this sunny and warm day. Thankfully there was a cool breeze which blew fresh air into the hall. The Guides formed a guard of honour for the Cardinal at the entrance to the hall, and the solemn procession entered – His Eminence, followed by his entourage of deacons and sub-deacons holding his long crimson cape aloft, and Sister Stanislaus bringing up the rear – as the choir sang Elgar's Majestic 'Ecce Sacerdos Magnus'. This was a celebration of the new hall, just as the whole nation had celebrated the coronation of the new Queen, Elizabeth II, a few days before. But this coronation year also had a special meaning for St Anne's Convent: it was 50 years since its founding. At the luncheon that followed the Cardinal proposed the loyal toast.

~

The Story of Fátima

Sister Stanislaus had promised that the first public performance in this state-of-the-art hall would be the story of the miracle of Fátima. This dramatisation of the events in the little Portuguese parish of Fátima 30 years previously was prepared and produced by Father Agius of St Benedict's Priory. Father Agius had visited Fátima and spent some time with the parents of the three children concerned, and his first-hand commentary added to the interest of the production at which a large audience of parents and friends were present.

Mary O'Brien was one of four girls who formed a small choir trained and accompanied by Miss Arnold. They sang several hymns, including the Fátima hymn, for the assembled congregation who joined in the chorus.

The three Portuguese children were tending a flock of sheep outside the tiny village of Fátima, during the First World War when they first saw the angel. He was transparent, they said, and shining like a crystal. The angel, who identified himself as the "Angel of Peace" and "Guardian Angel of Portugal", taught them prayers, to make sacrifices, and to spend time in adoration of the Lord.

In the spring of 1917, something more extraordinary began to happen - visions that would put the three children on the path to sainthood and transform Fátima from an ordinary village to the site of a Catholic shrine, venerated and visited by millions.

The prophecy reported by the children related to secrets; the first of these told of the end of World War I and the beginning of World War II, as well as possibly more World Wars in the future. The second was to do with the rise and fall of Soviet Communism. The original apparitions took place during the six months preceding the Bolshevik revolution in Russia, and supposedly the Lady talked to the children about the need to pray for Russia. These apparitions at Fátima were officially declared worthy of belief by the Catholic Church in 1930.

The third secret was written down by Sister Lucia and delivered to the Bishop of Leiria in 1944. Mary can never have known it as it was revealed 13 May 2000, after she had died. The Vatican described this secret as a vision of the 1981 assassination attempt on Pope John Paul II.

The activities of the school seem rooted in the wider geo-political world; in the description of Fátima and with Father Peyton, the Rosary Rally and his involvement with the CIA.

~

Novitiate

Now fully confirmed in her faith, Mary considered a further step. She had often witnessed robing ceremonies at her school: deeply moving occasions when one of her fellows made the commitment to take the veil and give her life to Christ. Mary regularly sang at these rituals as part of the school choir and it was a step that she also considered taking.

Mary's decision was perhaps influenced by the discovery that her screen idol, June Haver, was intent on leaving Hollywood to take holy orders and become a nun.

Junie Stovenour was just a kid in Rock Island when Rudy Vallee predicted she would grow up to be a famous singer. She was already emceeing a radio show called 'Juvenile Theatre' and had sung with famous bands when they visited her home town. Soon Junie changed her last name to Haver and became one of Hollywood's best-known stars.

Mary's first encounter with June Haver was as a shimmering blonde goddess. She was already well-established in a contract with 20th Century Fox and earning $3,500 a week. Mary searched for June's story in the pages of her movie magazines and found much more. When still just a teenager, June had been signed to sing with Ted Fio Rito's band. She went to the beauty salon, got a fancy hairdo and – Hey presto! – she was changed from a cute bobby-soxer to a glamour girl. Her rise to the top was incredibly fast, going from a $75-a-week job with the band to her golden Hollywood contract.

Mary and her mother saw almost all the 20th Century Fox musicals that starred June Haver, from 'I Wonder Who's Kissing Her Now' in 1947 to 'The Girl Next Door' in 1953. Mary's fierce ambition to be a famous singer and dancer started then.

In 1966 she recalled:

I used to love the pictures. I was brought up on the pictures. I was brought up on 20th Century Fox musicals. June Haver was my idol and I always dreamed of being like her and dancing and singing my way through a wonderful world of music and Technicolor.[64]

Mary read about how June's fiancé, John Duzik, a dentist, died suddenly as a result of haemophilia during an ulcer operation in 1949. After that, she spent more and more time in Catholic charity work and her Catholic faith deepened. In the summer of 1950, she went on a

---

64 Alan Smith, 'Dusty Goes Back to Own Childhood', *New Musical Express* (15 July 1966).

pilgrimage to Jerusalem and Rome, where she had an audience with the Pope. Movie magazines gave Mary a direct line to her idol, and she read how, during the filming of 'The Girl Next Door', June fell and injured her back doing a dance routine on a whirling table. She wasn't able to work for months after that, and in February 1953 announced her plan to leave Hollywood and begin preparations to become a nun.

Stunned by the realisation that the strength of June's faith was such that she was prepared to abandon her fabulous career to take vows as a nun, Mary was thrown into confusion: what would her response to this have been? Mary craved a career as an entertainer, just like her idol. But when she learned about June Haver's decision, she began to question whether it would be the right step for her.

She wrote later:

There was even a short time when I seriously considered becoming a nun. One day I went to visit a novitiate. I thought it was a really inspiring place, but when I started to grow up, my ideas changed. It wasn't only that I became so absorbed in music, I just felt that I didn't have the strength of character to lead that sort of life.[65]

Reflecting on this life of abstinence and what it would mean for her, and with all that was happening in her life – her love of singing, her burning desire to be a star and her growing awareness of her own sexuality – she knew this would not be the right path for her.

~

Twyford Abbey

On 8 December 1954, Mary was part of the choir that set out by coach for Twyford Abbey. The girls were accustomed to their travels being fraught with incidents, but on this day, London had been hit by a tornado. It tore the roof off the underground station at Gunnersbury and ripped down walls in Acton. However, they pushed on through the storm; the sky was lit by brilliant flashes of lightning while rain and hail smashed against the coach windows

The previous December Pope Pius XII had ordered the Marian Year – a year devoted to glorifying Mary Mother of God. Throughout the world

---

65 Dusty Springfield, 'Fame has a Flipside too', *Woman's Own* 1965 in Dusty Springfield Bulletin No. 65 July 2008.

there were Marian initiatives in abundance, and at St Anne's the choir sang Mass on all the feasts of Our Lady. Now the choir had prepared some sacred songs to sing for the Alexian Brothers: 'Panis Angelicus' and 'Cum Jubilato' were chosen for the Mass.

The coach turned in through the gates and drove past the lodge at the entrance of the drive. The Abbey, just visible through the trees at the end of the avenue, was a striking building in the Gothic style. The setting, between landscaped gardens on one side and a walled garden on the other, was incredible. Inside the ceilings were painted with religious scenes, the stained-glass windows let in a dappled light and the bells could be heard ringing in celebration.

This occasion celebrating Mass with the Alexian Brothers was particularly poignant for Mary as it was the last time she would sing with the choir at the Abbey. To be part of Mass in these special surroundings was a joy for her; the Alexian Brothers always gave the choir a warm welcome, and a particular pleasure of these trips was the generous banquet laid on for them once their performance was over. Growing girls were always hungry and food was an important part of school life.

~

Mary's Musical Heroes

Mary had found her song-and-dance heroes in 20th Century Fox movies: people like Judy Garland, Betty Grable and June Haver. She spent hours scouring through the latest copy of her film magazine each week, searching for every scrap of information she could find about her heroines. Over the years her collection of these magazines grew and they were stored in an old tin trunk under her bed, with her parents given strict instructions to never throw any of them away.

Mary's favourite singers, at that time – Judy Garland, Peggy Lee and Ella Fitzgerald – all had one thing in common, their singing careers began when they were very young.

Judy Garland was a child star, first performing onstage at just two and a half years of age. At seven she toured the vaudeville circuit with her sisters as the Gumm Sisters, and when she was 13 she was signed by MGM. Her best-known role, as Dorothy in 'The Wizard of Oz', came in 1938, when she was 16.

Peggy Lee was seventh in a family of eight children and just four when her mother died. Her loving but alcoholic father quickly remarried. Her stepmother treated her with great cruelty, and her father was unable to stop it. She developed her musical talent and took several part-time jobs so that she could get away from home to escape the abuse of her stepmother. Both during and after her high school years, she earned small amounts of money, singing on local radio stations.

Mary later recalled:

When I was growing up, I had a gigantic crush on Peggy Lee's voice, I thought it was the coolest thing I'd ever heard: very sultry and laid back. I wanted to sound that way but never quite could. [66]

Ella Fitzgerald's story was just as desperate. She had a troubled childhood and at first wanted to be a dancer. However, when she was 17 she entered an amateur contest at Harlem's Apollo Theatre and won the first prize of US $25.00. This was her earliest and most important singing performance.

In the hours she spent listening to the radio, Mary discovered more musical heroes, and one in particular. She was listening to the Home Service one Saturday when she heard an unknown voice that made her exclaim 'Who is *that*?'. Nothing would ever be the same for Mary again. The tone, not even remotely like any other, the rhythm, the swing – it was a knock out. This was Jo Stafford, and Mary was blown away when she heard her for the first time. One track played that morning was 'I'll Never Smile Again'. Singing a capella, the Pied Pipers, led by Jo, sang with Frank Sinatra. And there, again, was that tone, shaping the chords that the group's four voices made together. It almost seemed that she wasn't singing at all; as if she just opened her mouth and her beautiful voice emerged. Sinatra's contribution to the record was great, of course, but the real impression Mary was left with came from Jo Stafford.

After that, Mary was determined to discover everything she could about this incredible singer. What was it that made her sound so special? Maybe it was her sense of pitch, the way she projected with hardly any vibrato, her breath control or her phrasing. In effect it was all of these things: the whole package. She had virtually perfect pitch, with

---

66 Brant Mewborn, 'Dusty Springs Back', *Rolling Stone*, After Dark (June 1978).

a beautifully clear and cool style and a unique vocal colour to warm it up. Everything she sang appeared effortless, and her wide range of styles included the blues, pop, jazz, country, comedy, folk and spiritual. She also recorded popular duets with Frankie Laine and Gordon MacRae, and the hillbilly song 'Tim-Tay-Shun' with Red Ingle. Jo Stafford performed this incredible range with ease, and her breadth of ability and styles was something that Mary would later seek to emulate.

Jo released 'You Belong to Me', in 1952. It was a number one record with a tour de force performance. The first song by a female singer to top the chart in the UK, it was Jo's biggest hit. In its famous introduction, she vocalised the lead part in the trombone choir. In 1954 she was presented with a diamond-studded plaque to mark 25 million record sales. Later, her 1960 comedy records as Darlene Edwards would earn her a Grammy Award.

Mary's transistor radio was her lifeline, with Radio Luxembourg and British Forces Network essential listening. She was driven mad as she fiddled with the dials and searched through the static and noise in her attempts to tune into the station. Jo Stafford had a regular programme on Radio Luxembourg: 'Time for a Song' was broadcast at 6.30pm every Sunday. She played top British wartime acts, such as Ted Heath, Anne Shelton and Vera Lynn, and Mary heard the music of Stan Kenton, Louis Armstrong and Duke Ellington, among others. Jo included some of her own songs in a random mix of artists, talked about the records and gave some Hollywood news. Another regular feature on Radio Luxembourg was 'Hollywood Calling!', which introduced the stars of MGM. Mary was fascinated by film stars, so a programme that gossiped about them was essential listening.

Jo Stafford also hosted programmes on Voice of America. Searching through her movie magazines for more information about Jo, Mary read that she described herself as 'a short, hungry dumpling in horn-rimmed spectacles'. It was a description that Mary could identify with; it could just as easily apply to her. She was surely encouraged by the thought that, if Jo Stafford could make it as a singer, so could she. In another interesting twist of fate Jo converted to Catholicism before her marriage in 1954, to her musical director, Paul Weston.

Once she discovered Jo Stafford, Mary played her records and listened to her on the radio constantly. She wanted to learn more about Jo's full rich voice and how she produced it. Through singing in the choir and performing in school concerts, Mary's voice had begun to develop and mature, and now she wanted to expand her understanding of the technical side. It is likely that Jo spoke about the book she had written on singing technique. *Easy Lessons in Singing* was published in America in 1951. Foyles bookshop, in Charing Cross, was listed in the school magazine, and it's likely that if Mary was to find a copy, she will have gone there to make enquiries and perhaps place an order. The book gave helpful advice on correct breathing, singing in tune, good diction, finding an individual style, group singing, microphone technique and how to interpret a song, as well as advice on personal appearance.

Meanwhile, Dion's influence on Mary's musical development was immense. His natural ability allowed him to play both piano and guitar by ear. He had bought Mary her first guitar and taught her some simple chords. The siblings started making music together when they were very young, using a range of homemade instruments: a cigar box filled with marbles, a battered old copper frying pan, a cracked pair of maracas. Their father helped out by recording their efforts on an old tape recorder so that they could play them back and analyse their performances. Both were lovers of Latin American music and they would jam together, Dion on guitar and piano and Mary providing percussion using hairbrushes, milk bottles, saucepans, and even a coal scuttle.[67] The siblings made use of their father's skills with electronics when he set up a broadcast system for them. Neighbours were invited to come in to hear them play: they performed in the kitchen while the performance was relayed through a loudspeaker into the sitting room. Later, when Mary entered a talent contest in Ealing, Dion played the piano for her as she sang Judy Garland songs from Easter Parade that she had slavishly copied – numbers like 'I Love a Piano' and 'When the Midnight Choo Choo Leaves for Alabam'.[68] They even made little 78 demo records of these songs when she was young.[69]

Kay and OB were bemused and gratified to know that their children expressed their love of music in their desire to play and perform. They

---

67 Peter Jones, 'We're Catching up America', *Record Mirror* (9 November 1963).

68 Alan Smith, 'Chart Topper Dusty Left Holding the Monkey!', *New Musical Express* (22 April 1966).

69 Just Dusty: The Real Dusty Springfield (DVD), Odeon Entertainment (2009).

had to get used to finding musical instruments lying around the house, and giving up the kitchen to be used as a rehearsal room. Kay said:

There were always musical instruments lying around. I remember I would push open doors of the rooms and instruments of all sorts would fall over. [70]

Mary spent hours and hours with her guitar, teaching herself to play the music she loved. She began to improve as she learned new songs totally by ear, listening and playing along to the record. She would record her attempts on her reel-to-reel tape recorder and play them back, over and over again, until she thought she had it right. With Dion's help, she began working on arrangements too.

~

Feast Day Celebrations

Given her love of music and performing the Sister Stanislaus Feast Day Celebrations at St Anne's provided the perfect opportunity for Mary to develop both. There was always some kind of musical production happening at the school, and Mary took every chance she could get to play her guitar and sing.

The feast day celebrations for Sister Stanislaus were held on or around 13 November each year. Sister Stanislaus took her name from St Stanislaus Kostka whose liturgical feast day is celebrated on that day. Each form at the school contributed a performance, as well as a wide range of individuals and groups. 1952 was Angela, Jean and Mary's earliest attempt, and they needed to find a suitable song.

This was during the time that Mary was fascinated by Jo Stafford, and so she searched through her song catalogue looking for one that would suit the trio. And then she found it: the perfect song. 'Scarlet Ribbons', a beautiful child's lullaby, tells a miraculous tale of a father who hears his little girl pray before she goes to bed, for 'scarlet ribbons for her hair'. It is late, the shops are all closed and there is nowhere the father go to buy the ribbons; he is distraught all through the night. At dawn he peeps in to see his daughter and is amazed to see beautiful scarlet ribbons in 'gay profusion lying there'. He says that if he lives to be a hundred, he

---

70 Tony Bromley, 'Mary was a Tomboy', *New Musical Express* (2 July 1965).

will never know where the ribbons came from. Jo usually sang with an orchestra, but this version had a stripped back arrangement with very simple vocal backing and an orchestra that was scarcely audible.

Mary decided this was the song they were going to sing at their appearance at the Feast Day Concert. The trio practised for weeks. They had to search out a quiet corner in the school, somewhere they could run through the songs and work on their harmonies. They were often seen in the cloakrooms, even though it was against the rules to hang around in them during breaks. They had no choice, as the classrooms were most definitely out of bounds. Fortunately, Sister Stanislaus turned a blind eye to this rule-breaking and they were left in peace.

The great day finally arrived, and Mary's trio was given a rousing reception by the whole school. A former pupil recalled:

There were always concerts and things like that and Mary and her friends were well known. We looked forward to what they were going to do, because they were very, very good. I don't suppose we appreciated how good they were, we just knew that we liked listening to them. [71]

On the concert for Sister Stanislaus, the school magazine declared: 'The school gave her a concert, which we hope she enjoyed as much as we did in performing in it. The gasp that greeted Form VI's appearance can only be regarded by them as recognition and appreciation of true genius.'[72]

By the time Mary was 14, her ambition to be famous was already fully formed. She was going to be a singer and she was going to be a star! She didn't really know why, and she didn't know how she would or could, but the hunger and drive were there: she was determined to achieve her goal.

For the Feast Day Concert the next year, she chose 'The Three Bells', also known as 'Little Jimmy Brown'.[73] Originally a French language song, it was the 1951 version by The Andrews Sisters that is likely to have

---

71 A former pupil of St Anne's School: interview with author

72 St Anne's School Magazine 1952

73 Originally 'Les Trois Cloches', recorded by Edith Piaf with Las Compagnons de la Chanson, it was a major hit in 1946. The song was written and composed by Jean Villard Gilles in 1939. The first English language version with lyrics by Bert Reisfeld was recorded by the Melody Maids in 1948.

grabbed Mary's attention. The Andrews Sisters were an American group and Mary had heard them on the radio singing mostly boogie-woogie, but this song was not their usual style. A ballad that told the tale of a simple village dweller, it marked his birth, marriage and death by the ringing of chapel bells in his little valley town. The trio, accompanied by Gordon Jenkins' Orchestra & Chorus produced a very moving, harmonious rendition. They had high hopes for their recording, but unfortunately, it didn't reach the heights predicted by Billboard. Mary bought a copy of the record and worked on an arrangement that she could perform with her friends at the Sister Stanislaus' Feast Day Concert.

Speaking more than 60 years later, Kate Davies, Mary's classmate, recalled the performance. She said:

I was trying to remember last week this song that they sang, it was 'Little Jimmy Brown'. 'The Three Bells'. Mary played guitar; she was a very good guitarist. We always used to look forward to their performances. She was one of us, she was well liked, there was nothing to dislike. She was just different from us because she had a lovely voice. People just liked her as a person, and also, I was in awe of her singing. I loved it. I could listen to her all day. As a kid I can still see myself sitting on that chair and I got goose pimples when they sang that song. [74]

Later recorded by The Browns in 1959, the song reached number one on Billboard's Country and Western chart and the Hot One Hundred. It was a massively popular song which, in time, would be recorded by a vastly diverse range of performers, including Roy Orbison, Nana Mouskouri, Johnny Cash and Andy Williams. It was also recorded in Dutch, Italian and Spanish.

~

Mary's Sexual Awakening

One time after assembly, there was a strange spectacle in the school. A number of the older girls were seen standing at long intervals along the corridor. They were silent they were spaced in such a way that they weren't able to talk to one another. They were there when the girls went

---

74 Kate Davies, former pupil of St Anne's Convent School for Girls: interview with author

to their classrooms and they were still there when they broke for lunch. It was a puzzling sight and no one was sure what it was all about. Clearly, these girls were being punished, but no one knew why.

Later, Sister Stanislaus announced that the group had been late back to school after lunch the previous day and were being punished for their lateness. The Sister named all of them, but their misdeeds weren't described exactly, other than to say that they had missed assembly.

The rumours about what had happened spread quickly round the school. It seems that one member of the group had a terrible crush on an older girl, who was in Clayponds Hospital recovering from an operation. She had wanted to visit this girl and take her a little present, it was decided that they would all go. But the hospital was farther away than they had imagined and the return trip took longer than expected. By the time they got back to school the afternoon session had already begun. When Sister Stanislaus heard about this, she scolded the girls and made their punishment very public.

It wasn't unusual for girls to form romantic attachments to other, usually older, girls. Close friendships often contained a simmering undercurrent of sexual tension, which might sometimes spill over into a more physical expression of feeling. It was not encouraged by the nuns and teachers, but neither was it discouraged. Mary knew that liaisons between girls were quite common, and this mixed messaging from the nuns was confusing. Her confusion was made stark for Mary one year at the annual school fete.

The fete in 1954 followed the usual format, but this year there was something unusual. Sister Stanislaus announced the winners of the children's fancy dress competition and introduced Miss Nancy Spain who was there to present the prizes.[75] There was reported in the *County Times and Gazette*:

Later in the afternoon the fete was visited by Miss Nancy Spain, the novelist and broadcaster, who judged the children's fancy dress competition in the school hall. There were a large number of entries and Miss Spain found her task a difficult one. [76]

---

75 St Anne's School Magazine 1955.

76 'Fathers built the sideshows for the fete', *County Times and Gazette*, 19 June 1954.

The person Mary saw bound up onto the stage that afternoon was a most unusual miss; clad in trousers. In the 1950's and early 1960's, Nancy Spain was well-known as a star columnist for the *Daily Express*, *She,* and the *News of the World* and was a regular contributor to *Woman's Hour* and *My Word!* on the radio. She loved taking part in activities normally reserved for boys, and would regale listeners with lively accounts of her adventures, whether on a dockland crane, rock-climbing or rally-driving. She wrote a number of campy detective novels and later became one of Britain's first TV celebrities on talk and game shows like *Juke Box Jury* and *What's My Line?*

By the 1960's, Nancy Spain was a ubiquitous figure on BBC television, but before then she was known only through the articles she wrote and her radio broadcasts. Mary and the other St Anne's girls were unlikely to have ever seen her. So, her appearance at the fete must have come as a surprise for them. In Mary's world, women and girls dressed neatly in conservative skirts and tops and wore sensible shoes; either that, or they were nuns who spent their days encased in the black and white tunic and wimple of their habit. They didn't present themselves as this woman did, in trousers and shirt with a cravat.

The sight of Nancy will have helped confirm in Mary the realisation that girls didn't have to submit to the fate reserved for them. It was clear that Nancy Spain shunned the usual restrictions placed on women at that time, and Mary realised then that she could too. But she was faced with a dilemma: while she admired the bohemian ways and free spirits on display, 'she knew she would never want to be seen as butch' [77]. Nancy Spain had little regard for her appearance and her usual style of dress was best described as 'natty gent's sportswear'. While her sexuality wasn't publicly discussed, it was fairly obvious that she was a lesbian. On one occasion a woman, in a shoe shop, was overheard to say to her daughter (perhaps the girl was holding out for the wrong type of shoes) that she didn't want to grow up to be a 'Nancy Spain'. Mary also dreaded being seen in that way.

It is likely that, with the onset of puberty, Mary began to realise that she was attracted to girls rather than boys. It must have been a struggle

---

77 Dusty Springfield, Ray Connolly, *Evening Standard,* September 1970

for her to understand those feelings and her place in the world. Girls growing up gay know about the fuzzy warmth they feel in the pit of the stomach when the object of their desire is nearby. Her attraction to Judy Garland and later June Haver, when she saw them on the big screen, are symbolic of her attraction to women. Then there was the feeling of peace when faced with the serenity of Sister Marie Louise at the convent in High Wycombe.

It might have passed without note in school when a girl had a crush on another girl. But, for Mary, it would be difficult to escape feelings of guilt, and fear of being found out drove her to stay silent. She quickly realised that when those girls grew up and left school, news would come back that they had met a suitable young man and were engaged or married with children. Acceptance of a close emotional bond between girls in school wasn't expected to continue into maturity. Young Catholic girls were not meant to question their role as women in the 1950's. Instead, they should accept the world as it was; it seemed there was no way to change it. Women were expected to get married, start a family, and warm their husband's slippers by the fire, or else take vows and devote themselves to Christ. Everything in Mary's world pointed her towards that 'normality'.

Mary's confusion most likely continued and was compounded. It would be difficult to know who she could talk to about the way she felt? One resource was the agony aunt in her girls' magazines. This woman always counselled that it was perfectly normal for young girls to feel close, even attracted, to their female friends, but that would fade as they got older. Perhaps Mary was reassured by these words.

~

Dion and the Pedini Brothers

In 1950, when Dion was 16, he left the Royal Grammar School in High Wycombe, his formal education was over. He was expected to find a job and secured a place in a bank, but not long after that he moved on to Lloyds, where he worked as an underwriter. All through this time his mind stayed focused on music.

National Service was an unavoidable fact of life for young British men in those days. Late in 1952 Dion was called up and joined the Army. First, he was sent for ten weeks basic training where he endured the routine humiliation suffered by new recruits: the endless polishing, parading, running, jumping and climbing. Then when Dion's facility for languages was noted, he was assigned to the Joint Services School for Linguists, in Coulsdon Surrey. This government Cold War initiative trained thousands of young men in Russian, in preparation for a feared conflict with the Soviet Union.

Coulsdon was a fairly short train ride from Ealing, which meant it was easy for Dion to get home at weekends, when he would entertain the family with grimly amusing tales of his National Service life, both in basic training and later at the Russian School. He described the cold huts, with the only heat coming from coke stoves, and the food that came with a fine dusting of coal dust. The doctor and dentist were found in the Guards Depot next door – the aptly named Captain Blood, Lieutenant Butcher and Captain Savage. The casual dress of the language recruits was in stark contrast with the Guards who maintained a strict discipline and dress code.

The boys at Coulsdon had to gain a basic understanding of Russian quickly. They spent five or six hours a day, Monday to Friday, with their teachers. For homework they had to learn the Semeonova grammar, translate passages and learn lists of vocabulary every day. Liza Hill, the director of the JSSL throughout its working life,[78] decreed 50% oral work: grammar in classes of about 25, alternated with conversation in groups of about eight, where no English was to be spoken by the instructor.

Dion, in common with the other recruits, had to be sure he would keep his place on the course. They had to pass weekly tests to avoid the prospect of being returned to unit. Work to learn Russian may have been hard, but he had no wish to go back to this brutal regime, nor to be sent to fight in Suez, Korea or Malaya. But the schools were run by the Army and the men in charge could be savage.

---

78 Elizabeth Hill. This redoubtable lady came from a family that had been trading coal for 200 years. Her mother was a member of the Russian nobility and her father was educated at Lancing College. By the age of eight she was fluent in four languages. The Revolution brought the family from a sprawling Russian apartment to the brink of destitution in two rooms with a gas ring in Earl's Court. Liza's determination and her languages helped her to gain a teaching post in a girls school in North Wales and from there to battle her way into the heart of this critical undertaking.

One officer's party trick was to keep the squad standing to attention to see how long they lasted before fainting. One recruit lasted 75 minutes and was by no means the last to go down. [79]

The teachers at the JSSL were clever émigrés who entertained their charges with tales of their passions and drilled them in complex Russian swear words. They were an incredible bunch from a mix of professions and walks of life; there were landed gentry, diplomats, officers and lawyers, and even a prince, a baron, a couple of counts and a senator.

A talented pianist and musician, Dion formed a group with Tony Cash (who had been playing the clarinet for three years when he joined the Navy), Malcolm Brown (who had a guitar he was learning to play), Roy Smith on trombone and Brian Mulligan on trumpet. As Coulsdon was close to London it meant the boys had easy access to everything the city had to offer. Jazz in the early 1950's was growing in popularity among young Britons and players didn't need a great deal of skill to perform the simplest forms of the genre. This led to an increase in the number of new bands. Tony and Malcom heard that Ken Colyer, who had pioneered the popularity of jazz in the UK, was on his way home from New Orleans and was going to lead a new band formed by Chris Barber and that included Monty Sunshine and Lonnie Donegan.

In Coulsdon, the group aimed to copy the Colyer line-up. They gave the occasional performance in the NAAFI and the five of them even went up to London to make a record – just for fun, not for sale. Dion was really the only thoroughly proficient musician in the group and inevitably they weren't very proud of the sounds they produced.

But the students at the JSSL didn't just learn Russian. They were offered a cultural feast of Russian literature, movies and plays - some of which they performed themselves - from which they derived much more benefit. They had been brought in to help defend their country, but they learned to love Russian culture and, above all, its music. The choir in Coulsdon was held in the NAAFI and welcomed all students: auditions were held and Dion was one of those who attended. The Coulsdon choristers learned many touching Russian lullabies. This is where Dion learned the Russian boating song 'Styenka Razin', which he later

---

79 Tony Cash and Mike Gerrard (2012) *The Coder Special Archive*, Hodgson Press, p.123.

adapted to 'The Carnival is Over'. Recorded by The Seekers in 1965, it was a massive number one hit for them.

At home, a favourite haunt of Dion's was the social club at St Benedict's Church. His friends there were Peter Priechenfried, Peter Miles Johnson and Nick Bowyer, and sharing a love of music, they formed a kind of barbershop quartet called The Pedini Brothers. The songs they sang came from all over the world. In the evenings the four of them practised in the kitchen at 2 Kent Gardens. They sang Latin American, early 1900's popular songs, and barbershop songs as well as some Russian songs adapted by Dion from those he learned at his Russian studies. Their Latin American performances included percussion instruments such as maracas, claves and bongos. Barbershop and ballads were sung a capella and sometimes at gigs Dion would play ragtime piano solos. The others didn't play while they were performing. The group even made half a dozen vinyl recordings. Nick Bowyer recalls: 'Gawd only knows where they are now. We played them until there was more scratch than music.'[80]

As Mary watched the Pedini Brothers practising, she picked up ideas she could use with her trio at school. She listened to their harmonising, and while the group rehearsed, she took every chance to join in. Along with his great love of Latin American music, Dion was passionate about Carmen Miranda. As a child he used to obsessively draw her shoes. He loved platform shoes and his drawings of them were really good. Speaking later to the *Village Voice*, Mary said:

My family were big fans of Twentieth Century Fox musicals. My earliest memory would be of Carmen Miranda's band, which was called O Bando da Lua. It was rather sophisticated Rio Carnival music, actually.[81]

Relief from the strictures of the language school at Coulsdon also came in the form of a special coronation year variety show at the St Benedict's social club. 'Coronation Cream' involved performances by many local lads and lasses and The Pedini Brothers accompanied Simone Grimaldi's sinister 'Voo-doo' dance. They stood with solemn faces tapping out a monotonous rhythm in support of Monica Sweetman and showed their

80 Nick Bowyer, writing on the Tom Springfield page of www.mikepratt.com

81 Stacey D'Erasmo, 'Beginning with Dusty', *The Village Voice* (29 August 1995).

versatility performing the Edwardian ballet 'Wait Till the Sun Shines, Nellie'. The Pedini Brothers were given a special mention for their fine performance, including some original musical numbers.

Once the language course was complete, Dion will have spent the next three months on a Russian Radio Voice Intercept course. Then he had several weeks at Maresfield with the Intelligence Corps, with the most basic accommodation: cement block rooms, each with a cast-iron stove in the centre, eight to a room. Alan Bennett later described it as the foulest camp he had ever been in.[82] Recruits spent their time with 'Top Secret' intelligence tasks like translating the football pages of the Soviet Army newspaper *Red Star*. Chores included peeling potatoes and black-leading ovens in the cookhouse, as well as reading the Soviet newspapers.

Dion's final destination will have been West Germany on signals intelligence work, listening in to Soviet military radio traffic, recording and logging it long-hand for onward dispatch to GCHQ where it was analysed to discover Red Army movements and intentions. All very secret, of course. [83]

Ultimately, the JSSL achieved far more than was ever intended. It trained potential interpreters and translators – but it also changed people's lives, not least that of Dion O'Brien.

In the ten years of its existence some 5,000 young men were trained with competence in Russian. It is rare to find a school – especially run with military discipline and intensity – whose Old Boys speak of it with almost universal respect and affection. For many, including the dramatists Alan Bennett and Michael Frayn, the years at this school were indeed some of the best of their lives.[84]

---

82 Alan Bennett (born 9 May 1934) is an English playwright, screenwriter, actor, and author. He was born in Leeds and attended Oxford University, where he studied history and performed with the Oxford Revue. His work includes *The Madness of George III* and its film adaptation, the series of monologues *Talking Heads*, the play and film of *The History Boys*, and popular audio books.

83 Tony Cash, author of *The Coder Special Archive*: email to author

84 Geoffrey Elliott and Harold Shukman (2002) *Secret Classrooms*, London, p. 3.

When Dion was finally released from his National Service, he pursued his interest in performing in earnest. He was determined to build a career in music and show business.

~

Theatricals

Iolanthe

At assembly early in 1954, on the stage of the brand-new school hall, Sister Stanislaus announced that the next school production was going to be a Gilbert and Sullivan operetta – *Iolanthe*. Mrs Irwin, the speech and drama teacher, and Miss Asquith, the music mistress, would be responsible for producing the show, which would be performed at the end of the summer term. It was to be the most ambitious production mounted so far in the school hall. Mary and her friends knew right away they wanted to be part of this new adventure.

When she joined the school a little more than two years before, Mary had been a shy and nervous 12-year-old. Now she was older and growing accustomed to her life in Ealing, she had begun to enjoy her time at St Anne's Convent School. It was fun and along with her friends, Jean and Angela, she performed regularly at school concerts and fetes. Musical theatre presented a fresh opportunity for them.

All of the girls hoping for a part in Iolanthe, gathered for the auditions. Miss Asquith and Mrs Irwin were there ready to conduct them.

Mrs Irwin handed out copies of the libretto and gave the aspiring actresses an introduction to the plot and a description of the fairy opera. Gilbert and Sullivan wrote a series of comic operas. *Iolanthe*, their fourth, included memorable musical numbers that made them household names. The political party system and other institutions are mocked and satirised. But mixed with bouncy, amiable absurdities it all comes across as good fun. The comedy revelled in the supernatural, here the usual order was turned upside down; women held the power in this society.

Iolanthe, the character who gave the operetta its name, had spent 25 years in exile for the capital offence of marrying a mortal. Now she was to be allowed to rejoin her sisters. She told them about her son,

Strephon, born of her marriage to her mortal husband. But this son was fairy only down to his waist; he could make his top half invisible and pass it through a keyhole, but his mortal legs were left kicking behind.

The Peers were led by the Lord Chancellor, and only he could give permission to marry a Ward of Court. Strephon, an Arcadian shepherd, was in love with Phyllis, the Lord Chancellor's beautiful and much sought-after ward, and was determined they would marry even without gaining consent first. Phyllis loved Strephon but she had no idea that his mother was a fairy. He was faced with the task of persuading the Lord Chancellor to allow them to marry. In order to pursue his goal, Strephon asked his mother and the other fairies for help. But when the Peers saw him in the company of a young and beautiful woman, they formed the belief that he was unfaithful and wasted no time convincing Phyllis of this. Strephon struggled to convince Phyllis that this beautiful young woman was in fact his mother.

This is a world where the power lies with the Queen of the Fairies. She takes control and decides who will be elected to the Parliament; Strephon is made an MP, and now he can marry Phyllis. Iolanthe is pardoned, and reconciled with the Lord Chancellor. In the meantime, the fairies all fall in love with members of the House of Lords. The Fairy Queen had a political and moral mess to deal with but in the end the tangled plot unravels and all live happily ever after.

The three friends were certain of good parts in this production. They were already well known in the school, and the mistresses were aware of their acting and singing abilities. Miss Lehman had taught them the rudiments of movement in preparation for the annual dancing displays. Maybe they weren't the best dancers but they had learned enough to give a reasonable performance.

The girls waited for the announcement with excited anticipation, and when the day finally came, they discovered they had been given leading parts: Mary was to play the part of Strephon, the half-man, half-fairy son of Iolanthe, Angela would be Phyllis, Strephon's sweetheart, and Jean was given the part of Earl Tolloller. The rehearsals were fraught and exhausting. It meant that everyone got cross and irritated at different times. There was rarely a full cast in attendance, and that caused problems.

There were all sorts of reasons for not attending; this one had a cold, that one was at netball, and a multitude of other excuses. But in the end, by some miracle, it all worked out.

Dress Rehearsal

The dress rehearsals were an opportunity for Mrs Irwin to give last minute instructions to the cast. All practised their songs with the help of Miss Asquith. The Peers, strutted through their marching song in their elegant blue and scarlet cloaks with sparkling coronets. The Fairies went through their steps, thrilled with their blue taffeta dresses that were decorated with pink roses, and flowered headbands. The main characters, of course, had the most beautiful costumes, nearly all of which were made by the sisters. The choice of costume for Strephon had been difficult, Mary hated the idea of tights and instead wore white breeches with a tight-fitting green doublet. Angela, for her role as Phyllis, was dressed demurely as an Arcadian shepherdess.

FIGURE 2.5 PROGRAMME FOR IOLANTHE (COURTESY OF MARY MCGRATH)

The Performance

Then came the performance. The stage, set with an Arcadian landscape, had a river running around the back with a rustic bridge crossing it. 'Wizard Prang' (Mr Prangly), the janitor and handyman, had built the set, which had been dressed by Mrs Scott, the art mistress, with help from many willing volunteers.

The hall was filled with the parents, pupils and staff of the school when Mrs Irwin walked onto the stage to introduce *Iolanthe*. The lights were dimmed and slowly the hall fell silent. Miss Asquith at the piano played the opening bars of the overture. Mary and Angela stood in the wings waiting to go onstage. Behind the curtain the fairies were arranged in their proper places, ready for their entrance.

The curtain is raised and the fairy Celia runs onto the stage, searching for her fellows, she calls on them to join her. One by one they come skipping onto the stage, singing the opening number. They raise the first laugh from the audience as they sing their comic song. Then begin a wistful lament about the long absence of Iolanthe, begging for her to be brought back to them. The Fairy Queen agrees that Iolanthe should be pardoned and calls her from her watery exile. Strephon then heard Iolanthe tell the fairies about her life since she left them. That was Strephon's cue to enter and tell his mother of his plan to marry Phyllis, even without the Lord Chancellor's consent.

Strephon comes on stage singing:

Good morrow, good mother!

Good mother, good morrow!

The Queen and fairies depart, singing as they go. Iolanthe makes her affectionate farewell and Strephon is left alone on the stage.

His sweetheart, Phyllis, appears singing and dancing and playing the flageolet.

Good morrow, good lover!

Good lover, good morrow!

The dialogue that follows between the lovers shows Strephon to be the more ardent of the two. Phyllis isn't convinced that their marriage will make them happy forever, and fears penal life servitude for Strephon if they marry without the Lord Chancellor's consent. She suggests they should wait the two years until she is of age. But Strephon is horrified at the thought of waiting: what might happen in two years? She might fall in love with the Lord Chancellor, and half the House of Lords were sighing at her feet. Strephon wants them to marry, the sooner the better.

Mary and Angela had practised their parts many times, and they knew how important it was to get the right comic timing. Mary remembered Mrs Irwin's advice about emphasising their dialogue and she knew they had nailed it when she heard the laughter from the audience.

They sang their duet, 'None shall part us from each other', then left the stage to clapping and cheering. Mrs Irwin was there beaming, as they came into the wings. Mary's nerves had left her now.

Mary went through the rest of the performance almost in a trance. The enthusiastic reaction from the audience as they took their final bows, assured them that the production was a success!

The school magazine of 1955 printed a report of the show:

The first night performance was a great success and it was the same for two more glorious nights. The last, however, was the best. After the speeches and presentations, the cast sought out friends in the audience, and had fun listening to the criticisms and congratulations.

Afterwards a grand feast was laid on for the performers in the Junior School building. They celebrated with cakes, cider, songs and games before bringing the venture to an end with a toast to the success of the show.' [85] Several days later a glowing review of the production was published in the local newspaper under the heading 'Convent pupils in "Iolanthe":

The girls of St Anne's Convent, Little Ealing, must have worked very hard for their production of 'Iolanthe' on Monday and Tuesday, and their audience on the opening night was most enthusiastic. It was perhaps a rather ambitious programme, since Gilbert and Sullivan is not so easily sung as many people think. Mary Yeoman took the most onerous part of Iolanthe and sustained it well, while Angela Patten looked charming in her shepherdess costume as Phyllis and she and her sweetheart Strephon, Mary O'Brien, were at their best in the scene where Strephon confesses he is a fairy. Anne Perks, as the Lord Chancellor, has a strong

---

85 St Anne's School Magazine 1955

part in which the humorous dialogue fitted her rather better than the singing role.[86]

~

St Louis Blues

The performance by Mary, Jean, and Angela at the Sister Stanislaus Feast Day concert in 1954 has become the stuff of legend. There is much debate over what actually happened, stories abound of the 'St Louis Blues' debacle at the Feast Day Concert, and much of the confusion comes from Mary herself.

The three friends knew this would be their last performance at the concert and they wanted it to be special. It was important for them to find the right song, so they searched for something other than their usual sentimental repertoire, but nothing seemed to fit.

This was around the time when Mary's love of the Blues began. She was a great admirer of Bessie Smith and had heard her singing 'St Louis Blues'. She decided they would sing it at the concert, but how could a trio of school girls do justice to Bessie's version of the song? They would have to find something more up-tempo. There was the Hall Johnson Gospel Choir's a capella rendition, sung by a solo voice that emerged from the complex call-and-response backing, and then there was Gilda Grey, accompanied on the piano by Liberace who performed the song while dancing the 'shimmy', but perhaps the most persuasive version was the one by Lena Horne.

Mary was determined this was the song they were going to sing. It was a challenge, but she didn't think about the meaning of the lyrics. 'St Louis Blues' was one of the first blues songs to succeed as a pop song. It was written in a bar in Memphis, in 1914, by W C Handy, who had had a chance meeting with a woman on the streets of St. Louis, tormented because her husband had left her. He heard her anguished cry; 'Ma man's got a heart like a rock cast in de sea.'

Kay and OB must have been sick of hearing the record, played on repeat by Mary until she knew the song by heart. Once she had the words and the melody, she played around with the chords before

---

86 Convent Pupils in Iolanthe', *County Times and Gazette* (24 July 1954).

working on the arrangement and deciding on the harmonies. For Mary, this performance could never be just 'good enough'. She knew she wanted it to be perfect and she hoped her friends would want that too. The group worked together, rehearsing at every opportunity. The cloakrooms were, as always, their last resort as a quiet place to practice in.

Miss Cheriton, the geography mistress, came to the dress rehearsal. She was there to vet their performance and ensure it was suitably decorous. She listened to the singing. They had put so much effort into getting this right – the tight harmony, the solo voice and the guitar blended together – and they sounded good! But she was not happy. She saw the atmospheric purple lighting, heard the lyrics and declared 'Oh no, this won't do at all. It is most unsuitable. It is just too erotic.'

In an article she wrote for the school magazine some years after she left, Mary said: 'I will never forget performing in this trio at Sister's Feast Day when we sang a dreadful version of 'St Louis Blues' with purple "mood" lighting.'[87] On another occasion, Mary said that their appearance was cancelled at the last minute: 'We were going to do 'St Louis Blues' with some purple lighting effects to help us along. But the geography mistress put a stop to it. Said it was too erotic! But the nuns loved it ...'[88]

Then, later she said: 'I had my first group when I was still at school. One day at an end-of-term concert we sang 'St Louis Blues' against a weird background of purple lighting. I thought it very exotic and the nuns enjoyed it too, but oddly enough the other mistresses at the school were horrified.' [89]

Angela Patten said that Mary chose the song and did all the arrangements, the guitar and harmonies. Her memory was that the headmistress and five of the nuns walked out in disgust.

Yet others say that while Miss Cheriton thought the group was too risqué, the younger staff overruled and allowed them to perform. At this point in time, with memories growing dim, the truth is almost

87 St Anne's School Magazine 1963 article by Mary O'Brien

88 Peter Jones, 'We're Catching up America', *Record Mirror* (9 November 1963).

89 Dusty Springfield, 'Fame has a Flipside too', *Woman's Own* 1965 in Dusty Springfield Bulletin No. 65 July 2008.

impossible to discern. What we can be sure of is that 'St Louis Blues' was arranged by Mary and practised by the three friends, and that some kind of performance took place.

~

Twelfth Night, December 1954

Mary was involved in one more hugely successful production before she left school. *Twelfth Night*, directed by Mrs Irwin, included girls from the IV and V forms. With St Anne's being an all-girls school, it was necessary for girls to perform in male parts, and one of those was Mary. *Twelfth Night* was presented to the school on the last four days of term, before the start of the Christmas holidays. The costumes were beautifully hand sewn by Sister Mary Lourdes, the scenery of vast blue Italian skies and white villas under the sun was painted by Mrs Scott, and Miss Asquith provided the music. A double cast produced excellent performances; Mary played a swashbuckling Sir Toby Belch, a part she shared with Pauline Stacey.

An amusing incident in St. Anne's Convent School's production of "Twelfth Night." The players are Elizabeth Fenton, May Fairchild, Jean Macdonald and Mary O'Brien as Sir Andrew Aguecheek, Feste, Maria and Sir Toby Belch.

FIGURE 2.6 TWELFTH NIGHT – MARY ON RIGHT
(*MIDDLESEX COUNTY TIMES AND GAZETTE*, 25 DECEMBER 1954)

Many years later, a former pupil went to see a production of *Twelfth Night* while on holiday in South Africa with friends. She told them that the last time she was involved with the play she had played Viola while Mary was Sir Toby Belch:

> *I just happened to say the last time I saw Twelfth Night, or was aware of it, Dusty Springfield was in it as Sir Toby Belch. My moment of fame. But, of course, she wasn't Dusty Springfield then, she was Mary O'Brien.*[90]

---

90 Sylvia Clayton, Former pupil of St Anne's Convent - interview with author

The St Anne's School magazine reported in 1955: 'Others particularly noted for their acting were Jean MacDonald, the coyly vivid little Maria. Sylvia Clayton and Pamela Moore shared the presentation of a young Viola of fluent charm and outstanding dramatic ability. Elizabeth Fenton presented a whimsically absurd Sir Andrew; Rosemary Abdullah and Sheila Newman played the capricious, low-voiced, self-possessed Countess Olivia; Denise Cunliffe and Mary Fairchild got the clown and his songs across and Doreen Rulton and Alison Devenish, who shared the part of Malvolio, saw that his presumptions were suitably punished. The production was a success, and that was mainly due to the painstaking patience and diligence of Mrs Irwin. She spent many hours of her time preparing and encouraging the actors.'

~

Leaving School

Mary was sixteen in 1955, and it was settled that she would leave school at the end of the summer term. She had no clear idea of how she was going to earn her living, but one thing was certain: she was going to get into show business. Later she wrote about her thoughts at that time: 'I talked of nothing but show business to all my friends till they must have been bored stiff. I remember so well one of the last afternoons before we left the convent. We had just come in from playing hockey and were changing in the games room. We were all about 15 years old then and preparing to go out into the great big world. Like most schoolgirls we got to talking about a reunion. 'In five years' time,' I remember a girl called Elizabeth saying, 'let's all meet on the steps of St-Martin-in-the-Fields in Trafalgar Square.' 'Wonderful,' I replied quickly, 'but it might be difficult for me. You know, getting away from recordings and rehearsals.' The other girls shrieked. 'Hark at old big head,' they teased. [91]

In fact, it was true, and Mary really did try to make it. The girls had planned to meet on 21 June, five years later, but by that time Mary was with The Springfields, performing at Butlin's Ocean Hotel in Brighton; she couldn't get away!

---

[91] Dusty Springfield, 'Fame has a Flipside too', *Woman's Own* 1965, in Dusty Springfield Bulletin No. 65, July 2008.

Mary was singing in West End clubs even before she left school, landing her first job performing in the Montrose, in London's west end. Dion had a regular gig there, and one St Patrick's Day when the whole family were there, he told the manager, Sylvia Jones, that his sister was a singer too. Sylvia was sceptical but decided to let her do a number. She recalled:

She was terribly young but extremely good. Of course, she didn't have the black eyes and beehive then. She was 16, self-possessed and had lovely auburn hair. I had to obtain her parent's permission to allow her to perform.' [92]

Mary wowed the audience and was offered a job. Seventeen and sixpence a night seemed like riches then! This was her dream – this was showbiz![93]

And so it began. She was given a regular spot, sometimes singing on her own and other times with her brother. But Mary was still a pupil at St Anne's and singing in clubs at night didn't fit too well with the demands of school.

Anna Scott remembers meeting Mary not long before she left school:

I was a real newbie but she would chat away comfortably, unlike a lot of the senior girls. One winter afternoon I went into the main cloakroom on the way to the loo and saw her sitting on a low bench wrapped in her coat that hung on the peg behind. I went over to ask if she was alright. She said she had been up all night and was out of it. I think she was singing then with her brother in the clubs and pubs. She patted the bench and I sat down and wrapped myself up too. I wish I could remember what we talked about...but it has gone. She was a very nice person indeed.[94]

After a time, the audience seemed to stop noticing her. Mary sat in a corner with her guitar, playing and singing, and they just went on eating and drinking as if she wasn't there.[95] In an interview she said of them: 'They were small drinking clubs for upper crust debutantes and their

92 Anton Antonowicz, *The Mirror* (4 March 1999).

93 Dusty Springfield, 'Fame has a Flipside too', *Woman's Own* 1965, in Dusty Springfield Bulletin No. 65 July 2008.

94 Anna Scott, former pupil, St Anne's Convent School for Girls: email to author

95 Dusty Springfield, 'Fame has a Flipside too', *Woman's Own* 1965, in Dusty Springfield Bulletin No. 65 July 2008.

young officer escorts. Quite hideous! I spent the early part of my career singing to their backs.'[96]

Mary and her brother sang songs from the many artists they had loved listening to when they were growing up, from Peggy Lee and Jo Stafford to Frank Sinatra and the Andrews Sisters, as well as the Latin American music of Carmen Miranda and more. They drew on the Great American Songbook, including standards by George Gershwin, Cole Porter, Irving Berlin, Jerome Kern and many others – all of the popular songs of the day – as well as early 20th-century American jazz standards and popular songs.

Mary is remembered by her schoolmates as a bubbly, red-haired tomboy, a million miles from the statuesque singing superstar with a towering blonde beehive and kohl-laden eyes that she became. But this change didn't take place overnight; rather; it was a gradual metamorphosis.

A former pupil of St Anne's, Yvonne Messenger, recalled: 'It was no secret in the school that Mary wanted to become a singer and indeed that she already performed with her glamorous-sounding brother. At the time we didn't know whether this was just a hobby or if there were already public performances. Of course, we did not imagine how her dream would be realised.'[97]

Sharing her memories of Mary, she talked about how hard she found it to relate the person she saw on TV to the girl she had known at school. But then towards the end of Dusty's life she saw an interview on TV and there she was, 'the girl on the stairs'.

---

96 Brant Mewborn, 'Dusty Springs Back', *Rolling Stone*, After Dark (June 1978).

97 Yvonne Messenger, former pupil, St Anne's Convent School for Girls: interview with author

Part 3: The World of Work:

1955 - 1958

Where to Now?

'What Did She Know About Railways' was a very risqué song sung by Marie Lloyd on the music hall stage in 1890. The innuendo in the words of the chorus is clear – 'never had her ticket punched before'. This was the rather racy song that Mary claimed to have sung at her first audition after leaving school. Her tale of practising for three months in the green-painted loos of the Co-op Insurance building in West Ealing raised a laugh from her Talk of the Town audience in 1968.[98] Was she so naïve that she didn't realise the meaning of the words?

When Mary left school in 1955, she had to decide what she was going to do next. She had no interest in anything to do with academia and anyway she was aiming for a career in showbusiness. It's not that Mary wasn't bright. The problem is she didn't believe it herself. She said later, 'my brother seemed to sail through all his exams without swotting at all, while I had to work really hard to get anywhere.'[99] In another interview she reinforced this, saying:

'I wasn't very good at anything at school. I was at a convent school and the nuns were very strict and the standards terribly high. My brother passed fourteen subjects with honours. I left at the first moment I could. I just wasn't that kind of bright.' [100]

Her most immediate problem was how to combine her bid for stardom with the need to earn a living. She had to find a job but had little idea of what she could do – the certificates she gained at school didn't qualify her to work as a nurse, a secretary or a librarian, and she soon

---

98 Dusty Springfield live at the Talk of the Town, London, July 1968.

99 Dusty Springfield, 'Fame has a Flipside too', *Woman's Own* 1965 in Dusty Springfield Bulletin No. 65 July 2008.

100 David Evans (1995) Scissors and Paste: A collage biography of Dusty Springfield, Britannia Press publishing UK, p. 8

discovered she wasn't exactly cut out for office work either. That job with the Co-op Insurance in West Ealing was short-lived and she soon moved on to Squire of Ealing music shop, opposite the ABC Forum cinema on the Ealing Broadway, where she was a shop assistant. They sold pianos, radiograms and gramophone players. The basement was a record shop with soundproof cubicles equipped with headphones and turntables. Records could be played at the right speed; old fashioned 78s, singles at 45 or modern LPs at 33 1/3 rpm. Customers came to the shop to buy the first long player records: Humphrey Lyttleton playing Bad Penny Blues and Walther Geiseking playing the Grieg piano concerto. The shop stocked many varied styles and genres of music, from classical to jazz and pop. It was Mary's job to organise the discs by category and then alphabetically, and she spent many hours dusting the shelves. Here she could indulge her passion for music: it was the perfect place for Mary.

In those years her life was a combination of work and music. All she could think and talk about was singing, music and films. Her mother thought her an 'odd bod' and wondered why she showed so little interest in boys; she put it down to her obsession with music. Mary would sit at home in the evenings, strumming her guitar or playing records. Her parents struggled to work her out, but they already knew that her one wish, her one dream, was to go into show business. But she asked herself 'how anyone so shy and gauche, with wire-rimmed specs and short-cropped hair, could ever in a thousand years hope to become a pop singer?'[101]

Following her success in drama and musical productions at school, Mary briefly toyed with the notion of an acting career. She joined Peggy Batchelor's drama classes at the Questors Theatre and was an enthusiastic member of the group. Her teacher, Peggy Batchelor wrote 'Dusty Springfield was a difficult pupil but hugely talented.' [102]

She thought that maybe drama school and a career in acting was the way to go. But, Kay's memories of travelling with the dance troupe had left her with a very jaundiced view of the theatrical world, and it's likely she persuaded Mary against that ambition, or perhaps Mary simply

101 Dusty Springfield, 'Fame has a Flipside too', *Woman's Own* 1965, in Dusty Springfield Bulletin No. 65 July 2008.

102 Carole Hawkins (2012) Never a Dull Moment: A biography of Peggy Batchelor, Authorhouse UK, p. 128.

realised that she had a voice and if she was going to make it at all it would be as a singer.

Whether through acting or singing, Mary's single-minded ambition was to be rich and famous. She had no idea how she was going to achieve it, but she just had a sense that somehow it was going to work.[103]

~

St Benedict's Social Club

Mary and Dion were frequent visitors at St Benedict's Social Club; it was their refuge and a place where they could relax, mostly free from their parents. It also gave them a space to practise singing and playing their music. Dion had been a regular there for several years, but when Mary was younger, she was only allowed to go if Kay was available to chaperone her. Kay was very aware of the atmosphere of barely repressed sexual tension at the club and knew about the predatory young men. Now that Mary was older, Kay was less protective and she was allowed to go to the club with Dion.

On Sunday mornings, groups of young people wandered from the steps of Ealing Abbey to Castlebar, headed for St Stephens Road. Passing through the gate set in a high brick wall, they arrived at the club: a large three-storey Edwardian house set in a massive garden, with two red cinder and clay tennis courts and space for people to watch from deck chairs. Mary enjoyed a few games of tennis, although her short-sightedness made it almost impossible for her to see the ball, and her vanity wouldn't allow her to be seen wearing glasses, even in those days.

From the tennis courts, steps led down through French windows into a semi-basement club and bar room. Members flocked into this smoke-filled bar to quench their thirsts. It was a place where young Catholics could meet under the watchful eyes of adults; virginity was sacrosanct. This was long before the advent of the contraceptive pill, and of course, any contraception was considered a sin. Fear of pregnancy stopped Catholic boys and girls from giving in to their lustful desires. The girls at the club were husband-hunting, but the boys were just hunting, and they took every chance they could find. But it was no great issue for

---

103 Brant Mewborn, 'Dusty Springs Back', *Rolling Stone*, After Dark (June 1978).

Mary, who was still quite naïve. In any case, the boys didn't interest her and the girls were definitely off-limits.

But the club wasn't just for Sundays, Mary and Dion often went there on weekday nights too. Upstairs on the first floor there was a dingy room with an old upright piano that had seen better days. They took their guitars and practised there, sometimes enlisting the help of a volunteer to play piano with them. This was where Dion had met the two Peters (Miles and Priechenfried) and, along with Nick Bowyer, had formed the Pedini Brothers.

~

Clubs, bars and cafes

Once her singing career was underway, Mary performed in a variety of very smart supper clubs in Chelsea. Sometimes she appeared with her brother and at other times on her own. She was so young then, her cousin Angela Hunter, remembers Mary's father getting the last tube into the West End to collect her from wherever she was performing.

Le Rascas, an outrageous Belgravia club had a one-eyed-cook. He would come out and dance with the stars. Mary used to sing and play guitar in these clubs. She sometimes felt as though she got through a hundred songs in one night.

In an interview many years later, Mary recalled:

It was good training, even though no one was listening, and on a good night I could earn a guinea – this was the big time! After that I couldn't eat in a restaurant with a pianist or a guitarist – I had to listen because I felt so bad for them. To me it was the height of rudeness to turn my back on someone sweating it out in the corner or feeling degraded. It makes for a miserable evening – it's awful. I mean, it's a rotten job, it really is a rotten job. But it's a way to make a buck. No one really listened, apart from Michael Wilding and Jack Lemmon, to this day I love Jack Lemmon for applauding me. [104]

Mary had a great facility for picking up the sounds of many languages and she quickly learned to sing in Turkish and Spanish, and in Portuguese with a Brazilian accent. Mary and Dion also performed to spoiled debs

---

[104] Dusty Springfield, The *Ultimate Interview 1993*, in Dusty Springfield Bulletin No.50 November 2003.

at debutante parties in Eaton Square. The mothers were lovely but the daughters were just vile.

At the Kensington Restaurant Club Mary was the main attraction. Local newspapers began to take an interest in her. At that time rock'n'roll and calypso were fighting one another for supremacy; customers enjoyed dancing to rock'n'roll, but they often requested calypsos. A report in the *Kensington Post* described Mary's voice as 'soft and deep as liquid honey'. In the article, Mary speaks about her ambition to be a jazz singer, and how she hopes to start her training soon. She is quoted as saying, 'Originally, I wanted to be a famous horsewoman and to compete in country shows – but I kept falling off, so I gave this idea up in favour of singing'. But horse riding was not on offer when Mary was at school and the local stables have no record of her being a pupil there.

FIGURE 3.1 CALYPSO GIRL (SHUTTERSTOCK)

Recording – 'Can't We be Friends?'

This was Mary's opportunity, as she performed to audiences who weren't really listening, her voice was maturing. She used the time to develop her skill; this was when her unique, husky sound emerged. She had loved listening to her brother practise with his friends in their quartet and decided now was her time; she was going to record a song herself. She knew what she wanted to sing and she knew who she wanted to sing it with her. One day, in the hall of their flat, she grabbed hold of her brother's friend, Peter Miles, and begged him to record with her. He described the scene:

> She said, 'Peter come in here 'cos I've got an idea that you and I can record one afternoon in a studio in Queensway, and we'll rehearse here. I'll tell you the full arrangement.'

Mary chose 'Can't We be Friends?'; the timing and arrangement were all done by her. She suggested the ad libs between some of the lines, so when she sang 'Who's to blame?' Peter replied 'Mostly you'. At the studio, after a quick run-through, they wrapped up the recording after just one or two takes. Peter said of the session: 'The arrangement she made was so good and so non-complicated, that we just went and recorded it. It was wonderful.' [105] The recording can be found on the CD 'Simply Dusty', and we can hear Mary's guitar playing skill as she accompanies the duo. Her voice demonstrates many of the qualities she was to become famous for. Peter Miles said she was a big part of his life, and he had clear memories of their friendship: 'I have a picture of Dusty in my mind in her sitting room at home. It was her last year at school and she still had straight red hair.'

~

Musical Development

Now that Mary was working and had some money of her own, she could buy records, magazines and books for herself. She had learned about classical music from her father, and he had given her the tools to understand how music was structured. Now she set out on the serious

---

105 Peter Miles: interview with author

task of discovering music, in all its forms, for herself. She read articles and books about the history of music and the artists who influenced her. She pored through every music magazine she could lay her hands on, and read and memorised every scrap of information she could find. Mary's knowledge and understanding of music broadened and deepened in these years.

If she wasn't working or performing in one club or other, most of Mary's waking hours were spent in her room playing and listening to the music she loved. She was already fairly accomplished on the guitar and now she began to appreciate how talented professional musicians were. She listened with a discerning ear, discovering nuances she had never noticed before.

Wartime music had been the backdrop for Mary's parents' generation: it wrapped around them like a warm blanket, comforting and safe, and carried them through the hardships of the war. The BBC presented the dance bands of Bert Ambrose and Ted Heath, which looked more like orchestras than pop acts, with the musicians divided into sections and the bandleader standing up-front with a baton. Singers were often an afterthought and were only rarely credited on recordings; they were, essentially, anonymous. The BBC, paternalistic and dull, had every intention of continuing to deliver this format of music to the public. These dance bands were the soundtrack of British life in the early days of the pop industry.

The change in popular music in the 1950's and 1960's was volcanic, and Mary didn't just live through it: she was part of the revolution.

~

To understand how Mary developed her expertise in music and musicology, it is important to appreciate the musical landscape she lived through as a teenager. It is already clear that in her younger life she was exposed to a wide range of styles of music and many interpreters of the craft. Jazz had been a part of that fabric of her life from her youngest days. One of the gifts OB gave to his children; it was an important feature of his wide-ranging taste in music. He introduced Mary and Dion to early New Orleans jazz by playing records from his extensive collection for them. But now her explorations took on a new intensity.

In the 1940's and 50's serious jazz enthusiasts were catered to by the Rhythm clubs that had grown up throughout the UK. They held record recitals, jam sessions and talks, they also offered guest appearances by professional musicians and critics. The BBC produced *Radio Rhythm Club*; a programme specially geared towards jazz fans, from a variety of class backgrounds; mostly these were seen as young and male. But though this programme was primarily the preserve of young men it didn't stop OB from encouraging both of his children to tune in to it.

Jelly Roll Morton was a fundamental part of Mary's early schooling in jazz. In an interview, later in life, she spoke about him. She said, 'my first introduction to black music was as a kid listening to Jelly Roll Morton singles, old New Orleans stuff.' [106]

An early jazz pioneer, Jelly Roll Morton developed his piano style playing in 'sporting houses'. He was the first great composer and piano player in Jazz. In those days 78 rpm records were restricted to three minutes. Morton was a talented arranger who wrote special scores that took advantage of this time limit. He would introduce himself by saying, 'I invented jazz.' He died young and so missed out on the Dixieland revival which rescued so many of his peers from musical obscurity.

~

Jazz in Britain

In the late 1950's, jazz nights in Ealing were held in the Feathers pub and Ealing Town Hall on Thursday and Friday nights. These were organised by Fery Asgari in the early days before the club became established in the basement opposite Ealing Broadway station. Mary could go there to hear live jazz.

At that time, jazz in the UK revolved mainly around a group of young musicians; John Dankworth and Ronnie Scott began the modern jazz or bebop trend. The movement in the opposite direction, New Orleans Jazz, was represented by Ken Colyer and George Webb.

Ken Colyer and his brother Bill had an immense influence on the post-war popularity of jazz in the UK, and it's likely that Mary heard his name

---

106 Chris Bourke (1990) 'Dusty in Private', *Rip it Up* (New Zealand).

on the BBC's *World of Jazz*, when his letters, smuggled from prison in New Orleans, were read on air.

In the UK jazz took on a vital importance from which, first skiffle and then rock'n'roll evolved. A relatively small number of young men were essential to the movement that was at the root of these changes in popular music. Ken and Bill Colyer, Chris Barber and Lonnie Donegan, and they were all indebted to Lead Belly. The British popular music scene of the 1950's and 1960's wouldn't have happened if it weren't for Lead Belly's influence.

Lead Belly was born in the late 1880's. His songs included a range of genres: gospel, blues about women, liquor, prison life, and racism; and folk songs about cowboys, prison, work, sailors, cattle herding, and dancing. He was a legend; a folk-blues singer, songwriter and guitarist. Famed musicologists, John and Alan Lomax who spent their lives collecting American Folk music, discovered him in prison in Texas while he was held there for murder. Among his best-known recordings are 'Goodnight Irene', 'Rock Island Line', 'The Midnight Special' and 'Cotton Fields', songs that Mary and her brother Dion would sing and record in later years.[107]

~

Determined to play the jazz of Bunk Johnson and Mutt Carey, Ken Colyer formed the Crane River Jazz Band with five other jazz enthusiasts. He longed to go to the place where this music had originated and signed on to the Merchant Navy hoping for a ship that would take him close to New Orleans where George Lewis and several members of Bunk Johnson's band were playing.

Ken was an unknown when he signed on with the Merchant Navy this time. But while he was away, interest around traditional jazz began to take hold in the UK. Ken was thrown in prison when his visa ran out. During his imprisonment he smuggled fascinating reports about his adventures in New Orleans to his brother, Bill, these were shared with

---

107 He also wrote songs about people in the news, such as Franklin D. Roosevelt, Adolf Hitler, Jean Harlow, Jack Johnson, the Scottsboro Boys and Howard Hughes. Lead Belly was posthumously inducted into the Rock and Roll Hall of Fame in 1988 and the Louisiana Music Hall of Fame in 2008.

the readers of *Melody Maker* and listeners to the BBC's *World of Jazz*. Mary is sure to have heard at least some of the reports from the US.

Chris Barber had formed a band that was in need of a trumpeter. They had been following Ken Colyer's adventures in New Orleans and knew he would soon return to the UK. After a series of meetings they decided to offer Ken a place in the band. He was delighted and agreed to join them. After a hero's welcome, he took up his place with the new band. Bill Colyer took on the role of manager, and the band was called Ken Colyer's Jazzmen.

Colyer was in the line-up when they made their official UK debut at the London Jazz Club in Bryanston Street; this became the band's staple gig. Tony Cash and Malcolm Brown, Dion O'Brien's fellow linguists from the Russian Language School, had leave that weekend. They grabbed the chance to attend the launch where, crammed in along with 500 enthusiasts, they witnessed the launch of the Colyer Band. Tony Cash remembers:

> *The interweaving front-line instruments were supported by the sprightliest of rhythm sections which included string, bass and drums. Along with the rest of the audience, we were entranced'.* [108]

Between them the Colyer brothers and Chris Barber created the foundations of jazz, and more generally, popular music in 1950's UK. Mary and her brother, Dion, lived through this musical landscape whilst on their own musical journeys.

~

The Evolution of Pop

In the 1950's popular music in Britain became a melting pot of sounds and influences. Jazz, skiffle and rock'n'roll, led the way towards the beat boom and Rhythm 'n' Blues.

Skiffle had developed as a way of giving the boys in the Crane River Jazz Band time to get their breath back after blowing their lungs out in the first set. They needed some kind of entertainment to fill the interval. Bill Colyer began by playing records from his extensive collection. Later some members of the band decided to play music based on country

---

108 Tony Cash and Mike Gerrard (2012) The Coder Special Archive, Hodgson Press, p. 133.

blues. They used basic instruments; washboard, tea chest bass, etc and sang whatever songs they felt like singing. Initially it was described as 'breakdown music'. Later the word 'skiffle' was introduced, and the Crane River boys were the first to play it on a regular basis. 'This was in 1949, in a corrugated iron hut, round the side of the White Hart public house in Bath Road, Cranford.' [109]

Some years later, Lonnie Donegan started performing skiffle as a banjo player with the Ken Colyer Jazz Band. He played along with two other members of the band during breaks. Ken Colyer's band were first to record skiffle, but in 1955, the Lonnie Donegan Skiffle Group released a fast-tempo version of Lead Belly's 'Rock Island Line'. This was a major hit for Donegan in 1956 and sold over a million copies worldwide; the first debut record to go gold in Britain. After that the fortunes of skiffle were transformed, it overwhelmed the British popular music scene.

~

The Rise of The Teenager

People in the UK started to talk about teenagers in around 1955. It was ten years since the Second World War had ended and now the restrictions of that time were easing. Young people were developing a cultural identity of their own, they were rejecting the social etiquette and inhibited lifestyles of their parents' era. Styles of dress, popular music and pastimes were all changing. The older generation didn't like it, they moaned about 'kids today!', were horrified by their fashion sense and complained that their music was 'just a noise!'

Skiffle didn't need amps or a drum kit. An acoustic guitar or banjo, a washboard, and a broomstick and tea chest bass was enough. Kids learned the three chords necessary to start performing, and after that skiffle groups were everywhere in the country, singing the songs made famous by Lead Belly and Lonnie Donegan. These children didn't understand what they were singing about, but the energy of the music gave it a vitality otherwise unknown in post war Britain. This was a teen revolution.

---

109 Pete Frame (2007) The Restless Generation: How Rock Music Changed the Face of 1950s Britain, London: Rogan House, p. 1.

So it was that skiffle groups erupted in Britain in the late 50's; sales of guitars soared to between 30000 and 50000. Musicians performed in church halls, cafes, and Soho coffee bars, like the 2i's, the Cat's Whisker, and nightspots like Coconut Grove and Churchill's. No great musical skill was required. This was how many up-and-coming stars learned their trade. Tommy Steele, Lionel Bart, Mick Jagger, Cliff Richard, John Lennon, Paul McCartney and many more. Mary and Dion took influences from skiffle too, and used them when they performed together. Early American skiffle groups and Jug Bands, and their later UK counterparts used washboards, jugs, tea chest bass, anything that could be shaken, rattled or hit, blown or plucked to create a sound. Likewise, in their early days of music making, Mary and her brother used to create rhythms with found objects like pans, scuttles and cigar boxes filled with peas.

And then rock'n'roll happened! In 1956 Bill Haley, James Dean, and Elvis Presley presented their brand of music to the world. The kids went crazy in cinemas watching *Rock around the Clock* with Bill Haley singing 'Shake, Rattle and Roll', and of course, the title song. Close on his heels, Elvis Presley's records came flooding into the country: 'Heartbreak Hotel', 'Blue Suede Shoes', and 'Hound Dog'. Now there was a sea change in the music that kids were listening to. The charts were filled with rock'n'roll stars; Buddy Holly's 'That'll Be the Day', Jackie Wilson's 'Reet Petite', and the satanic sex of Jerry Lee Lewis, with 'Whole Lotta Shakin' Goin' On', and 'Great Balls of Fire'. People were scandalised when he toured Britain in 1958 accompanied by his wife who was also his cousin and only 13 years old. It's not clear what caused more scandal: was it her age or because she was his cousin; perhaps it was the devil-like music he was playing.

Next, Britain began to produce her own rock'n'roll stars. These grew out of the skiffle boom that was centred around Soho coffee bars, particularly the 2i's. This bar had taken its name from its previous owners – the Irani brothers. When it was taken over by two Australian wrestlers, they kept the name as they didn't have the money to have a sign made. Trade was slow at the start; the street was jam-packed with other coffee bars; competition was fierce. That changed in July 1956. The Vipers were performing for the Soho Bastille Day parade when it started to rain. They took shelter in the 2i's, ordered coffee and started to play. They attracted a crowd and when Paul Lincoln, the owner, saw that he asked them to come back again. Soon they took up a residency and packed the place out every night. Two young guys were hired to decorate the basement and paid in beer. They painted the walls black with Egyptian eyes that stared out over the tiny stage – the black paint came off on people's jumpers. This was a haunt for kids, who would cram into the space hoping to see and be seen.

One night, in September 1956, the Vipers, performing at the 2i's, featured Tommy Hicks, a young rock singer, who sang his newly written song, 'Rock with The Caveman'. Showbiz agent John Kennedy was impressed with what he saw. He was looking for a new star, someone to set the West End alight. With help from Larry Parnes, he signed Tommy to a record deal with Decca, and with his name changed to Tommy Steele, his first record was released a month later and went to top 10 in the charts.

After Tommy Steele was 'discovered' at the 2i's, its reputation as the place where stars were made began to spread. It developed into a focal point for rock'n'roll. Harry Webb, who became Cliff Richard, the Drifters (later the Shadows), Vince Eager, Terry Dene, Wee Willie Harris (known as the British Elvis recorded 'Singing the Blues'), Joe Brown, Eden Kane, Screaming Lord Sutch, Tony Sheridan, Lance Fortune, Ritchie Blackmore, and Paul Gadd (Gary Glitter) were all either discovered at or at least played the 2i's.

Although Mary and her brother were performing in rather more genteel venues at this time, there can be no doubt that they knew what was happening in London's music scene. The 2i's was an iconic venue, where stars were made!

~

Six-Five Special

British people had turned to television at the time of the Coronation in 1953; an estimated 27 million watched the ceremony. Often, the whole population of the street squashed into one sitting room to watch the only set in the neighbourhood. Then, in the years leading up to 1960, television's hold on popular culture grew stronger. A second channel, ITV, was introduced in 1955, and reception was expanded to cover almost the entire country.

Mary regarded those early television programmes as bland and tedious in a way that is hard to imagine. They were all very worthy - cookery lessons from TV chefs like the wildly eccentric Fanny Craddock and the goatee-bearded Phillip Harben; gardening tips from the TV gardener, Fred Streeter; *Music for You*, where a conductor in a black tie was introduced with a few saccharine words by Eric Robinson. Live entertainment consisted mainly of desperately dull continental cabaret artists: Slav acrobats, Czech jugglers, and dancers in clogs or lederhosen.

Radio was still the centrepiece of the BBC; it reached the entire country with something for everyone. Mary was always keen to hear her favourite programme, *The Goon Show*. She knew she could listen to the music she loved on the radio, if not on the Light Programme, then on Radio Luxembourg, which was now playing six hours of new music a day.

In September 1955, the BBC's monopoly on television was broken when independent television companies were granted broadcasting licences. As the *TV Times* reported on 22 September 1955:

Television is at last given the real freedom of the air. Comparable to the law that kept motor-cars chugging sedately behind a man carrying a red flag. Now it's the 'go' signal the green light for TV too – with no brake on enterprise and imagination.

Now that the BBC had competition, its policy to close every evening between six and seven was challenged. This hour, known as the 'Toddlers' Truce', was intended to give parents time to put their kids to bed. Audiences didn't seem to mind too much either way, but ITV weren't happy with the policy, claiming it reeked of a nanny state. The BBC had a financial advantage as it was funded by the mandatory licence fee. In contrast, the independent companies relied on advertising revenues. They wanted to broadcast programmes in that slot – closing down for a whole hour, especially the one just before primetime programming, meant the loss of an hour's worth of lucrative advertising revenue.

Both channels stuck by the truce until the beginning of 1957. Then ITV began broadcasting series such as *The Adventures of Sir Lancelot* and *The Buccaneers*. The BBC presented a new light-hearted nightly magazine programme called *Tonight,* and decided that Saturday evenings would be given a modern programme aimed at the young: *Six*

-Five Special. The *Radio Times* described the show as 'designed for the young in spirit who like to keep abreast of topical trends in the world about them, with special emphasis on the world of entertainment'. Music would play a major role, with rock'n'roll, skiffle and traditional jazz all part of the mix.

Broadcast right after the *News at Six* on Saturday night, it was live, and even via the TV screen, the chemistry was tangible! The show opened with a driving skiffle number and film of a train racing along the track, and Pete Murray, the top disc jockey of the day, with his catchphrase 'Time to jive on the old six five'.

The programme, featuring Kenny Baker and his Half Dozen, Michael Holliday and the King Brothers, a sports feature by Freddie Mills and a star spotlight on Lisa Gastoni – started rather cautiously. By the third show, the BBC broadcast the earliest live performance from a rock'n'roll star: Tommy Steele. In his eight-minute slot he sang 'Rip It Up', 'Rock with The Cavemen', 'Hound Dog' and 'Singing the Blues'. This was the longest sequence given over to rock'n'roll up to that point. Kenny Baker played with his Half-Dozen. Freddie Mills went swimming and the film spot was from *High Society*: 'Now You Has Jazz' by Bing Crosby and Louis Armstrong. The star spotlight was with the actress Adrienne Corri, while Julian Bream played classical guitar. Russ Henderson and his Steel Band played 'The Banana Boat Song'. Mike and Bernie Winters, the only comedy duo with two straight men, performed a sketch which mocked rock'n'roll, involving a Mr Barris made up to look like Bill Haley.

The BBC had come up with the idea for the show, but *Six-Five Special* was mostly the vision of Jack Good. He was made assistant producer but wasn't given free rein. Production duties for the programme were assigned to Josephine Douglas, Jack Good was associate producer. Jo Douglas stuck more to the traditional, somewhat conservative values of the BBC.

A young Oxford graduate, Jack Good wanted to get into theatre and had been president of Oxford University Dramatic Society. After university he trained as a producer with the BBC. With time to kill one afternoon, he went to see *Rock Around the Clock,* the film that brought Bill Haley and his Comets to prominence, and was creating scandalised headlines. Newspapers reported kids being driven into wild frenzies by the music, and turning the stalls and balconies into a makeshift dance hall. The sight of these teenagers jumping up and down and climbing over the seats fascinated Jack. He was hypnotised by the buzz, and resolved, if he was ever to get the chance, to produce a show that would radiate that same kind of excitement.

From the start, Jo and Jack had opposing views about *Six-Five Special*. Jo kept to the traditional BBC pattern – Reith's commitment to 'educate, inform, entertain' – she proclaimed that they couldn't present a show that only featured music. A sense of moral rectitude was pervasive at the time and *Six-Five Special* was its mongrel offspring; a mix of pop, light entertainment, youth club worthiness and forced jollity. Jo's vision was of a magazine programme with features such as a piece about a sporting hero, an interview with a film star, or a clip from a recently released American movie, there was even a priest in a dog-collar who did the hand jive to prove that the church was still alive and kicking. Good's view was more simplistic. He just wanted excitement; he remembered the way those teenagers responded to the new, noisy, lively music.

Good started as associate producer, but soon he was given equal billing to Douglas, mainly because she doubled as the show's presenter. They took it in turns week by week to produce and direct. Pete Murray recalls, 'Jo's ideas were very worthy whereas Jack was 100 per cent music'. He saw Jack as an innovator, 'a very wild wonderful man with great ideas.' Jack wanted to produce an all-out music show with lots of movement; the audience up on their feet moving to the music and mixing with the performers. He emptied the studio space and filled it with fans and musicians. Rather than sitting in docile rows, watching and pattering their applause, the audience was part of the action, dancing and clapping along with the music. And it was intense – the performers were energetic and the music was loud and insistent. In 1957, *Six-Five Special* was all there was for teenagers, and it clocked up audiences of 12 or 13 million.

In spite of her antipathy to television, Mary is most likely to have seen several of the *Six-Five Special* shows, and will have discovered a somewhat unusual kind of programme. In addition to the studio-based shows, there were a number of outside broadcasts; the most impressive of which came from the 2i's coffee bar in Soho in November 1957. For this the crew laid miles of cable along the street and lugged the Marconi

III cameras, weighing 12 stones each, down the rickety stairs. The audience, the dancers, the presenters and the groups were squeezed into the tiny space, causing all sorts of problems for the technicians. The programme was a mix of skiffle, trad jazz, and rock'n'roll. It was spontaneous and lively with the heaving audience moving constantly to the music.

Featured on the show was Chas McDevitt, as well as Larry Page, Laurie London, the King Brothers, Wee Willie Harris, Jim Dale and Mike and Bernie Winters. Incongruously it also included Gilbert Harding - the 50-year-old grouch famous for his choleric appearances on 'What's My Line'. The film clip came from *The Golden Disc*, the Terry Dene film set in Soho. Wee Willie Harris, the pink haired rock god, performed 'Rockin' at the 2i's', together with the King Brothers and Mike and Bernie Winters. This show was opened and closed by Adam Faith and the Worried Men . The 2i's status as the epicentre of the teenage revolution was cemented.

Six-Five Special became one of the most-watched programmes by teenagers in the UK. Good was a passionate advocate of rock'n'roll and his name came to be synonymous with rock'n'roll on English television in the 50's. His programmes were a platform for the likes of Don Lang, Lord Rockingham's XI, Dickie Pride, Marty Wilde and Cliff Richard to name a few … Besides, he was responsible for starting Cliff's career, making 'Move It' into a national hit! Long before Associated-Rediffusion produced *Ready Steady Go!*, Jack Good pioneered this programme format. Later, when BBC bosses found him too hard to handle, he moved to ITV and produced *Oh Boy!'* for them.

~

Discovering the Blues

While Dion was away learning Russian, Mary had begun to find out more about blues music. She knew that it didn't have the same sound as most of the songs she had heard as she was growing up. Her father helped her to understand that this was because blues music used its own form of scale, different to the do-re-mi scale she had been taught at school. He demonstrated on the piano how the blues scale was based on just five notes, two of them flattened, and this is what gave the blues their distinctive sound. In fact, one of these flattened notes was actually

101

called the 'blue note', and once her father had pointed it out, she could hear it. With her first guitar, bought for her by Dion, she learned some basic chords, the simple blues forms that follow an AAB structure over 12 bars. This form became the foundation of jazz, pop, country and rock'n'roll over the years and it was the way Mary was introduced to the guitar. In an interview talking about her bond with the music of African American artists, she said, 'I feel more at ease with them than I do with many white people. I wish I had been born coloured. When it comes to singing and feeling, I just want to be one of them and not me. Then again, I see how some of them are treated and I thank God I'm white.'[114]

Along with absorbing the sounds of jazz, Mary was listening to the blues: artists such as Bessie Smith, Robert Johnson and Memphis Minnie. But she wanted to know what it meant to talk about the blues, and set out to learn about the origins and evolution of this musical genre. She discovered early on the important part the American Civil War played in this development. [115] The conflict, between the United States of America and the Confederate States of America, centred on the abolition of slavery. The Confederate States were defeated by the United States after four bloody years of war, and slavery was abolished nationwide.

During the period of Reconstruction that followed, slaves were freed and granted 'equal protection' of the Constitution and guaranteed the right to vote. But by 1877 Reconstruction had ended and most of the gains that African Americans had made after the Civil War were suppressed; millions of them were economically and politically disenfranchised. African Americans lived with harsh conditions in the southern cotton states: an endless cycle of debt, in-farm tenancy and sharecropping, serfdom, curfews and lynching. Some migrated to northern cities, where they faced other difficulties: segregation, substandard housing, subsistence wages, second class status and discrimination. But rural or urban, like other folk-art forms, blues and gospel came from the experiences of everyday life of African Americans.

Mary discovered that blues music had a multitude of African American sources, from Southern plantations, lumber camps, prisons and fields,

---

114 Ray Coleman, 'Dusty: Pop Probe', *Melody Maker* (21 November 1964).

115 Many years later she became a student of the American civil War.

black work songs, field hollers, chants and ballads. These all came together to create this unique music. The spiritual and musical forms of blues and gospel have influenced much of the American music since then. The 'blue notes' that are characteristic of the form came to be prominent in country music, rock and roll and jazz. The first rock'n'roll songs, from 'Good Rockin' Tonight' to 'Rocket 88' to 'Hound Dog' to 'Johnny B Goode' were based on this template.

Rhythm and Blues (R&B) developed from jazz, blues and gospel and was a form that fascinated Mary. The mixture of jump blues, big band swing, gospel, boogie and blues, moved it away from being distinctly African American music, and it formed the foundation of a wide repertoire of American popular music genres, most notably rock'n'roll.

In an interview discussing contemporary popular African American music, Mary said: 'I was getting imports while I was still with the Springfields. I was aware of early R&B before Motown was Motown and early Stax – those labels that came out of the Memphis. Those were my earliest real influences. Around '61, '62.'[116] But it is most likely that Mary began her quest much earlier, when she went in search of the specialist shops that stocked these obscure imports.

~

Ma Rainey and Bessie Smith

Blues greats were people like Ma Rainey, Bessie Smith, Robert Johnson, Memphis Minnie, Muddy Waters, Son House, T-Bone Walker, and BB King. Gospel stars were such as Mahalia Jackson, Sister Rosetta Tharpe, the Gold Gate Quartet, Sam Cooke, the Staple Singers and Clara Ward.

Ma Rainey emerged from the Deep South and the very early days of recorded blues. Her story is very much bound up with that of Bessie Smith, the first blues singer Mary's father had introduced her to. Between them Ma Rainey and Bessie Smith pretty much defined the sound of female recorded blues in the early 20s.

Bessie Smith was very young when she started busking with her brother. At just 14 she was taken on as a dancer by the Moses Stokes

---

116 Chris Bourke (1990) 'Dusty in Private', *Rip it Up* (New Zealand).

minstrel show, a troupe of travelling minstrels. Soon after that, she joined the Rabbit Foot Minstrels with Ma Rainey, a star of the vaudeville circuit. By the time Bessie Smith joined the troupe, she was the main singer for the show. She guided and influenced Bessie in show business.

Ma Rainey began singing as a member of the First African Baptist Church. Later she married Will Rainey and they travelled from city to city as part of a minstrel troupe. It was on these tours that she learned real country blues and began to use them in her act. She was one of the first to record the blues - simple, straightforward stories about heart break, promiscuity, drinking binges, travelling, working, magic and superstition.

Ma Rainey had a dazzling stage presence. Draped in long gowns and covered in diamonds, she wore a necklace made of gold coins, wild horsehair wigs, and her teeth were capped in gold that flashed when she sang. Her prop was an ostrich plume that she swirled around to great effect in her performances. Audiences were enthralled by her. Thomas A Dorsey, who organised her backing band, the Wild Cats Jazz Band, spoke about her – "When she started singing, the gold in her teeth would sparkle. She was in the spotlight. She possessed listeners; they swayed, they rocked, they moaned and groaned, as they felt the blues with her." When she sang a "moaning" song, which would soon be called the blues, she could captivate a room in no time at all. Famous in the first three decades of the 20th century, Ma Rainey came to be known as the 'Mother of the Blues'.

Mamie Smith, an early blues singer, was the first to record the blues in 1920. Her song, 'Crazy Blues', was a huge hit. Soon after that, Ma Rainey was recruited to record for Paramount and Bessie Smith for Columbia. Bessie's first record, 'Downhearted Blues', sold over 800000 copies. Bessie's presentation was subtler than the raw, more direct Ma. As she developed her style, she could sing almost any type of song convincingly, from traditional blues to pop music like, 'After You've Gone.' By the end of the 1920's, Smith was the highest-paid African American performer of her day, and was known as the 'Empress of the Blues.'

A selection of the many records released by Ma Rainey includes 'Bo-Weevil Blues' with Austin and her Blue Serenaders, 'Moonshine Blues' with Lovie Austin, 'Yonder Comes the Blues' with Louis Armstrong, and 'See See Rider'. Sometimes it could be difficult to make out the words of the songs Ma Rainey and Bessie sang. But listening carefully, the story of the tough life lived by these women gradually emerged.

One of Ma Rainey's records called 'Prove it on Me Blues' is likely to have spoken to Mary on a visceral level. She knew, by this time, that the tug she felt in her stomach - at school (or later on at work) – came when she was close to the girl she had a crush on.

From the book 'Black Pearls' by Daphne Harrison comes this quote about Ma Rainey: 'The good-humoured, rollicking Rainey loved life, loved love, and most of all loved her people. Her voice bursts forth with a hearty declaration of courage and determination - a reaffirmation of black life.'[117]

~

Sister Rosetta Tharpe

Sister Rosetta Tharpe was another powerful, early 20th century gospel performer. In 1915, When she was five, she moved with her mother, Katie Bell Nubin, from Cotton Plant, Arkansas, to Chicago. They joined Bishop Robert's Fortieth Church of God in Christ (COGIC) but also held street meetings on Maxwell Street. Rosetta sang, and Katie played the mandolin and delivered the Word. Rosetta became a star performer singing and playing to a thousand people in a Chicago church. In the early forties, she performed in the Cotton Club with swing bands, for a short spell. She emerged as a gospel music star when she picked up the guitar and became Sister Rosetta Tharpe.

Brought up in the Catholic Church with its very specific musical tradition and songs of celebration, Mary's experience was very different. The gospel songs of the Pentecostal Church were a revelation to her. She understood the immense importance this music had for its worshippers, similar to the effect the music of her church had on her. But the contrast was great and very powerful. Unsure whether she could ever properly understand the music from the COGIC, she nevertheless revered it. What she realised was that it had a significance that went beyond entertainment and into the realm of religious adoration.

---

117 Daphne Harrison (1988) *Black Pearls*, Chicago: Rutgers University Press, p. 40.

Mary would soon discover Sister Rosetta Tharpe. Her recordings started in 1938 and went all the way up to the late 50's. Her enormous repertoire included favourites such as 'Gospel Train', 'God Don't Like It', 'Mary, Don't You Weep', and 'Lonesome Road'. The songs she sang included– 'Silent Night', 'Down by the Riverside', 'Up Above My Head', 'Didn't it Rain', and 'This Train'. In Britain followers were lucky, her Brunswick recordings were the first ones issued here of true gospel singing. For Mary perhaps more important was her discovery of some of the memorable duets Rosetta recorded with Marie Knight. They toured together and recorded several call-and-response gospel songs for Decca that reached the rhythm and blues charts. They established themselves as one of the top gospel acts of the time with top ten hits in the US R&B chart at the end of 1948. Marie's solo version of Gospel Train" 'reached number 9 on the R&B chart in 1949. 'Didn't it Rain' was a big hit for Rosetta and Marie in the States.

Marie Knight also began by singing gospel as a child in the Pentecostal tradition. After her split with Sister Rosetta in the mid-1950's, Marie began singing rhythm and blues as well as gospel. Years later, taking her first steps into solo fame, Mary paid homage to the music of Marie Knight. She recorded 'Nothing (in the World)' on her first LP; a song recorded by Knight in 1961.

The records Mary discovered in these years included blues, gospel and jazz. They were fascinating and enthralling but always seemed so far away. The yawning gulf of the Atlantic Ocean between them must have seemed an impossible gap to close.

~

Rosetta on Six-Five Special

At the height of the jazz era in 1950's Britain Chris Barber was immensely popular. He loved African American blues music and started to bring these musicians to England. Chris introduced many great performers to UK audiences, including Sister Rosetta Tharpe, Sonny Terry & Brownie McGhee, Louis Jordan, Big Bill Broonzy, Muddy Waters and James Cotton. He wanted to learn jazz 'at close range, by example', and Sister Rosetta Tharpe was first. On November 23, 1957, Pete Murray and Josephine Douglas welcomed the Chris Barber Jazz Band onto *Six-Five Special,* along with the many Six-Five regulars. On this day Sister

Rosetta Tharpe appeared on the show, with Barber. It was an ultimate thrill for Mary to see and hear this awesome blues and gospel singer performing right there on her TV screen. Barber announced that Sister Rosetta was touring with his band and they were scheduled to appear in theatres all over England, with the last show in the Coliseum in London on the 15th of December.

As Gayle Wald states in, *Shout Sister Shout*, her biography of Rosetta Tharpe: 'She wasn't the first gospel soloist to tour Europe, her 1957 tour made her a preeminent heroine of the blues revival and its leading gospel protagonist.' [118]

Rosetta was quick to inhabit the role of gospel star. Everything about her exuded fabulousness: from her stuffed to bursting wardrobe bags to her wigs – variously described as blonde, auburn and 'flaming orange' – to the scent of her Arpège perfume. But what young blues fans noticed first was her guitar playing. They had no idea who she was, this great guitarist suddenly appeared and they went 'Wow, listen to that!' She was stunning. Not only were they not used to hearing blistering guitar, they weren't used to hearing a woman playing blistering guitar. She was ripping the wallpaper off. [119]

The tour started on a Friday evening at Birmingham's Town Hall, a venue that held about two thousand people. The souvenir programs billed Rosetta as "America's Sensational Gospel Singing Favourite," and that evening, she proved she was worthy of the title. [120]

Rosetta had the amazing ability to hold her audience's attention. Ottilie Peterson recalled that 'to hear her in the flesh was quite astounding. Her voice sounded fuller and rounder in person – a little more like Marie Knight's –than it had on record. It was quite astounding... The first time we heard her, there wasn't a person in the band who hadn't wiped their eyes for tears' [121]

Chris Barber gave this description of Rosetta: 'her guitar, by itself, was as loud as the entire band. It was beautiful music, it was enthralling,

---

118 Gayle Wald (2008) *Shout Sister Shout*, Boston: Beacon Press, p.171

119 Gayle Wald (2008) *Shout Sister Shout*, Boston: Beacon Press, p.173

120 Gayle Wald (2008) *Shout Sister Shout*, Boston: Beacon Press, p. 164.

121 Gayle Wald (2008) *Shout Sister Shout*, Boston: Beacon Press, p.160

totally enthralling and totally convincing. Sister Rosetta stole the show. Until now British audiences had only seen imitations of blues and gospel, but there onstage for the very first time was the real thing. She had a fantastic swaggering guitar style and that wonderful voice, the warmth and humanity that makes her the godmother of rock and roll. Remarkable performer. A force of nature, a fantastic performer. Remarkable musician.'

Ottilie Patterson, who sang with the Barber band, wasn't scheduled to do anything with Rosetta. But when she heard Ottilie performing, she insisted that they were going to sing together. The song was 'When the Saints Go Marching In'. Rosetta told her what to do and how to do it. When the time came, she fitted exactly into her role. It was thrilling for the fans to see Rosetta improvising with their own British jazz stars. 'They refused to leave the hall until the band played several encores; that is not different songs but repetitions of what they had already played.' [122]

George Melly, singer with Mick Mulligan's Jazz Band, described Rosetta: 'On stage her performance was splendid. When she actually started singing, her formidable bottom swinging like a metronome in time to her wailing voice and emphatic guitar, it was pure delight. She wore on stage a series of brilliant dresses with plunging necklines, and a great deal of chunky jewellery.' [123]

Ginger Baker, the legendary drummer who went on to fame as a member of Cream and Blind Faith, was born with fiery red hair. On tour in Scandinavia with Rosetta and the Diz Disley band, he recalled the first time he met her at rehearsal, 'she said, hey honey I love your hair colour, what dye do you use? Her hair was bright red'. When I told her it was natural, she said, you'll have to drop your pants to prove it!' [124]

Given the chance to see that show, Mary's head and her heart will have been filled with the sounds of the concert and the beautiful music she had heard. One day she determined she would perform this kind of music.

---

122 Gayle Wald (2008) *Shout Sister Shout*, Boston: Beacon Press, p. 165

123 George Melly (1965) *Owning Up*, London: Weidenfeld & Nicholson, pp. 544–45.

124 Gayle Wald (2008) *Shout Sister Shout*, Boston: Beacon Press, p.173

Dion

Late in 1954, not long before Mary left school, Dion's time in the Army, eavesdropping Russian comms, was at an end. He had no intention of being stuck in an office, working in a bank or with Lloyd's Underwriters. All that was firmly behind him, and now he set his sights on a career in the music business. He had joined the choir at the Joint Services School for Linguists and sang Russian folk songs, he also formed a jazz group with several other recruits.

The Pedini Brothers, the barbershop quartet that he had formed with his friends from the St Benedict's social club, was in the past. As soon as he was free of National Service, Dion began to chase bookings in West End clubs. In December 1955, as part of his plan to pursue his showbiz ambitions, he took part in a 'Help to professional artists scheme' at the Cote d'Azur Club, organised by Vincent Montefusco. After that he had regular appearances in the Montrose, La Rascas, the Society Restaurant and Annabel's. Sometimes Mary joined him and other times he performed with a partner.

But if he was going to further his career, Dion knew that he needed proper stage experience. An advertisement in *The Stage* for a guitarist 'in the modern style' seemed the opportunity he was looking for. He applied and was given a contract to join Follies on Parade in a summertime seaside revue in Skegness. He joined this end-of-the-pier variety show at the end of May 1957. This was entertainment for holidaymakers who went in search of sun, sea, and sand as a break from their humdrum lives at home. It was a proper job in the theatre where he would be performing onstage with a variety troupe. Dion's guitar performances were described as charming, and his cabaret manner almost informal. His simple production of 'Ain't We Got Fun' was excellent, and he was a big hit with the girls. He was also teamed with The Lehmiski Ladies in a snappy song-and-dance routine, 'Singing the Blues'.

After 12 weeks of twice-nightly shows, and Saturday matinees, the season came to an end, and Dion went home again. This was his first, and possibly only, solo seaside season.

~

Disaster

As with all siblings Dion and Mary fought all the time, nevertheless she idolised him, and looked to him for help and support. He was her second fiercest critic (she was the first), but she was bereft when he left for Skegness. Who could she do battle with now? In a perverse way she enjoyed their rivalry; the combination of competitive bickering and closeness that they shared. She didn't have that with anyone else.

Mary was adrift and convinced her show-business career was going nowhere. It had been two years since she left school, and she was in a rut. There she was, dusting the shelves in Squires Record Shop, organising the records, and playing the West End clubs several nights a week. But not really getting anywhere. She sat in those clubs, strumming her guitar and singing for hours at a time, but people never seemed to listen, and she felt demoralised; she had no clear idea of what she was doing and nor was she sure of where she was going.

Depressed, she began to think her dream of being a star was pointless wishful thinking; it was all too hard. Later she recalled this conversation with her mother: 'Through tears of frustration one night after the show she moaned 'I'll never make it'. Her mum counselled 'It's a tough life, maybe you're not tough enough.'

This should have been a challenge to spur me on, but it didn't. I decided to go back to selling. This time I got a job demonstrating toy trains in a store. But again, my passion for being the best was nearly my ruination. [125]

Having decided to give up on show business, Mary found a job in Bentall's department store. This time she would take it seriously; she was going to build a career in retail. But nothing ever works the way you think it will.

For one thing, she still bought her copy of *The Stage* every week and read it cover to cover, searching for...what? She didn't really know. Just something, anything, that would move her on from the mundane. Whenever she found an advert looking for a singer, she sent off a letter, hoping for a positive response. Usually nothing happened; they didn't even bother to reply.

---

125 Dusty Springfield, 'Fame has a Flipside too', *Woman's Own* 1965, in Dusty Springfield Bulletin No. 65 July 2008.

Dion, back now from his summer in Skegness, had hooked up with a partner, Georges Martinique, and together they were playing the West End clubs. They had a regular date at Helene Cordet's club, Cercle de la Maison de France. Dion wrote to producer, John Kingdon, at the BBC, asking to be considered for an audition, and to remind him of his appearance on *In Town Tonight* in May that year.[126] He enclosed a cutting from the *Sunday Graphic* with his letter. The short article about Helene Cordet's club featured a photograph of Dion and some talk of him performing little-known Andalusian melodies with his guitar.

John Kingdon arranged an audition for Dion and Georges in January 1958, at Studio B5, Broadcasting House. Two weeks later Dion wrote again to remind Kingdon about the audition and let him know they had added a third guitarist and were now a trio. Georges and Dion appeared on Ken Sykora's *Guitar Club* in March.

Meanwhile, Mary's despondency turned to disaster. One day, demonstrating a train set for a little boy, she fused all the lights in the entire store. That was the end of that retail career – she was given the sack immediately.

---

126 BBC Written Archives Centre, O'Brien Dion RCont 1, Letter from Dion O'Brien to John Kingdon, 30 December 1957.

Part 4: The Lana Sisters:

1958 - 1960

A Chance

Mary was in the depths of despair. Having more or less given up on her dream of a career in showbusiness, her plan for a successful life in retail was now over too. What could she do? She began searching *The Stage* with a renewed intensity. She scoured the wanted ads every week, determined to find some kind of opportunity.

One day she found something that looked interesting. Hidden at the bottom of the page, next to the 'In Memoriam' notices and the 'Artists Wanted' list, was an advert so small she could easily have missed it. It said, 'Wanted girl singer, "Modern," to join girl harmony act.'

This could be just what she was looking for. Searching out a half-decent photo, she wrote off right away and waited for a reply.

WANTED girl singer. "Modern," to join girl harmony act. Please state age, height, experience, if any, also salary required. Low voice preferred. Enclose recent photo. S.a.e. Knowledge of music an asset, must be willing to travel.—Box A2107, c/o "The Stage."

FIGURE 4.1 ADVERTISEMENT IN *THE STAGE* 9 JANUARY 1958

Audition

The reply to her letter arrived quite quickly, and it was good news. It came from the Lana Sisters, and on headed note paper it invited her, very formally, to attend an audition at the Max Rivers Rehearsal Rooms in Leicester Square.

On the appointed day, Mary caught the tube to Leicester Square, clutching her guitar and sheet music. This audition – her first professional audition – was almost a disaster.

It didn't help that she was late. It wasn't her fault, of course. There had been a hold up on the tube. Then, in her hurry to reach the rehearsal rooms, she kept slipping around on the slush covered pavements.

Iris Long and Lynne Abrams were in the studio, a pile of letters in front of them from young girls keen to break into show business. Mary's letter had gone to the bottom of the pile: they weren't sure they wanted her; they didn't think she looked right. But now all the girls had been auditioned and, yes, they may have been pretty, but none were suitable because they couldn't sing.

Iris was despondent. Her eyes flitted from the letter to the photograph of Mary O'Brien. She didn't think this girl was going to be any good. She wasn't glamorous enough. But they had seen all the other girls and had no option: they would have to at least give her a chance.

When she finally arrived at the Max Rivers Rehearsal Rooms, Mary was already 20 minutes late. Iris and Lynne were sitting inside this desolate and dilapidated old building feeling a mixture of impatience and despair. The room stank of stale cigarettes from the countless butts stubbed out by chain-smoking rehearsal pianists, and the familiar odour of sweat from generations of dancers. These traces of desperation were left by endless showbiz hopefuls. And here was Mary, just one more in that long list.

Lynne and Iris were dressed in smart matching outfits, they looked glamorous and sophisticated. They watched Mary clump across the stage and gasped, 'oh my god'. This girl was short and quite ungainly; with her guitar in one hand and her fake fur coat down to her knees she looked unprepossessing. She started to apologise, 'I'm sorry, I'm ever so sorry I'm late. I got stuck on the tube.' But Lynne said, 'forget all of that, forget about that, don't worry, just get on.'

Iris picked up her guitar and said, 'these are the songs we sing.' She started to sing, 'Sugar in the morning, sugar in the evening, sugar at supper time.' Lynne asked, 'can you sing that?' With that Mary dropped her coat, and joined in; it was like a transformation. She sang the bottom harmony; it was perfect. Iris and Lynne looked at one another and

114

exclaimed 'Oh! Ohh!' They realised they had been wrong to judge Mary. This girl could sing!

'You'll do, you'll do', they said. 'But boy have we got to work on your artistry because you're pretty useless.'

They offered her the job right away. Iris said, 'that was great, I like your voice; I think it's a perfect fit with Lynne's top and my middle range.' Mary had a lot to learn, but the main thing was that they both liked her voice. Lynne said later, 'It is incredible to think of what she became, and we nearly didn't bother with her; we just nearly didn't bother.' [127]

This was Mary's chance and she grabbed it with both hands; she was going into showbiz! Maybe being jealous of Dion when he went to Skegness had given her the jolt she needed to seriously look for a job. The debacle over the train set at Squire's had pushed her over the edge – it *was* lucky after all!

~

Rehearsals

The Lana Sisters had been on a break from touring when their third member, Sheila, left; it gave them time to hold the auditions for her replacement. It also meant they had time to get the new girl trained – a lot of work was needed to get the act in shape when Mary joined.

Rehearsals were held in the Metropolitan Theatre in Edgware Road. Mary met Iris and Lynne there a few days later. This theatre was dusty inside, the boxes on either side of the stage held up by plaster models of naked ladies painted gold. Most of their rehearsals were held in the chorus room, and they only occasionally went onto the stage itself.

Iris and Lynne had already decided that they should start with the trio's usual repertoire of songs. Mary soon realised that even though the Lana Sisters seemed to have an air of refined sophistication, they rocked! They began by working on numbers such as 'Rock Around the Clock' and 'Shake, Rattle and Roll' – the music that had been shaking up the older generation, and the film that had had the kids tearing up seats in the cinemas two years before. Now rock'n'roll was accepted as part of the musical scene. They practised the Charlie Gracie hit 'Butterfly', the R&B

---

127 Lynne Essex: interview with author

number 'Kansas City' and the fun, high-energy 'When Mexico Gave Up the Rhumba'. To complete their act, they rehearsed the semi-religious song, 'In the Beginning', which would bring the audience back down before they finished with 'My Mother's Eyes', a sentimental number loved by audiences everywhere. It was enough to get them started; there would be plenty of time later between bookings to learn more.

~

Becoming a Lana Sister

Mary had so much to learn about pitch and modulation and volume in those early rehearsals. She had to know how to project – to feel the sound coming up from her belly, not stuck in her throat; how to pace herself; about stagecraft; and work as part of a unit. And there were basics, such as how to get on- and offstage without seeming awkward. Singing was the least of it; that was the easy part that she had been doing all her life.

No one can recall why Mary's name was changed to Shan, but that is how she was known for the whole time she was with the Lana Sisters. It could be that it was close to Sheila, the name of the girl she replaced.

A priority for the sisters was to work on Mary's style; they took her to their hairdresser, and instructed her to cut and colour Mary's hair to match theirs. Next, they asked a dressmaker to alter Sheila's dresses to fit Mary. Lynne's natural elegance put Iris and Mary in the shade, and as their style expert and guiding light, she decided on the look of the group, insisting that their image must be glamorous and modern. She designed their costumes and had a brilliant dressmaker make them. Her sister also made some of their daytime clothes, as well as a beautiful duffel coat. Whenever the Lana Sisters appeared in public, both on- and offstage, they wore matching outfits, even including their sweaters and slacks at rehearsals. Lynne also taught Mary how to apply stage make-up so that it looked good under the lights without being tarty.

In their first incarnation, the group had been known as the Iris Long Trio, and for a short while they were the Long Sisters. Then, about a year before Mary joined them, their name was changed, to the Lana Sisters. As the Iris Long Trio, the girls had hauled instruments around with them: Sheila on piano, Iris guitar, and Lynne double bass. By the time the group were known as the Lana Sisters they had ditched the instruments, and

116

presented a slick, contemporary style. Iris sometimes played guitar, but mostly now they just sang, accompanied by the theatre orchestra. Their influences came from American girl groups and included quite a few rocky numbers. They wanted to be a bit different, to present a slightly risqué alternative to some of the more wholesome sister acts. Unlike some of those other acts, the Lana Sisters worked on their own harmonies. Their performances were planned to include a combination of high-energy numbers alongside ballads and comedy songs.

Lynne was the innovator – she worked out performance routines and found props they could use in the act; she was always searching for something to make them stand out. During rehearsals and after performances, the girls would spend hours talking through new ideas. Lynne suggested songs they could sing and ways they could present themselves, but Iris was more conservative and had to be persuaded to accept these ideas. The aim was always to be more 'with it'. The group was very successful; despite never making top of the bill, they were quite well known.

Now Mary was adapting to life in the Lana Sisters. Whenever a song was suggested, she didn't have to be told how to harmonise. It was in her blood, completely and utterly. She was right there with it, getting into the rhythm and giving it an edge. In the school choir she had spent a lot of time learning harmonies, and now she picked them up quickly and got a kick out of working on them during rehearsals. Iris insisted the group worked best as a harmony trio, singing in unison, and was completely opposed to the idea of any of the three taking the lead vocal. This meant that none of them ever sang the melody line.

When the girls performed with instruments, it had been hard for them to include much movement in the act. Once they finally gave them up, Lynne knew that they needed to dance, and they needed choreography. She worked out a dance routine for each song, and the girls practised until the moves were second nature. In the first of these they used straw hats when they sang 'Dixieland'.

Mary wasn't a good dancer. Despite Miss Lehman's best efforts at school, she always struggled to move well, and she found even the simplest routines quite hard, getting tangled in her own feet as she learned the moves. Lynne took her through the steps again and again, but sometimes it seemed as though she was rooted to the floor, her feet refusing to cooperate. Her short sight didn't help – she could hardly see her hand in front of her face, and had a nasty habit of tripping over everything that got in her way. One day, exasperated, Iris suggested she get contact lenses. Mary resisted, but Iris nagged until she finally gave in and agreed to get them. Eventually, after lots of practice, Mary was able to sing and dance at the same time. Slowly, they began to improve.

Rehearsals were long and tiring but Mary wasn't fazed by that, she had always given everything to her singing. For her, it was important to understand the mechanics of a song, to get the feel of it. Once the numbers were planned out, the group worked on the harmonies and choreography for each song. With a TV appearance in a couple of weeks, and their first stage show soon after, they had to keep working to get their act to the right professional level.

1958

Not long after Mary joined the Lana Sisters; Lynne Abrams (Essex) remembers her incessant chatter about Burt Bacharach. Long before she became famous in her own right, Mary worshipped him. It was the start of a lifelong passion.

In 1958, two songs were back-to-back number one singles in the UK. Michael Holliday's version of 'The Story of My Life' spent two weeks at the top in January. Straight after that, 'Magic Moments', sung by Perry Como, reached the top and stayed there for eight weeks. Burt Bacharach and Hal David met at the Brill Building in New York City; these two hit songs were the first of many written by the partnership.

First Performance

Mary was introduced to the world as part of the Lana Sisters on BBC TV, in an episode of *Show Band Parade* with Cyril Stapleton. The *Radio Times* described the show as featuring popular music of yesterday, today and tomorrow. They appeared alongside Dennis Lotis, Alice Babs, Bob Stevenson, Sheila O'Neill, Graham MacCormack, and the dancers and the show band singers, directed by Cliff Adams.

Liverpool Empire

This was going to be Mary's first appearance onstage with the Lana Sisters, and she was terrified. But Iris and Lynne gave her lots of support and encouragement and she was determined not to let them down.

By this time, she had heard some of the story of their years on the road together with Sheila Fuller. They had had seasons in Butlins, and one at the Palladium in Edinburgh, they had toured the continent and the variety circuit, and they had appeared on many radio and TV shows. They knew the business, and each knew how the other one worked. And now here was Mary, an awkward little amateur planted in the middle of them, not at all sure that she would be able to keep up.

After the many hours spent rehearsing their songs and routines, the schedule was arranged, and Mary was ready. The trio wanted to be sure they looked right – hair, make-up and clothes all had to be perfect. It was a baptism of fire for Mary! In time, the towns, the theatres, the appearances would become a blur, but that first theatre and that first time on stage burned itself into her brain. How could she forget her first introduction to an audience that had paid to see her perform?

The Lana Sisters appeared at the Liverpool Empire in an old-style variety show. Topping the bill was Peter Brough with his swivel-eyed wooden dummy, Archie Andrews, along with Jimmy Shand and his Band.

At this time the entertainment scene was going through a transition. In most theatres variety was still the established order, but with Lonnie Donegan in its vanguard, skiffle had exploded. There were groups of kids bashing at washboards and plucking at tea chests all over the country. These young hopefuls entered contests hoping for a chance to appear on TV, and in the early days, British rockers were put on a bill alongside variety acts. Those rock fans who went to see Cliff Richard in 1959 had no wish to sit through a succession of comedians, dancers, and jugglers before they got their 20 minutes of rock. The audiences who had come to see their regular variety performers were also unhappy with this compromise. They didn't want to be surrounded by bored teenagers waiting for the appearance of their idols.

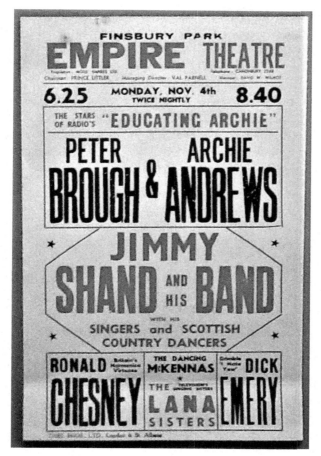

FIGURE 4.2 FLYER FOR EDUCATING ARCHIE
(THIS IS THE SAME LINE-UP AS THE LIVERPOOL EMPIRE)

When they arrived at the theatre, the first thing Mary saw was corridors lined with framed photographs and posters from days gone by; ghostly reminders of the many music hall greats who had performed there.

They checked in early in the morning, where the stage manager was organising the acts. Iris introduced Mary and explained that 'Shan' had taken over from Sheila. They were given a dressing room on the third floor but were warned not to use the lift as it constantly broke down. It had been known for people to hear their intro music playing while they were trapped in the lift, so the girls hauled their bags, stage clothes and equipment up the three flights of stairs. The other acts had already arrived and were practising. Somewhere from the bowels of the theatre they could hear the distinctive wailing of accordion music from Jimmy Shand and his Band. Back down on the stage, they ran through their numbers for the sound check. The stage manager gave them their cues and timings, showed them their marks and told them when they were on. As she stood on the massive stage, looking out into that huge empty theatre with its illustrated panelled ceiling, Mary realised this was it: she was about to perform for the first time on a proper stage.

Educating Archie was a regular feature on the Light Programme all the while Mary was growing up. Millions loved it and tuned in regularly to listen to Peter Brough, Archie Andrews and the team of characters. Archie, the ventriloquist's dummy, was haughty and imperious, elegantly dressed in a broad-striped blazer, and totally dominated his operator. The dummy was quite scary, and people often said they could feel its eyes follow them as they walked around the room. Peter Brough was a quiet and unremarkable little man, well-groomed and dapper. He had partly filed down his front teeth, hoping it would help him transfer his voice to the dummy, but it wasn't very successful. This was a ventriloquist who had become famous by means of a radio programme, which was a strange concept as the audience could see neither him nor his dummy and so couldn't tell whether or not his lips were moving. Of course, onstage he couldn't hide.

When the stage manager called 'five minutes to places', Mary felt a little rush of adrenaline, which kicked in even harder when he called the trio to their places, ready for their entrance. Ronald Chesney was performing with his harmonica; he had a remarkable way of speaking through it, and could make it sound almost like a full orchestra. It was almost possible to believe 'Sparky's Magic Piano' was on the stage. He even had a conversation with Archie Andrews. A piece of metal talking to a bit of wood, sounds crazy, but that's what happened! The act immediately before the Lana Sisters was Dick Emery, and they watched from the wings as he performed his stories, gags, and songs.

Then the Lana Sisters' music started. This was it – Mary was going onstage in front of a real live audience! Blinded by the stage lights, she could feel the energy from the crowd, but couldn't see them. When the performance started, everything was heightened. Mary was hyper focused on what she had to do, concentrating on remembering the routines for each number. The trio performed their much-rehearsed act, and threw in a bit of comedy. Before Mary knew it, they were taking a bow, and running offstage as the audience clapped and cheered. She had survived!

Mary always loved the boost of energy that came with being in the spotlight, and performing with the Lana Sisters for the first time gave her that thrill a hundred times over. Later, much later, in an interview she said, 'There's only one sound that excites me, and that's applause ... I just want to be noticed.' [128] And here it was, that joyful, addictive sound.

Lynne remembers sharing the bill with Jimmy Shand. 'He was sweet, at the end of the week he gave us all a huge box of chocolates and told us how much he enjoyed our act. He was so totally not like a showbiz person at all, even though he was a big star even then. He was a lovely man, just like an ordinary accountant.' [129]

~

A rookie mistake

A few weeks later, the Lana Sisters joined Archie Andrews and Peter Brough at the Savoy Cinema in Lincoln, and Mary did a terrible thing: she whistled in the dressing room. She didn't know it was unlucky. Lynne shouted at her to stop and ordered her to go outside, turn round three times and swear. Not knowing anything of showbiz superstitions, Mary refused. Lynne insisted that she had to do this to break the spell, but Mary stood firm, arguing that it was a crazy idea, and anyway, she didn't swear. By this time, they'd had their call to go onstage, and Iris and Lynne were both grumbling as they left the dressing room, but there was nothing to be done about it.

Well, Mary was wrong: it *was* bad luck. Descending the narrow stairs to the stage she tripped and fell, her knee bursting through her tight blue lamé trousers. She was horrified, but the opening bars had started,

128 Chris van Ness, Los Angeles Free Press, 20/03/1973

129 Lynne Essex: interview with author

and she was dragged unceremoniously onto the stage, where she had to go through the act with her bare knee poking through the hole in her trousers. Back in the dressing room, Iris was furious.

'Silly girl! Five years! Five years we have been slogging round the halls, getting known as a professional act. And you come along and in one appearance you make us look ridiculous.'

Mary was mortified, she didn't know what to say. She gave them a grovelling apology and pleaded for a second chance. 'I'm sorry, really sorry, I didn't know that would happen, I won't do it again. Please forgive me.'

Mary may have wondered why Iris didn't throw her out of the group there and then, ending her short-lived showbiz career. But although Iris said they would never be booked at that theatre again; she did give Mary another chance. And Mary tried very hard not to do anything as stupid for the rest of her time with the group.

From the time of the audition Iris had realised that Mary was a rare find. Here was a vocalist with a talent beyond anything she could have hoped for, and there was no question of asking Mary to leave the group. Iris knew she was too much of an asset to them.

~

FIGURE 4.3 THE LANA SISTERS ON SIX-FIVE SPECIAL (COURTESY OF NOLA YORK)

In April 1958, the Lana Sisters were booked to appear on *Six-Five Special*. Jack Good had left for ITV by then, Pete Murray had gone, and Jim Dale now presented the show. BBC bosses, nervous of rock'n'roll, were glad they could now take control. Mike and Bernie Winters provided the comedy, and the Squadronaires with Ronnie Aldrich – originally a band of Royal Air Force musicians that performed in Britain during and after World War II – topped the bill. As always, Don Lang and his Frantic Five played the theme song, and they also provided musical support for the Lana Sisters. The trad jazz component was supplied by Mick Mulligan's band with lead singer George Melly.

In his book, Roots, Radicals and Rockers, Billy Bragg mentions the Lana Sisters appearance on the programme. By that time, he says it had given up any pretence of being a rock'n'roll show, now skiffle was the only teenage music on the show. By the summer of 1957 it seemed every school boy (and many of the girls) in Britain was in a skiffle group, and the 'Great Skiffle Contest', a money-making talent show set up by London-based agent Stanley Dale, offered cash prizes and the chance to appear on live TV.

Rehearsals for *Six-Five Special* were non-stop throughout the day on the Friday, and there was just one complete run-through on Saturday before the show went out live that evening. Once the rehearsal was over the boys from the bands seemed to melt away, and the studio went strangely quiet. It was only later that the girls found out what was going on. The pub across the road had a television set above the bar, tuned into the show. The boys sat and enjoyed a pint while watching for their cue on the TV. They then left their pints on the bar and strolled across to the studio, they went back to finish their pints when their set was over. They kept this up all through the show.

This was live TV, and once the programme started the studio was chaotic. The floor manager in charge of the running order showed the girls where to stand, and with the space filled with cameras and cameramen, lights, microphone booms and instruments, the performers had to fight to keep their places. Just before the broadcast started the audience swarmed in and filled up any space that was left. By the time the programme went out, the studio was crammed with people and under the lights the temperature would rocket. The crew sometimes struggled to find a way around fans who got in front of the cameras, and microphone booms could end up in shot – it all got quite messy at times! But the programme was lively and fun. The kids clapped and danced to the music, and there was a mild air of anarchy. Once transmission started, the TV bosses had no control over what happened, and while the chaos created headaches for the technicians, somehow it all worked.

The Lana Sisters had one more appearance on *Six-Five Special* before the BBC called time on the show. Jack Good had been snapped up by

ITV, where he was given a free hand to produce his type of show, and his new music programme, *Oh Boy!* became an enormous success. The competition was too much for the BBC, and *Six-Five Special* was cancelled.

~

Between Tours – Birch Green

Lynne Abrams family had been evacuated to Birch Green at the start of the war. They never returned to London and were allocated a council house where they were still living when Mary joined the Lana Sisters. During breaks in touring the girls needed a convenient base to polish their act. Renting a flat in London and hiring studio space would be very expensive, so the solution was Lynne's parents' council house. Birch Green is just 21 miles outside London; There was a piano and space to rehearse. While Sheila was with the act she had lived there with Lynne and her parents, Fred and Ellen Abrams, so it seemed only natural that Mary should move into the house between tours too. That worked out quite well, though it's not clear how they were persuaded to have this stranger move in with them. But that is what happened. Lynne's family was warm and loving; they enjoyed each other's company and had a lot of fun together. Mary knew her mother and father loved her, but they weren't able to show it in the same way.

The girls' days were filled with rehearsals, when they would sing the same song over and over again. It must have driven Lynne's parents mad, but they never complained. Evenings were spent talking about showbiz. The act, the act, the act; it was all they could talk about. It was such a closeted life that very little intruded from the outside world. Sometimes Lynne would sit and watch the television, but Mary wasn't interested so she would drift away, and sit on her bed strumming her guitar.

In 1939, Birch Green was a tiny hamlet of just 12 or 13 houses. That year, five-year-old Lynne Abrams and her brother and sister were among hundreds of thousands of children evacuated from the cities at the outbreak of the war. They were taken to this tiny village in Hertfordshire while their heavily pregnant mother stayed in London, awaiting the birth of their little brother.

Lynne described the scene in the school hall, the evacuees were lined up and waited to be chosen by people from the village. Her family came from London's East End, so people thought they were from the slums. Lynne and her brother and sister waited for a long time, until eventually her brother was picked. Lynne and her sister were last, and they were fostered by a very strange couple. The lady had a glass eye that really frightened her, and the husband tried to make her laugh by doing tricks with his false teeth. Being younger, Lynne had to spend a lot of time on her own with this couple, and she felt it was like being in a horror film – she was clearly very unhappy. After a time, the lady who had chosen their brother – a lovely family – decided to take in Lynne and her sister too.

After their younger brother was born their mother brought him to Birch Green, where the family could all be together while her father was sent to fight in the war. They were allocated a little ivy-covered cottage in a terraced row. It was the kind of cottage that looked idyllic, but wasn't! It was tiny, with two bedrooms upstairs and two rooms downstairs. There was no cooker, no running water, no electricity, and the toilet was at the end of the garden. Lynne recalled the anguish of being caught short in the middle of the night! The four kids had to share a big double bed. During the Blitz, Lynne's mother's relatives were bombed out, so they moved into the cottage as well. Lynne said she honestly didn't know how her mum managed it. 'Amazing, amazing!'

~

Birth of The Lana Sisters

Lynne Abrams was just six when she met the girls who lived next door to their little cottage in Birch Green. They talked endlessly about singing and showbiz, and when they sang songs by the Andrew's Sisters and Judy Garland, Lynne joined in. She loved harmonising with them, singing songs such as 'Apple Blossom Time', this is where she first got the singing bug!

After that, she sang everywhere, just as Mary did as a kid. Lynne drove her mother and father to distraction with her constant singing and laughing. She was crazy about singing, which seemed completely natural to her. Encouraged by the penny offered as an enticement, she attended church every Sunday, where she joined the choir and was selected for voice training. Of course, this training concentrated on classical songs like 'Ave Maria', never pop songs.

At 15, Lynne went to college to learn shorthand and typing, and then found a job in Roche Products in Welwyn Garden City, first in the typing pool and then as secretary to the advertising manager. But she was young and restless and knew there must be more to life than this. When her boyfriend told her he was leaving for a job in Newfoundland it was a pivotal moment – she wasn't going to just sit there and die of boredom. She scoured *The Stage* and found an advert by a woman in Sheffield looking for a young singer. She applied and got the job. Despite Lynne's young age, her mother allowed her to go and her father drove her all the way up to Sheffield where she found digs with a lovely family.

The lady in Sheffield had puppets, and didn't need a singer so much as someone to work the puppets. There were great long scripts that Lynne was supposed to learn, and she hated the huge, ugly puppets. She knew she couldn't do it, but she was determined not to give up and go home, even though she was upset and homesick. After all she had left to become a star. The family she lived with were very kind and helped her find some work singing in working men's clubs, which was okay for a time, but it wasn't what she wanted to do.

Lynne searched *The Stage* again and found an advertisement for a hostess in a private holiday camp in Weymouth, owned by a Mr Humphries. On arrival, Lynne found the bookings in chaos. So, at just 17 and because she was used to office work, she ended up organising the accommodation. She was supposed to be there to entertain but instead was in charge of the bookings. Lynne remembers: 'It was madness! I was doing 90 per cent and the man that owned it was away with the fairies, he had no idea.'

The campers liked her singing though, and when Mr Humphries saw that she was swamped with all the additional work, he decided to advertise for someone to help. Iris Long spotted the advert, applied and got the job. That was when Iris and Lynne first met.

Iris had a similar story to Lynne. [130] Bored with her work in a typing pool in London, she landed a job as a Redcoat looking after the campers at

---

130 45 Cat, The Lana Sisters

Butlin's holiday camp in Filey, where she was also the announcer on Radio Butlin.

One day, travelling back to Filey on the train, she spotted a large trolley stacked with musical equipment. She put her guitar and amplifier on top with the rest of the equipment. When the woman, who seemed to be in charge, asked her what she was doing, Iris apologised. The lady asked if she happened to play. Of course, she said yes and explained she was on her way to Filey. This was Ivy Benson, who was also going to Butlins with her band. She told Iris to leave her instruments on the trolley and go with them. The 20 girls that made up the Ivy Benson All Girl Band had reached the heights of fame between the wars, playing classics, dance music, pop and jazz, Field Marshal Montgomery had personally requested that they perform at the VE Day celebrations in Berlin in 1945. Ivy loved diamonds, playing the fruit machines and enjoyed a drink or two after the show. Iris became very friendly with Ivy and tagged along with the band. Ivy took Iris with her when she went to meet agents, and Iris quickly got to know them and who the good ones were.

In Filey, Iris played records behind the glass bowl console of Radio Butlin and announced Ivy Benson and Her All-Girl Band's performances in the ballroom. She also played guitar with the band and soon joined them as a member, playing all over Europe and Egypt.

By the time she came back to the UK, Iris was set on forming her own all-female trio. She replied to Mr Humphries' advert in *The Stage* and went to work with Lynne in Weymouth. She had a great deal more experience in showbiz than Lynne, and realising that they would work well together, she described her plan to start a trio and asked Lynne to join her. Lynne's ambitions were much the same and she was quick to agree. Iris wanted to model her group on the Hedley Ward Trio, a very famous band with three fellas that played guitar, piano and bass. They had formed in 1948 and had a spot in radio's *Educating Archie*.

The girls put an advert in *The Stage*, and they found Sheila. This was the start of their trio. They were known as the Iris Long Trio. Like the Hedley Ward Trio, they played piano, bass and guitar, and they travelled all over the continent playing in night clubs, and on US Air Force bases. Iris played guitar, Sheila piano and Lynne double bass – that was the main reason they were booked on the US air bases.

Broadcast & Televised by
THE "IRIS LONG TRIO"

FIGURE 4.4 THE IRIS LONG TRIO (COURTESY OF NOLA YORK)

This novice act needed some polish, and their agent said they should sort themselves out, get some experience and perfect their act. So they went to Scotland, where they were booked to play seven or eight weeks at the Palladium in Edinburgh. On the same bill were Chic Murray and Maidie. It was a slow process, but gradually the act improved.

The Iris Long Trio first appeared, in October 1953, at the Chiswick Empire in London. They were described in *The Stage* as three attractive young ladies, who had already signed TV and radio contracts.

A string of stage, TV and radio performances followed, with appearances on BBC TV in *The Benny Hill Show Case,* and on *Henry Hall's*

Guest Night, as well as tours of European clubs and US airbases on the Continent. They went to Chelsea Barracks for *On Parade,* in 1956 and later that year they appeared on *Camera One* with Don Rennie. By the beginning of 1957, Iris chose a new name for the trio; they would now be called the Lana Sisters. The group appeared with Ted Ray and June Whitfield in *The Spice of Life,* in February 1957.

~

Organising the act

Over the years, Iris and Lynne had developed an uneasy relationship, with each taking care of the varied aspects of the act. Iris mostly focused on the business side: organising the bookings, arranging the travel and finding places for them to stay when they were on the road. Most importantly, she looked after the money. Lynne's input was more on the performing side: she came up with the ideas of the songs they should sing, and their presentation onstage.

Iris had got to know all the agents through her friendship with Ivy Benson, and she kept in contact with them to be sure of regular work for the trio. She regularly wrote to the Entertainments Manager at the BBC, sometimes asking to be remembered for future shows, and other times to tell him that the act had changed its name, or had changed agent. In the very early days, the trio's agent was Cecil Buckingham, and then between 1955 and 1956 they moved on to Johnny Riscoe, a well-known eccentric and joker, who had once managed a revue called 'The Nude Look'. Whenever it was due to visit a town, the local papers were inundated with letters from an organisation called the Purity League, denouncing the show. The result was a full house every time, and it was only later that people discovered the Purity League consisted of just one person – Johnny Riscoe!

When Mary joined the Lana Sisters, their agent was Al Berlin. They had been with him for several years, and he was still getting them good bookings in variety shows. But during Mary's time with the group, Iris changed agents almost every six months. In September 1958 she had decided to move to the Will Collins Theatrical and Vaudeville Exchange, looking for a change. Six months later they went to Evelyn Taylor, and after three months they switched again to the Tito Burns Agency. A month and a half later they were back with Evelyn Taylor, and shortly after that Iris decided to take over the task herself. She was dedicated to the business.

The group travelled to dates around the country in Iris's ancient shooting brake. In the early days they had needed a vehicle big enough to transport all their gear, including the double bass. But this car had seen better days – it broke down constantly and the girls were never quite sure it would get them to their gigs.

While Iris drove, the other two entertained themselves in the back seat by singing, but pretty soon the hypnotic effect of the wheels rumbling on the road sent them off to sleep. Unfortunately, Iris was hopeless at directions and they might drive all night on their way to their next job, only to find she didn't have a clue where she was going. Sometimes Lynne or Mary woke up in the dark of the night to find Iris feverishly checking the map and road signs, searching for the right road. Iris hated having to pay for petrol and they often ran out. Lynne had vivid memories of that time: 'My stomach would be turning over like this, something shocking because you had to get to the theatre – the show must go on. You have to be there for the band call!'[131]

FIGURE 4.5 IRIS AND MARY WITH THE TRUSTY TRANSPORT
(COURTESY OF LYNNE ESSEX)

131 Lynne Essex: interview with author

Lynne was never sure they would make it. It was something of a conundrum – Iris was so totally focused on the act, and was determined to make a success of the trio. Yet she could be so casual about directions and would allow the car to run out of petrol.

Travelling and appearing all over the country meant the trio had to find lodgings. Summer seasons were in seaside resorts, where they enjoyed sunshine and balmy weather, and mostly their digs were reasonable. Sometimes, though, they could be awful. In the winter they travelled further afield, always up north where there were audiences who wanted to be entertained. Lynne recalls arriving at their destination very late one night, unable to find digs and being forced to sleep in the van outside Old Trafford. They still had to report for band call the next morning, and then look glamorous for their appearance in the evening. Mary was learning some hard lessons about the tough life of show-business. Lynne said, 'It was a glamorous life you know, showbiz.'

Over the next two years Mary would get to know Iris and Lynne well. With them, her life took on a new direction and it was fun. They travelled all over the UK, performing in theatres and cinemas, and she saw the realities of life as part of a professional stage act.

~

Mass

While the group were touring, it was easy for Mary to find a church on a Sunday where she could go to Mass. In every town and city, a Catholic church was close at hand, but Birch Green was a tiny hamlet and the nearest church was miles away. Still a devout Catholic with a strong faith, Mary needed to go to Mass, it helped to keep her stable in her unfamiliar world.

The nearest church to Birch Green was in Welwyn Garden City: The Catholic Church of Our Lady, Queen of Apostles, and it would take almost an hour and two buses to get there. Lynne was amazed to discover her father, Fred, offered to drive Mary to the church, despite always refusing to drive her anywhere. He told Lynne that she knew her way around and could manage well enough on the bus. But with Mary it was different, and while she was staying with Fred and Ellen, he drove her to church, waited until the service was over and brought her home again.

The Glasgow Empire

At the beginning of May 1958, the Lana Sisters spent a week at the Brighton Hippodrome with the American comedian Mickey Katz. This was followed by a week at the Glasgow Empire. Iris's wheezing old car wasn't going to make it up the hills and through the traffic jams in the towns and cities on the way, so they travelled to Glasgow by train.

Starring at the Empire that week was Russ Hamilton, who Mary discovered was a sweet guy with a gentle nature. He had released a new disc, 'We Will Make Love', a romantic ballad he had written himself. It was a lovely, innocent song that reached number two in the charts. The B-side, 'Rainbow', a pretty self-penned ballad, was most appealing because Hamilton couldn't say his r's. Pushed hard in the US, it made the charts there and stayed for four months, even climbing to number four. Hamilton's records were so successful that he was invited to appear on *The Big Record Show* with Patti Page. America! This was Mary's dream – and Russ had made it to the top ten there! Unfortunately, commitments at home meant he had to postpone his visit until October, and by then the moment had passed.

Russ had led a skiffle group while he worked at Butlins in Blackpool. They were so good they were asked to perform for the staff at the Royal Albert Hall. Billy Butlin was looking for a record they could use to wake up the campers. Russ went to Oriole with his group to record it, and while in the studio, he asked permission to record his own number, which he offered to pay for himself. Jack Baverstock, the musical director, rated the disc so much that he persuaded the owner to sign Russ. Working at Butlins Ocean Hotel in Brighton gave him the publicity he needed to get some slots on *Six-Five Special*, and after that his song took off like a rocket. The record climbed the charts, reaching number two. Elvis Presley's 'All Shook Up' had been at the top for four weeks and Russ was set to replace him. The record company had been taken by surprise by the success of the record, and just as Russ's single was about to take over the number one spot in the UK, the factory ran out of copies, and at the same time, the plant closed for two weeks' holiday. While the plant was closed, 'We Will Make Love' dropped to number four, and then faded away. Paul Anka's 'Diana' took over from Elvis instead.

Russ did make it on to the Patti Page show, eventually. He also had an interview lined up with Ed Sullivan, but had to turn that down because he was booked onto *Six-Five Special*. This was a lesson for Mary on how fickle show business could be, and the importance of being in the right place at the right time.

The Glasgow Empire had a reputation. The girls heard that the audiences there could be unforgiving. They were relieved to learn it was mainly comedians who were targeted. Des O'Connor used to tell the story of pretending to faint on stage to escape what he thought was going to be the wrath of the audience. He said that as he was lying on the floor Bobby Dowds, the Music Director, leaned across to him and asked, 'Say Des, is this in the act?' Mary never knew how much truth there was about the tough reputation of the Glasgow audiences. It could simply be that it was fashionable to belittle the Glasgow crowds; to talk about how many of them would shout back at acts, especially cockney comedians. The Lana Sisters were given a great reception by the audiences who loved their act, especially their closing number, 'My Mother's Eyes'.

On tour with Guy Mitchell

Next, the trio went to Coventry for the start of a tour of one-night stands with Guy Mitchell, the pop singer Mary discovered when her friend Angela's father encouraged him to release 'She Wears Red Feathers' in the UK.

Guy Mitchell's real name was Al Cernik. Originally signed as a child actor by Warner Brothers in the thirties, later he supplemented his income as a saddle maker by singing in a country music broadcast. Mitchell's career took off in 1950, when he was spotted by Mitch Miller, signed by Columbia and adopted his stage name. Guided by Miller, Guy hit number one in the UK in 1950 with 'My Heart Cries for You'. It was paired with 'The Roving Kind', a more rousing number based on a European folk song, reaching the top ten in February ahead of versions by folk group The Weavers and country and western singer Rex Allen. The cutesy 'Feet Up (Pat Him on the Po-Po)', a minor hit in the US, was a top seller in England. 'She Wears Red Feathers' and 'Look at That Girl' topped the UK charts, while 'Pretty Little Black-Eyed Susie', 'Chicka-Boom' and 'Cloud Lucky Seven' made the UK top ten.

Several cover versions of 'She Wears Red Feathers' were recorded, and one featured in the opening scene of the 1989 film *Scandal*, which told the story of the Profumo affair of 1963. The circle was completed when Mary as Dusty Springfield sang, 'Nothing has Been Proved', the theme song for the film.

Mitchell ventured into rock with songs such as 'Heartaches by the Number', 'Rock-a-Billy', which reached number one in the UK, 'The Same Old Me', and his biggest hit, 'Singing the Blues'. One of the decade's biggest hits, it stayed at number one for over two months, from December 1956 to February 1957. It was at the top for more weeks than any of Elvis Presley's songs.

Guy Mitchell was at the peak of his career when the Lana Sisters joined him on this eight-day tour, and his popularity was such that police had to be called to hold back his screaming fans. He began his performance with 'Rock-a-Billy' and his stable of rock songs. Then he came onstage wearing a Stetson and whirling a lasso and raised the roof when he sang 'Home on the Range' accompanied by his guitar and four members of Dennis Ringrowe's band. His rendition of 'Singing the Blues' brought sighs and squeals from the girls. Also performing in the concert were three television singers, Group One, Alan Clive, comedian Joe Church and Dennis Ringrowe and his Orchestra, who also provided musical backing for the Lana Sisters.

FIGURE 4.6 WITH GUY MITCHELL, L TO R IRIS LONG, LYNNE ABRAMS, GUY MITCHELL, MARY O'BRIEN (COURTESY OF NOLA YORK)

When that tour was over, the girls spent a week in the Birmingham Hippodrome in an old-fashioned variety show with Mike and Bernie Winters. This time they shared the bill with singer Don Fox, Ross Harvey and his act with birds, a dart blower, unicyclists, jugglers and dancers.

The manager of the Hippodrome was Bertie Adams. He was old school; during the Monday morning band calls he would sit in the stalls wearing a carnation, and all the acts were required to come down to shake his hand and say good morning. There was a 14-piece orchestra directed by Arthur Roberts, a most charming man with immaculate grey hair. The stage manager, Ernie Clapham, was a fitness freak and muscle builder. He had converted part of the under-stage area into a makeshift gym, where he pumped iron all afternoon when the theatre was locked up and no one was around. During the summer he would walk around the theatre wearing a singlet, looking like an advert for the old *Health and Efficiency* magazine. Few acts argued with Ernie when he pulled them up for running over their time![132]

---

132 Information on the Birmingham Hippodrome taken from

www.arthurlloyd.co.uk/Birmingham/BirminghamHippodrome

Butlin's, Clacton-on-Sea

The Lana Sisters performed a Sunday concert at Butlin's, Clacton-on-Sea.

FIGURE 4.7 In Clacton on horseback (Courtesy of Lynne Essex)

Clacton-on-Sea had one primary role: to provide summer holidays for visitors. There was almost no work to be had in the town outside the holiday season. People came as day-trippers, or on holiday for a week or a fortnight. Few had private cars then, and so they arrived by rail or coach, or some still by the paddle steamers from Tower Pier, London. Next to the Town Yard and the Clacton Town F.C. ground in Old Road was an Eastern National Coach Station where visiting coaches parked for the day in Ellis Road, now the site of Clacton Police Station.

FIGURE 4.8 FUN IN CLACTON (COURTESY OF LYNNE ESSEX)

A Butlin's holiday provided something for everyone. Top-line stars such as Arthur Askey, Jimmy Wheeler, Dick Bentley, Derek Roy, Arthur English, Mike and Bernie Winters and the Radio Revellers appeared on *Sunday Night Showtime*, and the famous Butlin redcoats were always ready to help the holidaymakers.

~

Visiting Home

Life on the road was exhausting, and the girls had little time or energy left for anything else. But, whenever there was a chance, Mary took Lynne and Iris to visit her parents in Kent Gardens. Basking in her new career, she wanted her parents to see how well she was doing. Even better if Dion was there; he was so brilliant on piano and guitar and she wanted him to show off his chops. During these visits, Dion and Mary would play for the girls: Dion on guitar and Mary on bongos, and lost themselves in the rhythm. Iris and Lynne would join in, clapping along to the beat. Lynne reminisced about those times witnessing Mary and her brother jamming together:

> I heard her and her brother when I was in her mother's flat, in Ealing. I used to go up there a great deal. They would muck about, but it was smashing. I used to love listening to it, all Latin American. She could play the guitar and she was brilliant on the bongos; marvellous rhythm and they were really good together. [133]

Mary was aware that her life growing up had been somewhat eccentric and chaotic, but now she began to realise just how dysfunctional her family was. Living with Lynne and her parents in Birch Green, she discovered a warm, inclusive family. Here were people who supported and encouraged one another, where cuddles were just a part of everyday life. The O'Brien's weren't touchy-feely in that way. Mary knew her mother and father loved her; they just didn't know how to show it.

Kay O'Brien was a tiny little woman with a strong Irish accent, who seemed to live in a world of her own. She talked constantly on topics as diverse as Ireland and Rio, and she liked to sit up long into the night with a glass of wine in front of her. She shared her memories of visiting Rio when she was a young girl, telling tales of Corcovado, Copacabana, Ipanema, Sugar Loaf Mountain and the samba. She recounted the magical, spectacular parties and the streets filled with bands and beach parties that went on all day and all night. What memories she had of those times.

Other times she spoke about Ireland and Tralee. Kay's mother and father used to fight over politics, and they had fierce arguments on the subject of Irish independence. Her father, Maurice Ryle, favoured an Irish Parliament under the umbrella of Great Britain – a kind of devolution, while her mother, Bridget, believed that Ireland should be an independent country, completely free of British control. It was a constant battle between the two.

---

133 Lynne Essex: interview with author

Kay also spoke of the terrible poverty in the country. Her father had campaigned to improve the appalling living conditions of the poor. Using the pages of his newspaper, he battled against the oppression suffered by his countrymen and women. Kay and her family were lucky that they didn't suffer in the way so many of the people did. Her father had a good income and they lived in a grand house in Tralee.

Shy and diffident, OB appeared dour and his presence in the household was almost ghostly.

During these monologues Mary would sit and watch her mother, such an animated little woman, recalling the wild arguments they used to have. Kay's short-clipped hair was white now, but Mary remembered seeing photos of a young Kay with jet-black hair. Kay O'Brien always seemed quite remote, like someone who wasn't properly a part of the world.

~

Radio

Realising how much listeners loved light entertainment, the BBC began looking for programmes they thought would be popular. By 1943, a quarter of a million workers were singing and laughing along to *Workers' Playtime,* with comedians Elsie and Doris Waters and the comic Tommy Handley. *Workers' Playtime* had started as a way of boosting morale during the war, and continued for many years after. The production visited factory canteens all over the country to perform for the workers and broadcast to the nation.

Radio bookings sustained the Lana Sisters, and *Workers' Playtime* was an important standby for them. This programme, still popular in the 1950's, was a favourite with Mary's mother, Kay. The bright and breezy presenters introduced comedians and singers who sang and told jokes for half an hour. Listeners had no clue what it took to get that show on the road. The producers, the presenters, all the artists involved, had to find their way to the factory canteen, wherever it was. The crew had to move a massive amount of equipment from one place to the next three times a week. Variety artists were organised by the Entertainments Manager, whose job it was to ensure they were in the right place at the right time and on the right day. He had to be sure that they turned up for the morning rehearsals and were ready for the performance at 12.30. The singers, musicians and comedians would check in first thing in the morning, set up, rehearse and then present a half-hour performance for the workers.

Mary's first appearance on the show came in July 1958, when the Lana Sisters drove to a building material manufacturer in Higham, Kent. Sharing the bill with them that day were Max Geldray, Freddie Sales and David Hughes, and musical accompaniment was provided by the resident Worker's Playtime band. During her time with the Lana Sisters, Mary visited Peterborough, Kettering and Plymouth, Weybridge and Shepton Mallet, Nottingham and many other places too numerous to mention. They performed alongside Elsie and Doris Waters, Rosemary Squires, Chic Murray and Maidie, Pearl Carr and Teddy Johnson, Terry Scott, Alma Cogan, Max Wall and Cyril Fletcher, Jon Pertwee, Harry Worth and many more.

Aside from *Workers' Playtime,* the Lana Sisters had radio dates that saw them travel all over the country. *Midday Music Hall* was one – it came from the North of England, the Midlands and London. And then there were the Parades – *Air Parade* from a combined RAF and WRAF Recruit Training Depot in Wilmslow, Cheshire, and *Marine Parade* from the Infantry Training Centre, Royal Marines, in Lympstone, Devon.

When their other bookings went quiet, the Lana sisters always had regular slots on *Workers' Playtime,* and a host of other radio shows. It kept them ticking over, and they were glad of it.

~

Recording

Iris was ambitious, and determined the Lana Sisters would be noticed, and not just on the theatre circuits. She meant for them to make it big! One way to do that was to cut some records and get them played on the radio. They arranged an audition with Tony Hatch, Petula Clark's recording manager, who helped her score many hits. The Lana Sisters sang their song 'Down South' for him; Lynne had written the lyrics and they had all worked on the arrangement. There was talk of using it as a B-side of one of their records, but he turned them down. This didn't deter Iris, who persuaded their agent to get a record deal for the trio.

Fontana was a subsidiary record label of Philips, where Jack Baverstock, a former dance band pianist and pop paper editor, was the Artists and Repertoire manager. He came from Oriole, where he had built a reputation as a hit finder on the strength of 'Freight Train' by Nancy Whiskey and 'We Will Make Love' by Russ Hamilton. His task was to build up the new Fontana label from scratch. The Lana Sisters succeeded in getting an audition with him. Jack was a lovely gentleman, and it was really important that he liked their act. In 1958, Fontana issued the first of seven singles by the Lana Sisters.

'Chimes of Arcady'

On 12 September 1958, the girls went into the Philips Studio in London. Mary had been in a recording studio several years before, when she recorded the number, 'Can't We Be Friends?' with Peter Miles. But this was a proper professional recording studio, and it was quite different. In this great barn of a place the Ken Jones Orchestra sat in one corner, the backing singers in another and Mary, Lynne and Iris stood in the middle. They crowded round the one microphone that dangled in front of them; it had to pick up all the sounds from the various parts of the studio. The engineers were tucked away behind the console in the control room, listening on headphones and twiddling knobs to get the balance right between singers and musicians. The girls had to spend a lot of time standing around during the sessions, waiting for the engineers to set up. But once recording started, they got through it quickly; it really was a production line.

Mary will have had little input into the choice of numbers to be recorded: that was down to Iris and Lynne. On this record, 'Chimes of Arcady', (written by Percy Wenrich and Harry Tobias and first recorded by the Frank Luther Trio), was chosen for the A-side. Written in 1938, both the words and the tune were dated. It was modernised by increasing the speed slightly and it is reminiscent of 'Charmaine' by The Batchelors. The arrangement and production are well-considered, and it is interesting to note the use of male backing vocals; a refreshing change from the traditional girl singers. There is also a lovely chiming bells section and a glockenspiel that imitates the chimes of the title.

The B-side 'Ring-a-My Phone', was written by Lee Morris and James Lee and recorded by Brenda Lee with the Jordanaires (Elvis Presley's backing group), for release in June 1958. Like 'Chimes of Arcady', the track also uses male vocal backing and a glockenspiel. Dinah Washington had recorded the song around the same time, and the Lana Sisters' version is closest to hers, although the lyrics weren't exactly the same.

Don Nicholl of *Disc* gave the record a great review, and decided it deserved four stars. But this reviewer liked the B-side more than 'Chimes of Arcady'. He also said he preferred the Lana Sisters version to that of Brenda Lee. Their singing of this number reminded him of the Andrews Sisters.

A month later, *Disc* sent Mervyn Douglas to interview the Lana Sisters. We can imagine that they would have talked through their approach beforehand, and decided what they were going to say. Iris did most of the talking, and much of it was nonsense! As their business manager, Iris was a shrewd operator, and Lynne and Shan (Mary) weren't about to argue with her. But during the interview they were quite surprised by her story of how the group was formed. She told him that the three were at school together, and had formed a trio that performed at school functions. In fact, they had all grown up in different parts of the country and there was a marked difference in their ages, with Mary being the youngest, Lynne about four years older and Iris older again. Iris told him they had decided they didn't want to just be another sister vocal act, so they practised intensively to get their close harmony sound right. She said they shared a flat in London, though they were actually living in Lynne's parent's house in Birch Green. In spite of its many fictions, the article in *Disc* magazine gave them some much needed publicity for which they were very grateful. [134]

~

Television

The Jack Jackson Show

The Jack Jackson Show was an ATV production, a fast-moving mix of big band singers, vocal groups and stage performers. The Lana Sisters appeared on this show on 24 September 1958, just two weeks after 'Chimes of Arcady' was released. The host sat at his desk, relaxed and

---

134 Mervyn Douglas Disc Magazine, October 25 1958

pumping out a mixture of music and comedy. But this seemingly casual approach hid the hours he had spent planning and preparing his shows. He chatted to guests and introduced his company of comedians, including his cat Tiddles, who made regular appearances. A constant barrage of sounds —snippets of music and snatches of conversations — kept everyone on their toes. For the Lana Sisters, it was a treat to see Jack at work.

Rehearsals were held in a studio in Foley Street, and artists appearing in the show would wander in and out of the studios. It was amusing to see passers-by gawping when they saw the comings and goings of all these well-known faces. Regulars on the show included, Alma Cogan, Barbara Windsor, Paddy O'Neil, Judy Carne, Libby Morris, Bill Haydn and Glen Mason, and guest stars included Cliff Richard, Marty Wilde and Lonnie Donegan.

The show was broadcast live from the Embassy Club in Bond Street at ten o'clock on a Sunday evening. The studio itself was tiny, and the scenery only arrived at two o'clock on the day of transmission. With about 15 changes of scenery in a show, it meant that each prop had to be carefully positioned, right on the mark.

On their first appearance on the show, the trio shared the bill with Lonnie Donegan, Ray Ellington and the Mudlarks. When they weren't working with Lonnie Donegan the girls liked to perform his song, 'My Old Man's a Dustman'; the audiences loved it. Lynne had suggested putting some comedy in the middle to break it up and it worked well. Of course, when he was on the same bill, they couldn't sing that song.

Ray Ellington was a musician on *'The Goon Show'* who was sometimes written into the scripts. This surreal radio show was filled with bizarre sounding characters and outrageous, even unbelievable, adventures. It was one of Mary's favourite radio programmes, she loved listening to it, and she could imitate the voices too. Ray recorded his versions of 'The Three Bears' and 'Mr Sandman' on *The Goon Show,* and reproduced some of them with his Quartet on *The Jack Jackson Show.*

The Mudlarks were a trio: two boys and a girl, and they really were a family group, comprising two brothers and a sister. Their upbeat novelty style won them an appearance on *Six-Five Special* and a recording contract with Columbia. Their first record, 'Lollipop', went to number two in the UK charts; this was another number the girls made part of their repertoire. Later that year they had a second appearance on *The Jack Jackson Show,* this time with Joan Regan. And later still they were guests on the show with the John Barry Seven, Marty Wilde and Cliff Richard.

October saw their second appearance on *Six-Five Special.* The setup was pretty much the same as it had been the first time. Jim Dale hosted the Lana Sisters along with the Kalin Twins, Laurie London, Don Rennie, Joan Small, Jimmy Lloyd, Vince Eager, Craig Douglas and dancers: The Six-Five Dates. There was a bunch of talking heads from the music press - Maurice Burman (*Melody Maker*), Derek Johnson (*NME*), Gerald Marks (*Disc*) and Derek Hoddinott (*The Stage*) – and musical support came from Alan Clark and his Band. Also in the show were the Tito Burns '6.5-ers', Tony Osborne and his Brasshats and Martin Lukins and his Accordion Band.

The trio were snapped, in their matching polo-neck sweaters, by the *Disc* photographer when he came to the rehearsal.

FIGURE 4.9 REHEARSALS FOR SIX-FIVE SPECIAL
(RICHI HOWELL *DISC,* 18 OCTOBER 1958)

Stage

Lonnie Donegan

Back on the road in October, the Lana Sisters went to the St Albans Odeon with Lonnie Donegan and his Skiffle Group. The Lana Sisters were described as 'Britain's latest recording 'rock' stars. Sharing the bill were Cherry Wainer and Don Storer, the latest teenage rage Larry Page and the Pageboys, and Rory Blackwell and his Blackjacks. In 1956, Rory Blackwell had formed one of the first rock'n'roll groups in England, the Blackjacks. They played a bland version of American rock music, and as well as a resident season at the 2i's Coffee bar, the group appeared in concerts throughout the country. They were chosen as a representative British rock'n'roll group by the *Daily Mirror* to meet Bill Haley when he arrived at Southampton.

The following week the Lana Sisters returned to the Colchester Regal with Lonnie Donegan and his Skiffle Group, and Cherry Wainer, this time with the Jimmy Currie Trio.

~

West Side Story

The Lana Sisters had one further appearance on *The Jack Jackson Show* in November before a well-earned break. They used this time to work on new numbers and new routines. As the year ended, and before she went home to spend Christmas with her parents and her brother, Mary had another amazing experience.

Even before *West Side Story* came to London in December 1958, Dusty had read the reviews from New York. Her talk was constantly about the show and her friends were left in no doubt about her longing to see it. The Lana Sisters weren't touring then, so during their down time they were able to get tickets for the show.

When it opened in New York, Walter Kerr of the *New York Herald-Tribune* described *West Side Story* thus:

> *The radioactive fallout from West Side Story must still be descending on Broadway this morning.*

Director, choreographer, and idea-man Jerome Robbins has put together, and then blasted apart, the most savage, restless, electrifying dance patterns we've been exposed to in a dozen seasons. [135]

The programme described the precarious start to the production. In 1949, Jerome Robbins, Leonard Bernstein and Arthur Laurents had met with the aim of producing a different kind of musical – a modern retelling of Romeo and Juliet with religious conflict as the basis of the story. That idea came to naught, but Robbins was determined. Several years later the idea was resurrected when the three came together again. Now the nature of the conflict between the two houses would be gangs in New York's Upper West Side. The project moved ahead; they found a highly talented lyricist in Stephen Sondheim, and aimed to produce a lyrically and theatrically sharpened version of reality. When it transferred to the London stage, the *Guardian* reviewer wrote:

Jerome Robbins's choreography, that which sets before us not isolated dances but a flowing movement in and out of dance throughout. Leonard Bernstein's music, and Arthur Laurents's and Stephen Sondheim's words add up to a total work that demands comparison not with musical comedy as we have known it but with Menotti's operas or with Porgy and Bess. As a production, as a total work for the stage, West Side Story is superb. [136]

Her Majesty's Theatre in Haymarket was the iconic setting of this ground-breaking musical, and Mary was overwhelmed as much by the venue as by the performance. The opulent Louis XIV-style theatre had private boxes stacked three high on each side of the stage, and marble columns that separated the boxes from the stage and the rest of the auditorium. A massive cut-glass chandelier tumbled down from the ornate ceiling and the stage curtains, like the chairs, were of rich red velvet with paper of the same colour covering the walls.

Mary loved the show, filled as it was with the music of Latin America. This new Broadway musical was a departure from anything she had seen before. The reviews reverberated with words like 'vibrant', 'compelling', 'electrifying' and 'profoundly moving'.

---

135 Walter Kerr, West Side Story, *New York Herald Tribune*, 27 July 1957

136 John Roselli, 'West Side Story Hits London', *The Guardian*, 13 December 1958.

1959

Recording

January began with a trip to Kettering for *Workers' Playtime,* and at the end of the month the group laid down the tracks of their second single, 'Buzzin'. They collaborated with Billy Hooper to write the B-side 'Cry Cry Baby', It was recorded with musical backing from the Johnny Gregory Band and released on Valentine's Day.

'Buzzin'

This track was a good mix of unison and harmony singing with an early pop feel. The trendy electric intro, key change and sax break added to this, and *NME*'s reviewer saw plenty of precision and punch in the girls' performance. Don Nicholl in *Disc,* gave the record four stars and predicted that with this record the group would breakthrough to the top. He said: 'The girls come out of the groove crisply and with a knife-edge beat that leaves the number stamped on your mind.'

'Cry Cry Baby' on the flip side was described in *NME* as a medium-paced rocker, 'a little hymn of spite'. A jilted girl having got over her heartbreak could now get her own back. Iris, Lynne and Shan (Mary) were encouraged by this positive response to their disc, both from reviewers and the music scene in general. They knew they were good, but it was heartening to have it confirmed in this way.

Fontana's A. and R. manager, Jack Baverstock (below), goes through "Cry Baby Cry" with The Lana Sisters during a recording session at the week-end. The Sisters also waxed "Buzzin'."

FIGURE 4.10 WITH JACK BAVERSTOCK (RICHI HOWELL *DISC*, 24 JANUARY 1959)

Constantly on the look-out for ways to promote the group, Iris contacted the BBC, asking that they play their new record. Then an appearance on *The Jack Jackson Show* gave them the opportunity to showcase 'Buzzin'' on television.

Socialising

Socialising was always a sore point with Iris. Her great fear was that one of the girls might meet a young man and disappear suddenly from the group. In her time with the Ivy Benson Band, she had seen this scenario played out many times. Girls would vanish, sometimes overnight. For many of them, love and romance came before a career with the Ivy Benson Band, no matter how prestigious. It is impossible to know how many came to regret their impetuous decision.

Iris was determined this wasn't going to happen with her group, and one way she made sure of it was to put a ban on meeting other acts after the show. There wasn't a great deal of time for partying anyway. Their whole lives were consumed by performing, and they didn't really miss it. In the two and a half years Mary spent with the Lana Sisters she thought about little else, theirs was an incredibly insular life. They went to the theatre, got ready and gave their performance, and afterwards they cleaned off their make-up and changed back into their street clothes. They might spend some time analysing the act, talking over what went well and what they could do better, then they left. Generally, after a show they were in the car, whisked back to the boarding house and getting ready for bed before they knew it. There was never any thought of going to the bar to meet the other performers; they only occasionally talked to them and they never went to parties. Iris didn't allow them to fraternise, and woe betide them if they were to take a fancy to someone from another act.

~

Disc celebration party

Charlie Buchan was a famous footballer who produced football magazines. In the late 1950's he saw what was happening in the rock'n'roll scene and took a chance on producing a music magazine for the kids. The first edition of *Disc* was published in February 1958, and when it was a year old, he held a huge party to celebrate. On this occasion Iris relaxed her strict no-socialising rule because this party was properly organised and formal, with invites and all. The Lana Sisters weren't going to miss out, Iris knew how important it was to see and be seen at this kind of event.

What a night! There were around 400 stars gathered to enjoy the celebrations, and Johnny Gray and his Band of the Day swung like crazy, keeping people dancing all night long.

Enfield Tennis Club

The *Disc* party wasn't the only time Iris eased up on her rules enough to allow the girls to socialise, and when they weren't touring, she allowed them to relax a little. Iris was a member of a tennis club in Palmer's Green. She encouraged Lynne and Mary to dress up to the nines and took them to the club, intending to show them off. There had been a man, before she started the act – a member of the club – she had had a relationship with him and she talked about him, a lot. He had dumped her for a much older woman, Iris was mortified by the rejection. She took the girls there to parade them in front of this chap. It was the only time Lynne could recall her thinking about any kind of relationship. She was so dedicated to the business that it was all she thought about.

Other times, because Iris liked to put the girls on show, she took them to the Green Dragon, a large pub in Enfield that was her stomping ground. On these occasions, when asked what she wanted to drink, Mary always said that she didn't want any alcohol: she couldn't stand the taste of it.

~

Television

BBC TV's *Drumbeat*

On 25 April the Lana Sisters, backed by Bob Miller and the Millermen, made the first of three consecutive appearances on *Drumbeat*, the new programme for kids, launched by the BBC. First shown on Saturday 4 April 1959, it aimed to compete with *Oh Boy!*, ITV's successful pop music show. The show was broadcast live at 6.30 pm every Saturday evening from the Riverside Studios in Hammersmith, and occasionally from Lime Grove. These appearances gave the act much-needed airtime, and gave them a chance to promote their latest recordings; they sang 'Buzzin'' on the first show, and 'Tell Him No' on the last one. With no record to plug in the middle week, they sang 'Rock and Roll is Here to Stay'. *Drumbeat* was an offbeat and exciting show with great team spirit.

The John Barry Seven was the musical mainstay of *Drumbeat*. They had emerged in 1957, a group started by buddies from the army. The Seven debuted with a Sunday concert at a Rialto Cinema in York and, after Harold Feilding booked them for the Tommy Steele show in Blackpool there was no stopping them, the band enjoyed a rapid climb to fame.

Drumbeat had a strong resident team of solo artists: Adam Faith, Vince Eager, Roy Young and Sylvia Sands. The original compere was Gus Goodwin who was a bit of a comedian and a very nice and knowledgeable guy. He had three DJ programmes on Radio Luxembourg devoted to the big beat, and had made a mark with his *Rockabilly Show*. Adam Faith's career was launched by *Drumbeat*. Quiet and diffident off stage, he became a rock star in front of the microphone. Adam and Vince Eager covered the rock songbooks.

Interviewed for *The Saturday Sequence* in 1989, Mary said:

I always remember seeing Adam Faith on Drumbeat and thinking what a tremendously photogenic face he had. He really was quite beautiful. His face didn't seem to fit on his body. It was a big photogenic face that didn't belong on his body, but I know that feeling, my face doesn't belong to my body either.[137]

As a member of the John Barry Seven, Vic Flick appeared in every episode of *Drumbeat*. He described it as:

A *wonderful and exciting experience for me. Every week we were rehearsing our solo numbers, the backing for artists and any camera movements that we might be involved in. I have been involved with many TV series but never one that was as innovative, exciting and had such a team spirit.* [138]

Six-Five Special and *Oh Boy!* were given a great deal more attention but it should be noted that *Drumbeat* launched the careers of Adam Faith and John Barry as well as songwriters Les Reed, Johnny Worth and Trevor Peacock. This half hour show, produced by Stewart Morris, presented Sylvia Sands, the Barry Sisters, the Kingpins, the Raindrops and Bob Miller and his Millermen to *Music While You Work* listeners. While rock fans were offered Adam Faith, Vince Eager and Roy Young. The Lana Sisters didn't fit neatly in either camp. The *Radio Times* described it as; '30 fast-moving minutes of music in the ultra-modern manner, that will make the old-fashioned rug cutters feel like members of a knitting circle'.

The BBC produced an album to help promote *Drumbeat,* on which the Lana Sister's recording of 'Buzzin', with dubbed audience applause, was included.

~

137 Roger Scott, *The Saturday Sequence*, BBC Radio 1, 11 March 1989

138 *https://www.johnbarry.org.uk/index.php/jb7/drumbeat/drumbeat-general-page*

Saturday Club

On 13 June 1959 the Lana Sisters appeared on *Saturday Club*. There were to be many more appearances. This time they performed alongside Jim Dale, The Betty Smith Quintet, Dickie Pride and, of course, the Ken Jones Five, who accompanied them on many of their recordings. *Saturday Club* was to become one of the most important music programmes broadcast on BBC radio.

It had had a hesitant start. In early 1957, when the skiffle movement was at its peak, Jimmy Grant, a young producer from Plymouth, sent a note to BBC managers. It read, 'In London, the skiffle movement provides entertainment at several dozen coffee-houses, and skiffle repertoire includes blues, ballads, shanties, work songs, country songs, cowboy songs, railway ditties and even evergreen popular tunes.'[139] Grant's idea was to put on a modest series that would be called *Skiffle Session*. Skiffle, of course, was based on acoustic guitars and a variety of homemade instruments, including the ubiquitous tea chests and washboards. The plan was to showcase local London skiffle groups along with two or three singers. Grant suggested it should last 15 to 20 minutes and calculated the cost of putting on the show would be £51.10.0d.

At that time BBC management seemed determined to ignore the trends in popular music. They weren't keen on the idea of a show especially for teenagers, and their very definite ideas of the kind of music suitable to be broadcast to the nation didn't accord with skiffle; it threatened their comfortable monopoly. Music should conform to the musical tastes of the parents: after all, they paid the TV licence. However, in the end they were persuaded; it was only half an hour, which wasn't too much airtime. Auditions were held in March 1957, and several skiffle groups were considered.

With a weekly budget of £55, *Saturday Skiffle Club*, with Jimmy Grant as producer, was first broadcast on 1 June 1957 between 10 and 10.30 am and replaced half an hour of music from theatre organists. The fresh-faced 26-year-old announcer and newsreader, Brian Matthew, who regarded it as an experiment quite unlike anything that had been heard

---

139 Spencer Leigh (2006) Saturday Club: 'Hello Me Ol' Mateys', *Now Dig This*.

on radio before, was brought in to present the show. Chas McDevitt, the City Ramblers, the Vipers and Ken Colyer appeared during June, and soon it was the most popular show on the Light Programme.

While the kids loved the show, the BBC's management didn't like the American bias. 'Too many American work songs,' said one BBC executive, 'Doesn't anybody know any British work songs?' Jimmy Grant and his boss Don MacLean worked hard to find British music for the programmes, but many British folk songs are in 6/8 and had to be adapted to suit the skiffle style.

In October 1958, with the upsurge in rock'n'roll, the show was renamed *Saturday Club*, and extended to two hours. Matthew said when the show started, it was mainly a programme where they had to make most of the music. They had two hours to fill and were only allowed eight records, as the Musician's Union rules put a limit on the amount of 'needle time'. So, they made their own sessions with bands and groups and singers, and Brian, who was never what you would call hip, came to be known for his greeting; 'Hello me ol' mateys'.

All the stars of the 1960's, people like Cliff Richard, Adam Faith, Chris Barber, Humphrey Lyttleton, Marty Wilde, Terry Dene, Vince Taylor, Johnny Kidd, Michael Holliday, Bert Weedon and Clinton Ford made their early appearances on this programme. It was essential listening for teenagers and the audience for Saturday Club grew to 5 million, including many children as it immediately followed Children's Favourites. The Musicians Union had stopped overseas acts from performing, but when their ban was lifted, touring American artists including Eddie Cochran, Gene Vincent, Duane Eddy and Bobby Darin began to feature on the show.

The programme was recorded in the Playhouse Theatre, Haymarket, during the week, ready for transmission on Saturday morning, and the Lana Sisters always performed live.

~

Stage

The Enormous Package Show

By 1959 the music scene in the UK had changed out of all recognition. Jack Good was at the heart of these changes. His ground-breaking rock'n'roll shows on the TV – *Six-Five Special* for the BBC, then *Oh Boy!* for ITV – were different and dynamic, serving up rock'n'roll to the country's youth.

This year there was a marked change in the Lana Sisters' stage bookings. There were fewer variety shows, and now they were included in rock'n'roll packages. In March of that year, they were part of *The Enormous Package Show* in the Colchester Regal, with Cuddly Dudley and Vince Eager, a real rock'n'roll extravaganza!

Dudley Heslop had arrived in Britain from Jamaica in 1947, and by the mid-1950's he was recording for Oriole Records. He had begun to make a name for himself as one of the best rockers in the UK. His manager, Guy Robinson, promoted him as 'Bristol's answer to The Big Bopper', and he adopted a big grin, flashy suits and snazzy ties. He was also a co-founder of The Dominoes, with pianist Iggy Quail and vocalist Boysie Grant. He found fame with regular appearances on *Oh Boy!* and took on the name Cuddly Dudley. It really suited him – he was a lovely, cuddly guy!

Roy Taylor joined the caravan of mostly young boys on the pilgrimage to London seeking stardom. Roy and his group, The Vagabonds, were flat broke when they travelled from their home on the outskirts of Sherwood Forest for the finals of the World Skiffle Championship at the Locarno Ballroom. It was shown on BBC's *Come Dancing*, and they came second. Later, seeking out the tiny, sweaty cellar under the 2i's Coffee Bar, they used their second place in the championship to persuade the owners to let them play, after which they were offered a permanent spot. Soon, Roy was spotted by Larry Parnes, the impresario who developed the careers of Tommy Steele and Marty Wilde; he signed him up at once. Why not, he was a tall, blond, good-looking boy, and whenever he sang an Eddie Cochran number, he had the girls fainting. Larry Parnes always renamed recruits to his stable, and so Roy began his career as a pop star with a new name; Vince Eager.

Tony Marsh was the compere on this show and was infamous for his 'high jinks'. Mary hadn't come across him before and it's likely her sensibilities were deeply shaken by his behaviour. As a convent school girl she'd been sheltered from the more sordid side of life. One of his pranks was to stand in the wings with his trousers round his ankles, on display to everyone on stage.

In the music business the tales of his exploits as a formidable drinker and raconteur were legendary, and promoter Arthur Howes often travelled to a show just because he knew Tony Marsh was the compere. When Howes came along to see a show he said, 'I've come here to see ravers and performers like Tony Marsh and I don't want to be disappointed. There you have the secret of success. Don't disappoint the punters.' Arthur was the typical 'Mr Entertainment' and he believed that everyone should play their part in the great music hall of life, saying in his deep Cockney accent, 'You see, I love performers and Tony Marsh is a performer, on and offstage.' Many of the shows the Lana Sisters took part in were promoted by Howes.

'Tell Him No'

On 24 April 1959 the Lana Sisters went into the Philips Studios to record their third single. 'Tell Him No' was the A-side with 'Mister Dee-Jay' on the flip.

'Tell Him No' was written and recorded by the rock'n'roll duo, Travis and Bob, and charted at number eight on the *Billboard* Hot 100. The number was originally written about a boy telling a girl to watch out for another boy interested in her. But the Lana Sisters' version was presented as a girl warning a girlfriend against a boy. Reviewers thought it was a better performance than the other two versions.

On the flip side, 'Mister Dee-Jay', written by Buddy Kaye and Leon Carr, follows the lyric line of a request to the DJ to play 'our song'. This is a very clear, slick production. The song is a typical three-chord effort, but so were so many others at this time! There is a nice change of rhythm for the middle eight – quite imaginative. A catchy song, simple, mellow and easy paced, the song is very professional and the girls sound great performing this doo-wop number, with an American feel to it.

~

Cliff Richard Variety Package

On May 27 1959, the girls travelled to Blackburn to take part in the Cliff Richard Variety Package. Then moved on to Chelmsford and Woolwich. On the bill with them were The Drifters, who became The Shadows, Cherry Wainer and Don Storer, the Kingpins, Daley and Wayne, and the

159

Wise Guys, and once again Tony Marsh was the compere. In June, the three girls re-joined the Cliff Richard Variety Package at the Exeter Savoy, this time with the Monograms, Peter Elliot, Lisa Noble and the Tommy Allen Trio.

Cliff was a recently discovered singing sensation who had taken the first tentative steps on his path to fame in 1957. He toured Britain almost constantly throughout 1958 and 1959, appearing with rockers like Wee Willie Harris. The Lana Sisters originally met him on *The Jack Jackson Show*. With his greased quiff, curled lip and thrusting hips, Cliff was Britain's answer to Elvis Presley.

The trio appeared on Cliff's shows several times in those early days of his career. On one occasion after the show, with the fans at the front of the theatre going crazy and his manager fearing for Cliff's safety, the Lana Sisters were asked if they could take him home. There were no posh hotels at this stage of his career! He was going home to his parents' house in Cheshunt, Hertfordshire, just 10 or 15 miles from Lynne's parents' house. The girls smuggled him out the side of the theatre and into the back seat of Lynne's car. On the journey, Lynne and Mary discovered a very nervous young man who constantly bit his nails, until they delivered him to his mum's council house. Describing it later, Lynne said, 'I can see it now, that was Cliff Richard. He was very shy, a very nervous young chap.'

Between this engagement at the end of June and the middle of October, the Lana Sisters appeared several times on *Saturday Club*, *Workers' Playtime*, *Midday Music Hall* and *Air Parade*. They were also in the line-up for ATV's *Disk Break,* along with Lonnie Donegan and Bobby Darren.

Charity Concerts

In October the Lana Sisters performed in two star-filled charity concerts. The first was the Caxton Convalescent Home benefit gig, held in the Princes Theatre, Shaftesbury Avenue, where there was a 'show within a show' along the lines of *Oh Boy!*. The Lana Sisters appeared with a host of other stars, including Bernard Braden, the John Barry Seven and Sylvia Sands. Music was provided by Harold Collins and his Orchestra.

A few days later they took part in the annual Old Ben Concert at the Coliseum, which was organised by the Newsvendors' Benevolent and Provident Institution, whose aim was to support people living in the Metropolis and working in the print trade, who from infirmity, age or distress, were in need. The name 'Old Ben' came from the affectionate shortening of its name and the benevolence it gave. The long name had proved too much for many Cockney street sellers. Bill Pertwee introduced the first half of the show, and Johnny Downes took over to introduce a second half that got off to a colourful start with Gwenda Wilkins' lively piano accordion. [143]

~

'Seven Little Girls, Sitting on the Back Seat'

This was a novelty song written by Lee Pockriss and Bob Hilliard. In the US, Paul Evans and the Curls had a top ten hit with it, and the Avons reached number three in the UK with their version. The Lana Sisters and Al Saxon released their cover of the novelty song on 30 October 1959. The number shows a pronounced American influence – the car sounds big enough to be a limousine or one of those huge Cadillacs. Very aspirational for teenagers at the time, and slightly suggestive lyrics in places. The 'spontaneous' spoken lines are fun. The reviews were great, but sadly it didn't make any impression on the charts. They were never going to get anywhere with that record.

The B-side, 'Sitting on the Sidewalk', was written by Sid Tepper and Roy Bennett, the writing partnership responsible for many 50's and 60's hits, including Cliff Richard's 'The Young Ones'. For this track the girls are by themselves 'chanting a shuffler about a girl waiting for her boy. He's late! Catchy tune and prominent sax with words which tell a neat story. The vocal team is in good form and should have plenty of buyers for this one.'[144]

During their October appearance on Saturday Club, the Lana Sisters performed 'Seven Little Girls' with Al Saxon. In December of 1959, Brian Matthew took the Al Saxon part, in a rare foray into singing, not often to be repeated. In the *Sounds of the 60's with Tony Blackburn* pages,

---

143 More information can be found at http://www.newstraid.org.uk/

144 *Disc*, 31 October 1959

Brian Matthew's musical talents are discussed: 'Brian Matthew has a wonderful warm voice for broadcasting, but it's not necessarily the greatest vehicle for singing. If you have ever heard 'Trad Mad' - a song about a girl who digs Kenny Ball, then you'll know why Brian's singing career never took off.'

After a week with the Cliff Richard Variety Package at the Birmingham Hippodrome, the Lana Sisters went to ATV on Boxing Day for the highlight of their winter season – an appearance on the *Tommy Steele Spectacular*, performing 'Seven Little Girls' with Tommy Steele. Every star you could imagine was on the bill, and one of them was a good-looking young chap with a lovely tenor voice, Tony Dalley, who was a big name at the time. He asked Lynne out for dinner. But Iris, haunted by memories of the girls in the Ivy Benson Band, and the way they would suddenly disappear, was adamant – there was to be no fraternising, Lynne was not permitted to accept the invitation.

TOMMY STEELE with seven little girls in the back seat — THE LANA SISTERS and THE LIDDELL TRIPLETS with SHIRLEY SANDS—in one of the scenes you'll see in Tommy's Boxing Day show on ATV.

FIGURE 4.11 'SEVEN LITTLE GIRLS' WITH TOMMY STEELE
(*NME*, 18 DECEMBER 1959)

After a number of radio dates – *Music for Your Party* on Christmas Day, and *Workers' Playtime*, in Staffordshire, on New Year's Eve – 1959 came to an end.

1960

'You've Got What It Takes'

Early in January 1960, the Lana Sisters went into the studio to record their fifth single. 'You've Got What It Takes' was an original composition by guitarist Bobby Parker. He recorded it for Vee Jay records in 1958, as the B-side to his first solo single, 'Blues Get Off My Shoulder', and in 1959 Berry Gordy and his sister Gwen produced a recording by Marv Johnson for the emerging Motown label. This version reached number two on the Black Singles chart, and number ten on the Billboard Hot 100, early in 1960.

'You've Got What It Takes' was Mary's first encounter with Motown, although she wasn't aware of it at the time. In an interview on BBC's *Saturday Sequence,* in 1989 she said, 'I didn't realise I knew about it that early'.[146]

A cute string intro. The girls sing a mixture of harmony and unison. A nice short piano solo on this one. Perhaps it would be more effective as a solo song though? The *Picturegoer* reviewer took a rather Victorian view, describing the lyrics as provocative and more suited to a nightclub. It had, it seemed, little chance of success in the Hit Parade, but it was a Top 10 hit in Ireland for the trio.

The flip side of the single was 'My Mother's Eyes', and the Lana Sisters did an excellent job on the vocal, with good close harmony. Repeated piano chords underlined the rhythm and Ken Jones swirling strings added a bit of interest, but this was a very traditional song. Keith Fordyce, writing in the *NME,* said: 'I have never heard them sing better and it might not be a bad idea if this were treated as the A-side'.

~

Saturday Club Jazz and Rock Night

The trio were booked to appear in a BBC special, *Saturday Club Jazz and Rock Night*, to be broadcast from the Royal Albert Hall on 30 January 1960. Stars were Acker Bilk's Paramount Jazz Band, Terry Lightfoot's New Orleans Jazzmen, and the John Barry Seven. Also included in the

---

146 Roger Scott, *The Saturday Sequence*, BBC Radio 1, 11 March 1989.

vast line-up of talent were Adam Faith, Cuddly Duddly, George Chisholm, Sylvia Sands, Miki and Griff and Craig Douglas.

FIGURE 4.12 BACKSTAGE AT THE ROYAL ALBERT HALL: L TO R IRIS LONG, LYNNE ABRAMS, MARY O'BRIEN, SYLVIA SANDS, BETTY SMITH AND MIKI (OF MIKI AND GRIFF) – (BBC ARCHIVES)

Mary had been to the Royal Albert Hall before, but this time she had a more intimate view of this iconic theatre. While the Lana Sisters had appeared in some very special theatres, none compared to this one. This magnificent building with its domed glass roof, the great Henry Wills organ, and seats for more than 5,000 people was simply stunning. The huge but intimate hall is an exciting place to perform in.

That day, sitting at the side of the stage during rehearsals, awaiting their instructions from the producer, Brian Matthew came over to speak to Mary. He said he was sure he knew her, that he had seen her outside Ealing Cathedral.

Brian had performed 'Seven Little Girls' with the Lana Sisters in December, but he was always so busy and remote that there had been little chance of a conversation then. This time, Mary was surprised that he had taken the time to speak to her. This was the beginning of a long and warm friendship between Brian and Mary. He was such a lovely man, quiet, polite, respectful and not at all rock'n'roll! Everybody in pop knew Brian Matthew, and in the 1960's there were few acts who hadn't been interviewed by him. His relaxed manner put them at ease and achieved excellent results.

An electric atmosphere suffused the whole day leading up to this live *Saturday Club* show. Introduced by Brian, it started with rehearsals in the morning and built to a climax by the time of the actual performance. When Mary stood on the stage and looked out into the vast auditorium, with its banks upon banks of seats just waiting to be filled by the excited fans, she struggled to believe that this was real and that she would soon be performing in that venue, on that stage, in front of thousands of screaming fans.

~

The Brompton Squares

While Mary was touring with the Lana Sisters, Dion was still chasing bookings in West End clubs and sending letters to the BBC Entertainment Manager asking for more radio and TV spots. He appeared several times on Ken Sykora's *Guitar Club* with his partner Georges Martinique, and there were occasional solo appearances on BBC TVs *Twice Twenty* and the Light Programme's *Ten-Forty Club*. By the start of 1960, though, the partnership between Dion and Georges had ended. That was when he met and got to know Tim Feild, a young folk singer.

Tim Feild was born on 15 April 1934, into a seriously wealthy family. His mother, Esmé Violet (Mouse) Bentley, came from Woodlesford, where her family owned the Bentley's Yorkshire Bitter brewing company. She inherited a great deal of money when her mother died. Tim's father, Armistead Littlejohn Feild, was a publisher, who died after fewer than five years of marriage, leaving Mouse a widow when Tim was just three years old. She soon remarried, but Tim kept his father's name.

Tim was educated at Eton, and then, at 18, he was called up for National Service. It was generally believed that the Royal Navy did not admit National Service recruits, and although less than two per cent of those enlisted were sailors, Tim was among that number. It may have helped that his stepfather, Richard Arthur Hawkesworth, was a rear admiral in the Royal Navy. Once released from National Service, Tim set out to discover the world with a spirit of adventure but very little money. He took his guitar, and decided to see how far he would get, singing for his supper. He travelled all over the world, first spending a year in America and then heading off to other countries – Japan, Siam, Pakistan, Turkey and many more. He covered 20,000 miles and had some interesting times along the way, including teaching Liz Taylor's children to water-ski on the Costa Brava. In the Northern Provinces of Pakistan, close to the borders of Afghanistan, he met up with a Dervish Brotherhood (a Sufi fraternity) which sparked events that were to bring about a complete change in his life. In Pakistan, he became seriously ill and was forced to return to England. Once home and recovered from his illness, Tim entered and reached the finals of the 'Bid for Fame' TV series. But the top prize eluded him, and instead he found work as a singing waiter in Luba's Bistro. At the age of 21, he was in line for a substantial inheritance, but his stubborn refusal to give up his family name and his membership of the Communist Party, meant he was completely disinherited.[148]

In Britain in the 1960's, people's options when eating out were mostly limited to a choice between rigidly formal silver service restaurants and greasy spoon transport caffs. Wimpy Bars, Britain's answer to the American burger joint, were scarce, and there were very few Chinese and Indian restaurants. but cosmopolitan London was different, and by the early 1960's, bistros had begun to appear in the city. Small, informal, relaxed and fairly cheap places to eat, Luba's Bistro was among the best known.

Luba was a Russian émigré who had escaped revolutionary Russia as a child, and was raised in her uncle G. I. Gurdjieff's spiritual school in France, amid artists, intellectuals and politicians. The likes of Katherine Mansfield, Bertrand Russell and Franklin Roosevelt came seeking her

---

148 For information on Tim, later Reshad, Feild, see https://chalice-verlag.de/reshad-feild

uncle's insights into the riches of Eastern wisdom. She learned the secrets of the kitchen at the Prieure, taught by her mother and her eccentric uncle, and brought those skills with her to London, where she opened her first bistro. This bistro was unique, the place, the people, the rustic décor with loops of sausages and strings of garlic hanging from the ceiling, and paintings of Russian country scenes on the walls. A landmark in London for over three decades, Luba served everyone from starving artists to royalty with her generous heart and hearty fare.

Luba's was patronised by the great and the good of London's fashionable, artistic and music set: Helene Cordet and Peter Davis were regulars there, while Princess Margaret was known to visit. Terence Donovan, whose studio was next door, was another customer. He photographed the staff with Lison Lipnitzki for an *Evening Standard* fashion feature. Terence Keough, in *My Green Age*, describes eating there:

The bistro was remarkable, an unpretentious eating place in a made over garage on Yeoman's Row, a former mews, just off Brompton Road, a few blocks west of Harrods. The kitchen was open to the restaurant, in the Russian style, Luba herself could be seen at work there. The Russian dishes were basic; stuffed green peppers, goulash, galubtzy (cabbage rolls), and stroganoff, each garnished with one of the many variations of Luba's succulent red sauce. People sat wherever there was space at picnic like tables that held eight. Often there was a line-up at the door. A bottle of cheap Beaujolais could be bought at the Bunch of Grapes right next door to the Beatles' Manager's offices. Luba's staff uncorked it and provided glasses at no charge. The meals were cheap, four or five shillings for a main course. [149]

---

149 Terrence Keough (2009) *My Green Age*, Bloomington, IND: Trafford Publishing, pp. 195.

FIGURE 4.13 TIM FEILD PERFORMING IN LUBA'S BISTRO
(COURTESY OF MARINA C BEAR)

Stunningly handsome, Tim would sit in a corner tinkling away on his guitar and entertaining the diners with his folk songs. Dion is almost certain to have been a patron, and perhaps Mary was too. Could this be where Dion and Tim Feild met? Their paths would cross again at Helene Cordet's high society club where they both performed. There, they discovered a shared love of Latin American, African and folk music, and quickly decided to work together. Calling themselves the Brompton Squares, they proceeded to perform in clubs all over London's West End.

A cabaret act which made its debut at Quaglino's and the Allegro Room on Monday was The Brompton Squares. Tim Feild and Dion O'Brien, having already established individual reputations as cabaret entertainers, have now become a team which may be described as a two-man challenge to America's "Kingston Trio". Singing folk-type songs to their own guitar and bongo drum accompaniment, they are backed by Felix King's Orchestra.

FIGURE 4.14 THE BROMPTON SQUARES – TIM FEILD AND DION O'BRIEN
(THE *STAGE*, 18 FEBRUARY 1960)

The duo featured in a photograph printed in *The Stage* on 18 February 1960, in which they are shown casually leaning on a conga drum. The caption read: 'A cabaret act which made its debut at Quaglino's the Allegro Room on Monday was the Brompton Squares.' It went on to say they were a two-man challenge to America's Kingston Trio. They performed folk-style songs with guitar and bongo drums and were backed by Felix King's Orchestra, which had moved to Quaglino's after residencies at the Orchid Room and the Colony Restaurant, where King directed a nine-piece orchestra.

~

Disc Party

At the end of February *Disc* held another party, this time to celebrate their one hundredth issue. The Lana Sisters joined in the celebrations, as shown in this photograph.

Right: Not dancing, but enjoying themselves all the same were The LANA SISTERS and Fred and Mary Mudd of The MUD-LARKS. The lad in the background trying to break the camera lens is JOE BROWN.

FIGURE 4.15 DISC PARTY WITH FRED AND MARY MUDD AND JOE BROWN
(RICHI HOWELL *DISC*, 20 FEBRUARY 1960)

~

Radio

Saturday Club

The Lana Sisters next appearance on *Saturday Club* came on 2 April 1960, with Rosemary Squires, Dickie Pride, Dick Jordon, Gary Marshal, the Sonny Stewart Group and the Bert Weedon Quartet. As always, it was introduced by Brian Matthew and produced by Jimmy Grant.

Following the success of the previous live *Saturday Club*, the BBC presented the Sixth Annual Festival of popular music, *Big Beat*. Broadcast on 12 April, the show was headlined by Adam Faith, and as well as the Lana Sisters, it featured Craig Douglas, Duffy Power and Dickie Pride. The John Barry Seven, Bert Weedon, Johnny Wiltshire and the Trebletones, Rabin Rock Unit, David Ede, Lorie Mann, Colin Day and Ray Pilgrim were also in the line-up. Compere was Brian Matthew.

In the following weeks the Lana Sisters were busy with a mix of stage, radio and TV work. They spent a week at the Manchester Hippodrome during that month, and had guest billing on *Go Man Go* with David Ede and the Rabin Band. *Go Man Go* was a great radio programme, broadcast live every Monday lunchtime from the Paris Theatre in Lower Regent Street. This was a special holiday edition of the show, directed by David Ede, and along with the Lana Sisters he introduced the Rabin Band, Lorie Mann, Colin Day and Ray Pilgrim. At that time, the Musicians Union ruled that music performed on the radio had to be live, so rock'n'roll numbers heard on records from the US were played by the Rabin Band. The kids wanted to hear the real thing. The Rabin Band couldn't quite cut it and the performances weren't very successful.

At the beginning of May 1960, the trio spent a week at the Finsbury Park Empire in the show that closed the theatre. Emile Ford's 'Fast-Moving Beat Show' included Emile's band The Checkmates, Chas McDevitt and Shirley Douglas. Compere Tony Marsh was there with his usual outrageous behaviour, and the next week the show moved to the Brighton Hippodrome.

Emile Ford was the first black British male singer to top the UK charts, and with The Checkmates reached a million sales in Britain. His single, 'What Do You Want to Make Those Eyes at Me For?', stayed in the charts for six weeks, a feat made all the more remarkable by being achieved at a time when there were race riots in Notting Hill orchestrated by the far-right White Defence League. There were signs stating 'No Dogs, No Blacks, No Irish' displayed in boarding houses throughout the country.

Having arrived in the UK in 1954, when he was just 17, to study engineering at Tottenham Polytechnic, Emile took up the guitar and formed a small group to play pop and rock'n'roll songs. The band won a talent contest at the first Soho Village Fair, and their prize was a recording contract with Pye, a small record company enjoying success with Lonnie Donegan.

Also on the bill was Scots-born Chas McDevitt and his skiffle group with Shirley Douglas. A keen blues and jazz fan, McDevitt moved to London in 1955, when he had a spell playing with Ken Colyer's Crane River Jazz Band. He performed in coffee bars in Soho with his skiffle group, and won a talent contest organised by Radio Luxembourg. At the height of the skiffle boom he recorded 'Freight Train', which became a hit after Nancy Whiskey was added on vocals. After an appearance on *The Ed Sullivan Show*, the song was a million-seller and the Chas McDevitt Skiffle Group became an international success, the only British skiffle group other than Lonnie Donegan's to do so.

During the same week in May, the Lana Sisters also appeared on ATV's late-night show *Melody Dances*, with Jimmy Lloyd and the Bell Tones.

~

Nat King Cole – 14 May 1960

There was to be one very special high point for Mary in her time with the Lana Sisters, and it was huge. Jazz pianist and singer Nat King Cole was coming to London to headline several shows, and the Lana Sisters were booked to appear with him at the New Victoria Cinema.

Cole was the most successful American singer in the years between Bing Crosby and Elvis Presley. He had many hit singles and even Sinatra couldn't touch him. This handsome and sexy African American man defied the colour of his skin. Although his piano playing was superb, it was eclipsed by his smooth and liquid voice.

Nat King Cole had left America for a tour of ten European countries, and his last destination was London. The Royal Variety Performance was scheduled for Monday 16 May, and he was one of the stars of this show. The day before that, he topped the bill on *Sunday Night at the London Palladium*. But on Saturday 14th, he presented two concerts at the New Victoria Cinema, and the Lana Sisters were on the bill. It was a thrill for Mary to take part in that show!

What a night! The shows were sold out for both performances and Nat King Cole was treated to some of the wildest and loudest applause in the history of the cinema. He appeared wearing an extremely smart tailored blue suit and with his friendly personality and effortless way of entertaining, took control of the evening. The audience thrilled to the sound of his warm, fascinating voice in the more than an hour he spent onstage. With his piano playing he demonstrated his real feeling and understanding for jazz. The Cyril Stapleton Band provided musical backing, along with his own trio of guitar, bass and drum.

The Lana Sisters were dressed in brilliant pink tulle dresses made especially for the occasion, and they harmonised well as they sang 'When Mexico gave up the Rhumba', 'Sh-Boom', and 'My Mother's Eyes'.[150]

But although Iris, Lynne and Mary appeared with Nat King Cole that night, to Lynne's regret they didn't take the chance to watch him perform:

Sheer madness, we never even stood and watched his act. As soon as we've come off, Iris hurries us along, then the next thing we know we are going home. He's finished his act and we walked across the stage. Everybody's gone, you know what it's like backstage, it's dismal, and he's standing there with his wife and his daughter, young daughter, and he said, 'I loved your act girls.' He said, 'I loved it, it was great.' We never even asked for a photo, we never asked for his autograph. I have not even got a flyer of it.[151]

~

Change is in the Air

The group moved on to the Gaumont Theatre in Taunton next, where they were on the bill with the diminutive Jimmy Clitheroe in his own show. This time they joined Brian Budge, the Dagenham Girl Pipers and trick cyclists Los Dos Madrigales. When he was born Clitheroe's thyroid gland was damaged. He never grew any taller than 4ft 3in, about the size of an eight-year-old child. It meant that he could easily pass for a young boy, and he maintained that role throughout his life. His age remained a secret in case it spoiled the illusion, and he always performed in schoolboy's cap and blazer, even at radio recordings, for

150 Nat King Cole Scores Big Hit at London Concerts, *The Stage*, 19 May 1960

151 Lynne Essex: interview with author

the benefit of the studio audience. He appeared in publicity stunts for his local Boy Scout troop, continued to live with his mother after his father's death, and was never known to have a girlfriend. It all helped to maintain his show business career, which depended on the illusion.

The trio had just arrived in Taunton, and were getting ready to go onstage. In the packed dressing room, everyone was fighting to get to the mirror to touch up their make-up and check their outfits, and runners came to the door with instructions on the order of performance and a multitude of other bits of information. Mary answered a knock on the door and was surprised to find her brother standing there; she hadn't seen him for quite a while, and thought he was busy performing in Quaglino's with Tim. He asked her out for supper after the show, and of course she agreed, as she was both pleased that he had come all this way to see her, and intrigued to know why.

Dion had an idea that he wanted to share with his sister; the conversation between the siblings that night led to a complete change of direction for them both. His idea was to form a group with two boys and a girl singing a mixture of folk and pop, and he wanted Mary to join him and Tim in this new group. What an idea! Of course, there were other trios of two boys and a girl – for example, the Mudlarks, an English pop vocal group, and the Weavers in the US – but it was obvious he had been thinking about this for quite some time.

Dion sketched out the plan of how it would work, telling Mary that he and Tim had signed with a very successful and smart London agent, Emlyn Griffiths, who had been working in the business for many years. He had seen Dion and Tim performing in Quaglino's and he liked them. It was partly his suggestion to develop their sound by adding a girl singer. Dion had seen the Lana Sisters perform and knew that a trio was a great concept. And with such a talented sister who was well-used to singing with him, he knew she was the one. Griffiths had already organised a contract for them – a season performing in Butlin's holiday camps.

Mary had been enjoying her time as a member of the Lana Sisters – Iris and Lynne had taught her so much about showbiz and about stagecraft; though it had been a gruelling introduction to the highs and lows of life on the road and all the vagaries of show business. The rush of adrenaline when she went onstage and the roar of approval from the audience still thrilling now, almost as much as it had ever been. But, after more than two years with the group, the excitement had begun to wear thin. The constant touring and travelling, and the grind of performing had left her feeling weary. She wasn't given much say in the songs they sang, nor in how the act was presented, and it was clear that their records weren't making much impression on the charts. Basically, she was starting to feel dissatisfied. She wasn't too sure how staying with the Lana Sisters would help her reach her goal, and she was ready for a change. The rocky, poppy music she sang with them wasn't the kind she wanted to perform either, but she was committed to the act and at least it gave her a platform and visibility with audiences.

Excited by the offer from her brother Mary said yes straight away. She was thrilled by the prospect, and thought it was a brilliant idea; she wasn't too worried at the risk that they might fail. Dion told her the contract with Butlin's was due to start soon.

They had a lot of work to do to get their act ready. Dion and Tim found a guest house in Taunton and stayed for the rest of that week, meeting up with Mary every afternoon to rehearse the act they would take to Butlin's. It was challenging, Mary was still performing at night with the Lana Sisters, and spending her days practising with the boys was draining. They found a space in the town where they could meet and work on their routine. Mary was a perfectionist and insisted that they practise each song over and over again, until the boys groaned and begged to stop. She also told them they must look cheerful; she knew how important that was!

The rehearsals went well, and they knew they had something good that could bring them success. Although there was still a lot of work to do, Dion was confident that Butlin's would give them the time to polish their act. Their priority was to ensure they had prepared enough songs to get them started, and so longer-term decisions were shelved for the moment. They just had to be ready to give a half-decent performance when they arrived in Brighton, the first stop on their tour of Butlin's holiday camps.

~

Mary's suddenly long absences must have seemed strange to Iris and Lynne. Usually, when they were staying in digs the three would spend their days together. Mary went missing for most of that week, while she practised with the boys, and with the Butlin's contract only a month away, Mary knew she would have to tell her friends about the plan. She didn't look forward to the conversation, but at the end of the week of rehearsals with Dion and Tim, she broke the news to them.

Iris and Lynne were shocked – they hadn't considered the possibility of Mary leaving. Iris was caught completely off guard; she had seen the dangers of romantic liaisons breaking up the act, but not this. Their season in Blackpool was due to start soon and Mary was abandoning them. She gave them very little notice, and although they tried to persuade her to stay at least until the end of the season, she was resolute. The trio were expected to start in Butlin's in early June, and she hoped the Lana Sisters would be able to find her replacement before she left. In the meantime, she continued touring and performing with them until it was time to leave.

Although a lot of people think that Mary used the Lana Sisters, Lynne doesn't agree: 'It's true she had learned quite a bit and she was never truly unhappy with us. She never said, 'Oh, why can't we do this, why can't we do that? But she couldn't be happy stuck singing bottom harmony with us, even though it made us sound very good. She needed to grow.' Lynne felt that Iris was short-sighted in never allowing any of them to break from the harmony and sing the melody line, and if Mary had been given that chance the group would have sounded much better. With the polished act they had developed by then, Lynne often wondered how much more they could have achieved. Now Dion was offering Mary something very different – in this new trio she would be able to use her voice properly, which would free her to take her singing to another level. Lynne said, 'It would have been a tragedy if she hadn't left.'

'Someone Loves You Joe'

On 27 May, the Lana Sisters released two new sides. They recorded 'Someone Loves You Joe', by Norman Strassberg and Larry Kolber, and 'Tintarella di Luna' by Bruno de Filippi, Franco Migliacci and Sunny Skylar at the Philips Studios. As always, they were produced by Jack Baverstock, and backed by the Ken Jones Orchestra.

'Someone Loves you Joe', starts with a military drumbeat and the singing joins in with a forceful, deliberate lyric. The rhythm comes in, building in intensity right through to the end. 'Tintarella di Luna', is an Italian ballad about the colour of the moonlight, featuring twanging guitars.

~

Mary leaves

Looking at the evidence, it's possible to identify the precise date Mary left the Lana Sisters. She stayed with them for several weeks after she dropped her shocking news, and in that time a replacement was brought in, and began rehearsing with Iris and Lynne. There was almost no break in their appearances. Except, there was! From late May the group were on tour with Emile Ford and the Checkmates in his All-Star Show. Mary's last appearance with the Lana Sisters was most likely in Brighton on 6 June 1960. The Lana Sisters next booking was scheduled to start a week later.

Meanwhile, Dion and Tim were still performing in West End clubs. Their agent, Emlyn Griffiths, called the BBC booking manager early in May, to tell him that the boys were going to be in Butlin's for 16 weeks from the end of May. [152] In fact, the pair made an appearance in *Words and Music* on BBC TV on 7 June. Mary left Brighton and travelled home to London, where she met up with Tim and Dion. They were ready to start their season in Butlin's Holiday Camps.

~

The fate of the Lana Sisters

On 13 June the Lana Sisters spent a week with Adam Faith and Emile Ford in 'Seeing Stars' at the Globe Theatre, Stockton. This was the precursor to their summer season in Blackpool, which was due to start on 26 June. Iris must have been devastated by Mary's departure, but she didn't know how soon she would face another disaster. On the eve of their season at the Blackpool Hippodrome, Lynne was taken very ill in

---

152 BBC WAC, O'Brien Dion RCont1, Note by Patrick Newman about a call from Emlyn Griffiths, 4 May 1960

the middle of the night. The doctor was called, and she was sent straight to the hospital in Stockton – an old army establishment formed of Nissan huts – where appendicitis was diagnosed. Knowing that they couldn't appear without Lynne – the act just wouldn't work without her – Iris took the other girl and drove straight back down south, abandoning Lynne in this diabolical hospital more than 300 miles away from home. A report in *Disc* mentioned Lynne's emergency operation and *The Stage* printed an article about how the 'Delfont Jinx', which had already seen illness stop both Harry Secombe and Bruce Forsyth from opening their seasons in Blackpool had struck for a third time. When Lynne's illness meant the Lana Sisters couldn't make the opening of 'Seeing Stars', the Barry Sisters were drafted in at short notice to cover until Lynne was well again.

Iris was always afraid some young man might come along to tempt her girls to leave the group. Mary had been encouraged to leave by a young man, but not in the way Iris feared. When Iris left Lynne in hospital, she had no concern that an admirer would come calling, yet that's exactly what happened. A young man – a member of their group of friends – heard about Lynne's plight and drove north for a short visit in the hospital. When he left, he promised to write to her in Blackpool, and their relationship developed from there: they were married within six months. In just a few short months Iris had lost two important pillars of her group. But that wasn't the end, Iris found another girl to replace Lynne, and the group continued performing onstage and on the radio until 1963.

Mary knew nothing of this. Her time as a Lana Sister was over and it was the start of the next phase for her. Looking back, she knew how much she had learned from Iris and Lynne. In her time with them she discovered the realities of life as part of a professional group travelling all over the country to perform, and she had her first proper taste of being in a recording studio too. She found out what life was like constantly on the move from place to place, living out of a suitcase, staying in digs and eating on the hoof. More importantly though, she began to understand the mechanics of performing; how to get on- and offstage, how to harmonise, how to project, how to work an audience. And she discovered the rush – that feeling of elation from the sound of the audience clapping and cheering. Mary's life with the Lana Sisters had been hectic, but it was about to move into a higher gear.

In a radio interview in 1989, Mary reflected on her time with the Lana Sisters, saying, 'They were invaluable to me because, after all, it was the only training, and it was good training. When the Springfields were formed I was actually the only one of them that had any professional experience, rather than training.'[153]

~

Last Record

'Down South'

The Lana Sisters released another disc on 2 December 1960, quite some time after Mary had left the group. The record included 'Down South', written by Derek Warne and Iris Long, with lyrics by Lynne on the A-side, and 'Twosome', by John Shakespeare, on the flip. It is unlikely that these two sides were recorded before Mary's departure; it seems that her replacement is featured on this release.

---

153 Roger Scott, *The Saturday Sequence*, BBC Radio 1, 11 March 1989.

Part 5: The Springfields:

1969 - 1963

Getting the Act Together

Now things started to happen. Mary had thought a lot about the kind of songs she wanted to sing, and now that she was working with her brother, she was determined to have a say in their musical direction. There was so much to think about; their act, their look, their presentation, their musical style.

Mary and Dion both wanted their names to reflect this new beginning. Mary thought her name was just too ordinary and didn't suit a pop star! Dion's full name was Dionysius, but even when shortened to Dion people could never pronounce it properly.

Mary shrugged off Shan, the name she had adopted while with the Lana Sisters, and chose Dusty, a nickname she'd been given by her brother's friends when she kicked a ball around in the street with them. Dion decided on Tom, and from then on Mary was Dusty and Dion was Tom.

The group needed a distinctive name too. They chose The Springfields. Many questions have since been posed and theories put forward about the origins of the name. Tim's version − the apocryphal story told so many times it has almost become true − is that the group were rehearsing in a field in Spring and the name appeared in a lightbulb moment. In fact, they probably tossed many ideas around with none of them sounding quite right. In the end, the rather more prosaic likelihood is that the idea came when they realised that there are endless places in the UK and the US with that name. It was so familiar that people could recognise and identify with it easily.

~

Agent: Emlyn Griffiths

When Tom and Tim started working together early in 1960, they had signed themselves up to the Emlyn Griffiths Theatrical Agency. Welshman, Captain Emlyn Griffiths, was a well-known top theatrical manager in London's West End. His 6-foot-3-inch frame, monocle, military moustache, huge cashmere overcoat and rich fruity voice delivered with a slight stutter made him a memorable figure in the area. He promoted their musical act, the Brompton Squares, and organised all their bookings for them, including contacting the BBC to ensure they knew about the duo.

~

Butlin's

Griffiths had booked the group into Butlin's, sight unseen! Tom bought a dilapidated old Volkswagen campervan that was used to transport themselves and their stage gear, including Mary's stage clothes with their bouffant net petticoats.

Their first destination was the Ocean Hotel in Saltdean, five miles outside Brighton. As they pulled into the driveway that led them to the main crescent shaped building of this amazing art deco hotel, they were apprehensive and unsure of what to expect. They had had very little time to rehearse, and their brand-new act was pretty rough around the edges.

Billy Butlin had come up with the idea for his holiday camps after seeing bedraggled and despondent holidaymakers sheltering from the rain one afternoon in the 20s. Boredom and misery on their faces, they had nothing to do, and locked out of their guest houses, nowhere to go. Billy Butlin's idea was for a camp that would give people a holiday where it didn't matter if it rained all week. Somewhere that provided the holidaymakers with everything they needed, from a bed to lay their heads and a place to eat, with entertainment to fill their days, come rain or shine.

Billy Butlin attempted to recreate the atmosphere of the Grand Hotel on a budget. His holiday camps introduced redcoats to encourage the campers to have fun. The entire community of the camp existed inside the boundary fence, so there was never any need for people to venture outside.

Butlin's, from its inception, had been the proving ground for performers who went there to polish their acts. And it was so for the Springfields. The audiences were vital – a noisy bunch, unafraid to let the acts know if they were any good – and the trio used those weeks to discover their strengths and weaknesses.

The Springfields arrived in a world of brightly coloured buildings with exotic sounding names, set amongst wonderful flower gardens. Entertainments were organised by the ever-enthusiastic Redcoats: there were sporting activities, kids play areas, boating lakes, and a great range of bars, theatres and entertainment venues. Most of the activities were free; Billy Butlin pioneered the idea of the all-inclusive package, meaning holiday makers had no need to leave the camps during the whole of their stay, and could spend their days enjoying the facilities at no extra cost. The seemingly endless list of entertainments and activities, provided for the campers, all available for the equivalent of a week's pay, were a relief in the drab post-war years.

The Beachcomber bars first began appearing at all the camps during the early 1960's. The layout was based around a Hawaiian beach scene, with waterfalls and bridges and a 'volcano' which erupted once every hour. Others included the Crazy Horse Saloon, complete with Wild West paraphernalia, the Pig & Whistle with its famous revolving bar, the Regency and the French.

Ballrooms were always a major part of Butlin's life and each camp had a good selection to choose from, catering for a variety of interests, from modern or old time to jive. Each ballroom had its own resident band and separate facility.

Tom, Tim and Dusty will have been wakened in the mornings by the loudspeakers bursting into life with the famous 'wakey-wakey' call and the music calling the campers to the first sitting for breakfast. When they went to the Scottish camp in Ayr, their wake-up call came in the form of the bagpipes played by a local piper!

FIGURE 5.1 BUTLIN'S 1960 WITH CAROLE LUPTON
(WITH KIND PERMISSION OF JOHN LUPTON THANKS TO AUTHOR AJ MARRIOT)

During the Springfields time at Butlin's, Dusty's hairstyle stayed much as it had been with the Lana Sisters, although she did go back to her natural colour. Dusty's blazing red hair is on display in this photo, which was taken in the Saltdean Hotel in Brighton in 1960. It shows the trio with Carole Lupton, a redcoat who became a friend.

In the early 1960's, as a young boy, Sam was a regular at Butlin's in Ayr. He remembers his days spent sitting beside the swimming pool with his family, watching the live entertainment. There was always a comedian and a musical group and he has a particular memory of a trio with a girl singer. While most of the musicians were men, and not very interesting for kids to listen to, this group played bright and bubbly music and worked very hard at entertaining the campers. Sam's sister recalls identifying the group from television a few years later – she is convinced this was the Springfields in their very early days!

The Springfields travelled by campervan to camps all over the country, where they played two or three shows a night. It wasn't the most comfortable form of transport and driving the A and B roads was rough. With no motorways, there was no alternative but to negotiate a route through all the major towns on the way, and so traffic jams were inevitable, with the roads leading into the major resorts chaotic, particularly at holiday weekends. They soon learned that travelling in the daytime was a nightmare and so took to driving through the night to beat the traffic.

They all struggled with the challenges and privations of life on the road, bitching and squabbling as they went. This was a life of weary road journeys, cramped dressing rooms and dreary hotel bedrooms that got on their nerves. In an article published several years later, Tim spoke about how tempers were frayed to breaking point so that singing on stage was the only time they were in harmony. But before he became one third of the Springfields, Tim knew nothing of this. He said of that tour, 'You try travelling that far in that time with your dearest friend and see how dear that friend is to you at the end of it!'

From the age of four Dusty and Tom had been driven by their ambition; they were totally focussed on show business. Tim claimed they were four times quicker than him at learning a tune or perfecting a dance routine. They argued over every detail of the act, from the songs they sang to the engagements they should accept. Tim's approach was more laidback, he claimed that despite being a singer and guitarist in Britain's top pop group, he never really did learn to play the guitar properly.[154]

Once they had got started there was serious work to do; they had to decide what form the group would take, and inevitably the three of them spent many hours talking about the music they liked, what would be commercial, what the scene was like, and more importantly, what they were able to perform. They scrutinised the skills, influences and experience each of them brought to the group.

Dusty was gregarious, fiery and upfront, always needing to be centre of attention. She was driven, had amazing vocal abilities and was the only one of the three who had proper experience of performing on a stage, in a theatre. In contrast, Tom was quieter and incredibly shy, but still had a fierce determination and will to succeed. A real student of the American folk idiom, he wrote prodigiously and had a great facility with music: he was a brilliant songwriter and arranger. Finally, Tim was spiritual. His meeting with a Sufi fraternity on his travels in Afghanistan

---

154 Tim Feild, 'Why the Springfields are Splitting Up', *Sunday People*, 29 September 1963.

and Pakistan had a deep impact on him. A brilliant musician and incredibly handsome young man, he had learned a lot from his time as a travelling minstrel. He had a facility for entertaining, but was much more laid back than the other two.

So, there they were, a trio: two boys and a girl with varying backgrounds and levels of experience, their task was to pull together and form a successful act. What musical style would they choose – jazz, folk, country and western, Latin American or pop? What songs would they sing? In the end they took influences from all over the place. They could sing in many different languages. Tom was able to add his knowledge of music to his skill as a song writer and adapt traditional material to suit the talents of the Springfields. He was mostly responsible for the music, lyrics and arrangements and he took some chances experimenting with the various sounds. The Springfields were highly successful in their time together, with their folky/country and western style. But Dusty yearned to perform a raunchy R&B/gospel style of music. In the Springfields she was never able to properly satisfy this yearning.

The trio knew about similar groups and the music they were performing; for example, the Kingston Trio were an all-boy group that sang the type of songs the Springfields liked. Then there was the Weavers, a brilliant group whose lead singer, Ronnie Gilbert, Dusty admired. She wanted to sound sturdy and folksy, just like Ronnie.

In fact, the Springfields main influence, at least in the early days, came from the Weavers, as demonstrated by the many Weavers songs the trio sang and recorded. And the Weavers were interesting; they weren't just a folk group, they were political!

Pete Seeger, founder of the Weavers, had moved to New York in 1938, where the folk scene, included Alan Lomax, Woody Guthrie, Aunt Molly Jackson, Lead Belly, and others. By 1949 he began performing with his old partner Lee Hays, Fred Hellerman on guitar and vocals, and singer Ronnie Gilbert, a young woman with a powerful voice. Alan Lomax and the Library of Congress's Archive of Folk Song, introduced him to the wealth of traditional American songs. The group played their own arrangements of these songs as well as those written by Lead Belly and Woodie Guthrie and were signed to a record deal by Decca. The Weavers are famous for singing, 'Michael Row the Boat Ashore', 'It

Takes a Worried Man', 'Kisses Sweeter than Wine' and 'Wimoweh'. Their most popular songs were Lead Belly's 'Goodnight Irene' and the Hebrew folk song 'Tzena, Tzena, Tzena', songs that reached number one and number two, respectively, in the US Hit Parade in 1950. Ten years later the Springfields included these songs in their repertoire.

The Weavers were very successful. But they were blacklisted during the McCarthy era, because of their communist sympathies. They were dropped by Decca and their records were deleted from its catalogue. Other television and concert appearances were cancelled. Eventually they disbanded. They came back, in 1955, with a sell-out concert in Carnegie Hall. A brilliant show, it was recorded and released on a best-selling album.

Versatility was to become the trademark of the Springfields. They played a variety of instruments, including piano, guitar, bongos and conga drums, and sang songs that featured Hebrew, German, Greek, Czech and Russian, many of them composed by Tom. They could play to any audience and they shared Pete Seeger's philosophy; in a 1968 interview, in response to claims that record companies found the Weavers difficult to classify, he told the *Pop Chronicles* music documentary to 'leave that up to the anthropologists, the folklorists... For you and me, the important thing is a song, a good song, a true song... Call it anything you want.' [155]

Once they had decided on the kind of music that they would perform, Tom chose how he wanted the boys to look. His choice of beige suits, stripy ties and suede Chelsea boots were not exactly rock'n'roll, but that is what he decided on. It was more difficult for Dusty and a challenge she faced throughout her career. She spent a great deal of time thinking about how she should present herself.

---

155 Seeger & the Weavers: https://digital.library.unt.edu/ark:/67531/metadc19745/m1/#track/1

FIGURE 5.2 STUDIO PORTRAIT OF THE SPRINGFIELDS (ALAMY)

From this publicity photograph of the Springfields in the early days, it is clear that Dusty's stage clothes were still influenced by Lynne's styling, and her time with the Lana Sisters. Her skirts, voluminous and needing fourteen petticoats to fill them out, were paired with long-sleeved blouses, and a floppy tie fixed at the neck. She wore low-heeled court shoes and her make-up was muted, showing little evidence of the mascara-laden eyes and heavy pancake make-up that would later become her trademark.

~

BBC Audition

In early September 1960, once their Butlin's season was over, the trio began a season at Churchill's. They had also had a couple of appearances at the Earls Court Radio Show, a trip to Blackpool for a Sunday Concert and several bookings with the Harold Fielding Organisation. They knew how much their tour of Butlin's holiday camps had benefited them; the work they had done to improve their performance was evident. Now they all felt confident that they had a smooth and polished act. On the other hand, this period had been a roller-coaster of performances and rehearsals that left them exhausted. But when Tom suggested they should try for an audition with the BBC, Tim and Dusty readily agreed.

Over the years Tom, when he was known as Dion, had applied for auditions with the BBC, sending letters to John Kingdon asking that he and his partner, Georges Martinique, be kept in mind.

Tom got in touch with his contact in the Variety Department at the BBC to tell him about the group and ask for an audition. He learned there was a slot available and that they could do all the form filling at the same time as the audition. When they heard this news, their exhaustion was replaced with excitement. Butlin's had gone well and the audiences seemed to love them, but this was the BBC – getting regular appearances on radio, and even TV, would lift them to another level.

They went to Studio 1 in the Aeolian Hall on 9 September and were auditioned by John Hooper. For the audition they chose to sing, 'Good News', 'Unchained Melody', 'Whole World in his Hands', and 'Kisses Sweeter than Wine'. The audition report was very positive; it assessed them as well-rehearsed and professional with good intonation and diction, and although they were seen as a little square, their repertoire was rock/western and they were described as teenage in appeal. This meant that they were deemed to be a very marketable product with well-performed, excellent material.[156]

It was almost five weeks before the group heard the outcome of their audition. Emlyn Griffiths received a rather long and rambling letter from Patrick Newman, the Light Entertainment Booking Manager for the BBC, in which he grumbled about the fact that Dusty, Tom and Tim were now

---

156 BBC WAC, The Springfields RCont 1, Audition Report, 9 September 1960

known as the Springfields. Tom and Tim had previously broadcast with the BBC: Tom under his real name, Dion O'Brien, and Tim as Tim Feild. This broke the rule that said artists were not allowed to broadcast under two names, but he didn't seem to notice that Dusty had also previously broadcast as Shan O'Brien when she was a member of the Lana Sisters.

Having got those gripes off his chest, he went on to say that the reports were favourable so there would be little point in denying themselves the right to use the group, 'herewith, therefore, the glad tidings that they are available if any producer wants to use them.'[157]

~

Churchill's Season

The Springfields began their season at Churchill's Club in London, at the beginning of September, and although they had all been used to working in West End Clubs, they were now exposed to the seedy reality. The club had a floorshow of singers and dancers, which was where they fitted in. But the main function of the club was to serve the clientele, who were plied with drink by the hostesses. These girls just had to sit with clients, and they earned commission on the amount of alcohol they ordered, their collection of cocktail sticks showing how much money they were owed. Some also made private arrangements to engage in after-hours assignations. The group had worked since June without a break. Dusty recalled:

Those dreary back stairs where the hostesses used to sit chain-smoking night after night as they waited to be called to the tables. Those awful grey-faced 'night people' who spent so much money. The cramped little dressing room. We used to work until four in the morning and then catch the all-night bus back to Ealing. We walked the last mile home as we couldn't afford a taxi. Sometimes I could hardly put one foot in front of another, I was so exhausted.[158]

Tim Feild also described his memory of their time in Churchill's:

If we expected plush comfort after the hectic touring, we were much mistaken. We had to share a dressing room, which was nothing more

---

157 BBC WAC, The Springfields RCont 1, Letter from Patrick Newman to Emlyn Griffiths, 12 October 1960

158 Dusty Springfield, 'Fame has a Flipside too', *Woman's Own* 1965, in Dusty Springfield Bulletin No. 66.

than a long narrow corridor, with 32 other artists. These included two other vocal groups, 16 chorus girls, a whip-cracking act who were constantly rehearsing, and a lady fire-eater, who, for economy, used paraffin instead of spirit and smoked us all out.[159]

After the weeks of touring around the Butlin's camps and the season in Churchill's, the Springfields' career was slow to get started. But ultimately, if Dusty's life with the Lana Sisters had been hectic and all-consuming, it was nothing to the crazy schedule of touring, performing, recording, TV and radio work she was about to encounter as part of the Springfields. Dusty had learned a lot about stage technique from the Lana Sisters, now it was time for her to pass those lessons on to the boys.

First they were in the line-up for the annual Old Ben Concert at the Coliseum. The Springfields opened the show, which was a hard task. But they brought everything they had learned from Butlin's and Churchill's and delivered a good upbeat set. The *Stage* review said: 'Making a good impression in the difficult opening spot were the Springfields, two boys and a girl who sing tunefully and forcefully in the modern idiom.'[160]

Next, the group had two radio dates. They appeared on *Midday Music Hall*, an old favourite, with Frank Cook, Iris Villiers, Leslie Randall, Joan Reynolds and the BBC Variety Orchestra. Then the Springfields were guests on *Parade of the Pops*, a lunchtime show on the Light Programme that included popular music reviews and predictions of hits to come.

---

159 Tim Feild, 'Why the Springfields are Splitting Up', *Sunday People*, 29 September 1963.

160 Old Ben Concert at the Coliseum, *The Stage*, 27 October 1960.

191

1961

Charlie Drake

On 16 January 1961, the Springfields joined a variety show for what would be the first of several visits that year. Their tour with the Charlie Drake Show began with two weeks at the Southampton Gaumont, followed by a week each at the Gloucester Regal and the Ipswich Gaumont.

Charlie Drake was a popular comedian famous for his slapstick act, out-slapping the comedians of the silent film era. He was perhaps best-known for his nine-minute performance of the 1812 Overture, where he played every member of the orchestra, and he will always be remembered for his catchphrase 'Hello my darlings!', which was the result of his height that meant his eyes would often be directly level with a lady's bosom.

The Springfields took part in the full company presentations and were given their own spot as the penultimate act before the interval. They also performed with a comedy musical instrumental novelty act, Albert and Les Ward, singing 'Tea for Two', from the Broadway musical *No, No, Nanette*.

In March the trio went to the Churchill Club for a live show, broadcast on BBC radio as *London Mirror*. This was introduced by Wilfrid Thomas, who went backstage to dig up unusual personal stories. It included theatre news, a song of the week and London cabaret with the Bill Shepherd Singers and the BBC Revue Orchestra. The group also appeared numerous times on *Workers' Playtime*.

~

In the Recording Studio

In March of 1961 the group had been together for nine months, and they agreed that if they wanted more exposure, they would have to make a record. Mary's time in the recording studios with Iris and Lynne had given her an insight into the recording process, and more importantly, she had made useful contacts in the business. She contacted Jack Baverstock, the recording manager at Fontana, to tell him about her new group and ask for his advice.

Through Jack, the group made contact with the Philips recording manager, Johnny Franz, and were invited to his office for an audition. When the Springfields walked into the Philips recording studio at Stanhope Place, in April 1961, it was the start of their musical collaboration with Johnny Franz and musical director Ivor Raymonde.

Cockney record producer, Johnny Franz could easily have been mistaken for a bank manager. He was dapper in a deep grey, fifties-style pinstripe suit, with slicked-back dark brown hair and a pencil-thin moustache. One hand was buried in his pocket, the other held his ubiquitous cigarette which meant he was permanently swathed in smoke. His other addiction was sugarless tea. He recalled his first meeting with the Springfields: 'The three of them sat right here, right in front of my desk, and sang 'Dear John'. It was a new sound, a fresh sound. I signed them up on the spot.'[161]

Franz had such perfect pitch that he could spot a bad note from the other side of the control room. His production trademarks were a lush choir with big orchestras, provided by Wally Stott, Ivor Raymonde and Peter Knight.

Ivor Raymonde had studied music at Trinity College and started out as a professional musician playing jazz and classical piano. He had the chance to see his heroes play in the beautiful jazz clubs of New York during his spell playing jazz piano for the passengers on the Queen Mary's Atlantic crossings. Then he worked on various TV shows with the BBC, gradually reaching the role of musical director. Following his time at the BBC, Ivor Raymonde moved to Philips, where he became an in-house producer and arranger.

While Johnny Franz produced the Springfields, Ivor Raymonde was the musical director on all of their UK-based recordings. Dusty and the boys' first meeting with Raymonde took place then, and their partnership would continue for the life of the group. He forged a strong working relationship with the Springfields and subsequently with Dusty when she became a solo artist.

---

161 Alan Smith, 'Dusty Always Knew What She Wanted', *New Musical Express,* 19 August 1966.

In Stanhope Place the setup was complex; it included the studio, the control room and a separate machine room for the tape machines. The control room had big windows so that Johnny Franz and Peter Oliff, the engineer, could see into the studio. Roger Wake in the machine room looked through a little window, about three-foot square, into the control room. The engineer used a talkback button to speak to the studio and the machine room.

'Dear John'

The Springfields' first record, 'Dear John', was sung to the tune 'Marching through Georgia', with words by Tom. 'I Done What They Told Me To', was on the B-side. This was adapted by Tom from a number he had found – 'I Done What He Told Me To' – to suit the rhythm and blues style. A rhythm section supported them on the session, and guitarist Ernie Shear playing a banjolin.

The record was released at the beginning of May, to rave reviews from the critics. *Record Mirror* gave the disc four stars. The record was described as both folky and modern, with a catchy performance. Their brilliant harmonising allowed Dusty to have just some solo lines. The *Disc* reviewer said, 'I like it a lot and I'd like to see it rise.'

~

In May the Springfields were contracted to appear on *Bandbox* for a fee of 30 guineas (£750 in 2021). The programme was recorded on Saturday 27 May and transmitted on Monday 12 June. Letters sent by Griffiths were now signed on his behalf by Pat Barnett, who had recently become his secretary. She was often left in charge since her employer was generally either out or in his office sleeping off his Quaglino's pink gins. She was responsible for manning the phones, typing and signing letters, organising bookings, and arranging travel and accommodation for all of his clients, not the least of whom was the Springfields. Pat had most recently been working for a legal firm, and this role of secretary to a theatrical agent was a far cry from what she was used to.

Pat first met Dusty one day when the Springfields arrived in the office and demanded to see Emlyn. Dusty quickly realised that, if the group needed anything, Pat would organise it for them. From then on Pat became an important presence in Dusty's life. Later, at the start of her solo career, Dusty asked Pat to be her secretary and the two developed a close friendship which lasted for the rest of Dusty's life.

Pat's special interest was speed skating. As a member of the National Skating Association, she first joined the Brixton Falcons and then the North London Roller Speed Club and competed in many senior women's events. In this male-dominated sport Pat was known as the glamour girl of speed skating. In fact, there had only been one British Championship event each year for women, as opposed to three for men, until 1950. Pat often took Dusty to squad training sessions and in the 1960's asked her to present the trophies.

~

At the end of May 1961, the Springfields had their first appearance on *Thank Your Lucky Stars* at the ABC Alpha Studios in Birmingham. This show, hosted by Pete Murray, was recorded live on Sunday night for transmission the following Saturday, and it was their chance to promote their record, 'Dear John'. Appearing in the show with them were Johnny Kidd and the Pirates, Cleo Laine, George Chisholm and the Tradsters, Ronnie Hilton, Audrey Jeans and the Bird Twins.

During the first couple of series of the programme, teen idols such as Adam Faith, Craig Douglas and Billy Fury made frequent appearances. The artists didn't sing live – the idea was to promote their current record, which meant that performances were generally mimed.

Don Moss introduced the famous 'Spin a Disc' segment of the show, where a panel of 'typical teenagers' listened to the latest releases and awarded each of them marks out of five in a copy of the *Juke Box Jury* format. Janice Nicholls was a 16-year-old girl from Wednesbury. People of a certain age may have fond memories of Janice saying 'Oi'll give it foive', in a strong Black Country accent. This became a national catchphrase, although few people remember it now or know exactly where it came from.

Next, the Springfields took part in *Saturday Club,* along with Gene Vincent; followed by their overseas trip, to Holland, for a cabaret appearance in the Hague in June. They returned for an appearance on Dutch TV in a *Music Box* programme on Monday 12 June.

FIGURE 5.3 *DISC* ARTICLE, (RICHI HOWELL *DISC*, 27 MAY 1961)

The Springfields had been together for just over a year, and in that time, they had put a lot of work into improving their act. Now, following the release of their disc, everyone wanted to know them. By the end of May all of the main music magazines – *NME*, *Record Mirror*, *Disc* and *The Stage* – had sought them out, Richard Dingley invited them onto his Home Service programme *In Town Today*, and *NME* wrote an enthusiastic article about them. Suddenly it was all starting to happen.

In these articles the three youngsters chatted about their approach to music and about the particular talents they brought to the group. Though they all had a musical background, each of them had developed in different ways. Tom said they weren't seriously tied to folk music though they did aim to perform a type of folk music. They played a mix of folk and pop as they didn't want to be tied down to one genre. Their aim was to produce commercial folk songs that offered something of everything. So they included pop songs, such as 'Are You Sure', in their act. Often these had a country and western flavour. Tom said he was looking forward to recording the songs he had written himself. The Springfields act was becoming really polished, they were constantly adapting and improving the routines. And it paid off. Reviewed by *NME* the writer said: 'I firmly believe that those artists who possess a distinctive sound of their own, stand a far greater chance of success than the copyists. But their material is catchy in the extreme, as their current release, 'Dear John', amply demonstrates. I think this group is going a very long way.'[162]

~

Dusty's Image

Over the years the Dusty Springfield image has been the subject of much discussion. It was crafted with great precision by the woman born Mary O'Brien. She created Dusty Springfield by careful selection of her clothes, shoes and hair; her taste was impeccable. The heels and big hair made her seem taller than her 5-foot-2-inch frame, and she adopted Peggy Lee's habit of a sideways look halfway through a song along with a little smile.

The iconic towering beehive, black panda eyes and sleek column dresses, as seen in her BBC TV series, took time to develop. That look, with gowns almost to the ground, long sleeves and only simple details, came long after the Springfields. Dusty's hair was short and still red when the Springfields formed, and descriptions of her at the time spoke of the green-eyed, copper-topped sister of Tom, as seen in the sheet music photo for 'Dear John', in 1961.

162 'Springfields', *New Musical Express*, 9 June 1961

FIGURE 5.4 SHEET MUSIC COVER FOR 'DEAR JOHN'

In time, Dusty took her influences from Monica Vitti and French Vogue models: 'I based it on models with black eyelids in French Vogue.' she said. 'I thought, "That's what I want to do." But I never did it right. I still don't.' The prevailing look then was skinny, wide-eyed, coltish and available — as exemplified by Shrimpton and Twiggy. 'They were too beautiful. My body and face were wrong', she said. 'Honest to God, the bigger the hair, the blacker the eyes, the more you can hide.'[163]

When Dusty spoke about the way she wanted to look, she said, 'Obsessed as I've always been to get the right pop star image, I studied the models like mad in the early days of the Springfields. I read every

---

163 Dusty Springfield, 'You Don't Have to Say You Love Me', *Herald Sun (Australia)*, 10 June 1995.

beauty book I could find. I was determined to make the most of myself.'[164] On black and white television her natural red hair looked black, as though she was wearing a giant busby hat, which is why she decided to change her colour to light ash blonde. She would sit in the Vidal Sassoon salon for hours, in tears, while her hair was bleached. Two juniors stood on either side with hair dryers, blowing cool air onto her head, as this redhead was turned into a blonde. She went through a lot of pain to become Dusty Springfield.

~

The rest of June and most of July was taken up with appearances on BBC radio and television. The group joined Anne Shelton on her television request show *Ask Anne*, where viewers were interviewed by Patrick Feeny and chose songs to be played on the show. Radio programmes included *Bandbox* with Acker Bilk and his Paramount Jazz Band, and a Sunday mid-morning pop music show, *Easy Beat*. Introduced by Brian Matthew, the resident performer on *Easy Beat* was Bert Weedon, and it included a spot where members of the audience offered their opinion on three new records. The trio were spending more time working with Ivor Raymonde and his singers.

The Springfields appeared with Wilfrid Thomas in the international programme *Commonwealth of Song*, alongside their regular standbys on *Workers' Playtime*. These programmes followed the Light Programme blueprint – they were desperately conservative and did everything possible to avoid specifically pop and particularly rock style music. Ron Belchier, an ex-forces, old-school BBC producer, regularly produced these programmes. He believed in maintaining the status quo and was not at all happy about the direction popular music was going in. The atmosphere in these programmes was inhibiting. It is easy to imagine Dusty's feeling of suffocation and that she longed to break free from their limitations.

~

Television Special

One day Griff, their agent, contacted the trio with some important news. They were amazed to hear that the BBC had been in touch and

---

164 Dusty Springfield, 'Fame has a Flipside too', *Woman's Own* 1965, in Dusty Springfield Bulletin No. 66.

had noticed the impact the group were having on the pop music scene. They offered two TV specials that would showcase the talents of the Springfields. Griff told them that they were to be given two 15-minute slots, each of which would include six numbers from them and a couple of dance interludes. For two weeks in advance of the shows, *Disc* spoke of a busy time ahead for the group and trailed their upcoming performances.

On the appointed day, the Springfields met Ronnie Lane the producer, the dancers and the musicians in Studio 3 at the Aeolian. Starting at 10.30 they had just one and a half hours for the camera rehearsal. They had rehearsed the script and already had an idea of how to transition from one song to another, so the rehearsal allowed them to get familiar with the studio layout. Another 30 minutes let them check the line-up, and the actual recording was completed in the next half an hour. Musical support came from Ronald Hanmer and the Marimberos, and Bryan Ryman, and Audrey Gunner performed the dance interlude. It was soon all over, and when they left the studios, they could scarcely believe what had just happened.

These TV specials were a strange combination of musical styles and influences, mostly in the easy-listening vein. The first programme broadcast on 20 July was introduced by a clearly nervous Dusty. They sang 'Wimoweh Mambo' on this BBC session; it would later feature as the first track on their LP. The show included a live version of their recent release, 'Dear John'; 'The Green Leaves of Summer' from the movie *The Alamo*; 'Yellow Bird' a 19th-century Haitian song rewritten with English lyrics in the twentieth century. 'Brazilian Nonsense' was just that, and 'Ballin' the Jack', a popular song from 1913, introduced a popular dance of the same name; 'Gotta Travel On', was recorded as the B-side of a later single.

The second programme was broadcast on 27 July and opened with 'Cielito Lindo' a traditional Mexican song written by Quirino Mendoza y Cortes in 1882. It is one of the most popular songs widely known throughout the Spanish-speaking world as a symbol of Mexico; 'Come Back Liza' is a classic 'boy meets girl, boy misses girl' love song with a repetitive refrain and a classic Mento structure; 'Give Me the Simple Life' was a solo by Dusty; 'I'm Just a Country Boy', a solo by Tim and 'Lost Goldmine in the Sky' a solo by Tom. 'Melodie d'Amour', a popular folk tune of the French West Indies, was a standard among French singers, sung by Jean Sablon and Sacha Distel, among others. 'Eso Es El Amour' was a song by Los Chakachas, a group of Latin soul studio musicians. The song was a number one in Belgium in 1958, and along with 'Lonesome Traveller', it was included on the Springfields' Kinda Folksy LP. [165]

~

'Breakaway'

Back in the studio at the end of July, the group recorded their second single, which was greeted with enthusiastic reviews from both *NME* and *Disc*. The *NME* reviewer decided 'Breakaway' was different from the general run of chart music and he concluded that this was a folk song that would help them break into the pop charts. The *NME* reviewer praised their version of 'Good News', and approved of the gorgeous line 'excitable child', spoken in a sardonic George Sanders style. *Disc* reviewer, Don Nicholl, thought this record was even better than their first. The honky-tonk piano backing, provided by Ivor Raymonde, helped a lot. The track reached number 25 in the UK charts by late September. It wasn't quite the heady heights Tom, Tim and Dusty had hoped for, but it wasn't too bad for only their second release. The Springfields' second appearance on *Easy Beat* followed the release of this record.

Their next booking was on a new show, *The Cool Spot*. Now the BBC management had begun to accept the inevitable, and to recognise that young people wanted to hear their kind of rocky poppy music. *The Cool Spot* was presented by Jim Dale, late of *Six-Five Special*. Jack Good, that other scion of *Six-Five Special*, wrote about the show in his *Disc* column: 'There is a new bright ray of light. A programme called '*Cool Spot*' that set me back on my heels last Saturday night.'[166]

The Springfields appeared in the show several times over the next few months. This is where they met Reg Guest, who would become an important collaborator as accompanist and orchestra director for Dusty later in her career. In his column Jack Good describes Reg Guest:

At last, we got some beat that didn't sound as if it were transmitted through an amplified telephone. And the secret? Well, I have always

165 BBC WAC, TV Scripts, The Springfields, 20/07/61 and 27/07/61

166 Jack Good asks, 'Would these discs still be hits today?', *Disc*, 12 August 1961.

asserted vigorously in this column that the piano is the king of rock and roll instruments when it falls in the right hands. 'Cool Spot' is the first beat show on the BBC to swing around a thumping piano. And they've got Britain's greatest piano thumper at the helm, Reg Guest. [167]

Reg provided the R&B feel on records for numerous up-and-coming pop stars: Eden Kane, Adam Faith, Jess Conrad and Billy Fury. He also formed a group, the Nashville Five, to promote his kind of music. Jack Good noted:

Reg Guest is the heart that pumps all that is rhythmic in the best of British beat [...] Recently the 'Cool Spot' featured the Springfields. They are well on the way to being really 'something else'. Here is a group that digs the folksy stuff – only with a gospel beat. They fit the style of the Nashville Five like a glove, and to hear the two rocking together is a rare treat – rare in every sense of the word. [168]

The trio appeared on two further radio shows: *Steppin' Out*, a sometime holiday show with Don Lang and his Frantic Five, and *Blackpool Night*. They shoehorned this regular holiday show into their hectic schedule, travelling to the Jubilee Theatre in Blackpool for the pre-recording on 8 August.

In August and early September, the Springfields were booked into the Blackpool Opera House in a show headlined by Tommy Steele. The Lana Sisters had performed 'Seven Little Girls', with Tommy, on his ITV *Boxing Day Spectacular* in 1959. Now, Tommy's star had rocketed and he was celebrated across the country. He had already taken the leading role in four internationally acclaimed films and performed in successful stage shows in several countries. When Tommy bounced onto the stage, his huge personality was obvious to his audience. He could project himself across the footlights, into the camera or through the mic.

Two weeks later the group were on the Blackpool stage again, this time with Alma Cogan. Alma was a huge star in the 1950's, and she held a record of 18 chart hits by a female singer at the time. She topped the charts in 1955 with 'Dreamboat', and covered a number of American hits. By the late 1950's and early 1960's, she was also the star of her own

---

167 Jack Good asks, 'Would these discs still be hits today?', *Disc*, 12 August 1961.

168 Jack Good asks, 'Would these discs still be hits today?', *Disc*, 12 August 1961.

television show. She was 'the girl with the giggle in her voice' whose personality attracted as much attention from the press and the public as her singing. She showcased her powerful voice along with her bubbly personality, and dramatic costumes – a huge collection of luxurious dresses that she reputedly designed herself, hooped skirts with sequins and figure-hugging tops that were never worn twice. Alma Cogan topped the annual *NME* reader's poll as Outstanding British Female Singer, four times between 1956 and 1960, and her hits from this period include 'I Can't Tell a Waltz from a Tango', 'Why Do Fools Fall in Love', 'Sugartime' and 'The Story of My Life'. Written by Burt Bacharach, this was the number that made Dusty sit up and take notice when Michael Holliday had a number one hit with it.

~

Charlie Drake Season

Another appearance on *Bandbox* followed before the group embarked on their season with *The Charlie Drake Show*. This included appearances in Manchester, Liverpool, Birmingham and Newcastle, and reunited them with Charlie and the many regular performers on his show.

The Springfields become a quartet, 'aided' by comedian-singer Charlie Drake. (NRM Picture.)

FIGURE 5.5 THE SPRINGFIELDS WITH CHARLIE DRAKE
(*RECORD MIRROR*, 26 AUGUST 1961)

The Charlie Drake Show ran for a seven-week season. Presented by Bernard Delfont and produced by Maurice Fournier, it was a variety revue with the star appearing in various comic sketches and as himself. The bill also included Jack Rankin and the Hippodrome Orchestra, Albert and Les Ward, Patricia Bredin, Richard Allan, Sheila Holt, Tom Gillis, Tessa Davees and Michael Henry.

Following their TV specials and record releases, people were beginning to recognise The Springfields and their fanbase had begun to develop. Now whenever they stepped onstage the audience screamed with excitement.

The impact the group were having in Britain on TV and radio was celebrated in a *Record Mirror* article. In it the three talked about being perfectionists but said they were realistic enough to add a dash of commercialism. To make their sound stand out from any other two boy, one girl team, they concentrated on harmonic effects. A Christmas record was in preparation as well as an LP that would showcase their ability to sing in a variety of languages. Tom talked about the Latin-American band he had led in school at the age of 14. The first write-up he ever had was a WI (Women's Institute) report: 'Music was provided by 14-year-old Master Dion O'Brien, and knitted garments were presented to all present by Mrs Pringle'. It seems his wide experience, and his time spent as a Russian interpreter for the Intelligence Corps, was the key to the Springfields success. Their broad collective outlook shone through in their polished performances. The writer enthused: 'I honestly believe they are one of the most exciting groups to hit the home music scene for a long time.'[169]

~

Jimmy Young

In October the Springfields were booked as the resident act on a new weekly programme, *Younger Than Springtime*. In it, Jimmy Young introduced songs, strings and the sparkling piano of Johnny Pearson and his Strings in Rhythm. The group juggled this regular booking around their other appearances all the way through to March 1962.

Jimmy Young is probably best known for his hugely popular, long-running show, the *JY Prog*, on BBC Radio 2, which ran from 1973 to 2002. Jimmy Young had started in show business as a successful recording

---

169 'The Natives were Friendly', *Record Mirror*, 26 August 1961.

star. He was the first UK artist to have two successive number one hits on the *NME* charts, in 1955. 'Unchained Melody' reached the top in spite of intense competition from Al Hibbler, Les Baxter and Liberace. Next came his recording of the title song from the movie *The Man from Laramie*, which also reached number one. That year, Jimmy Young was second only to Ruby Murray as the UK's biggest-selling recording artist. His career as a radio presenter began in 1955 with two weeks on *Housewives' Choice*. His soft, easy-on-the-ear Gloucestershire accent and relaxed manner made him a natural behind the microphone. By 1961 he was broadcasting regularly on Radio Luxembourg and on BBC radio.

~

First Scottish Tour

Days after their appearance with Jimmy Young, the Springfields began a tour in the north-east of Scotland, where they were contracted to appear in several towns. Even though the dance halls they were playing in may have been small, the tours organised by Albert Bonici's company LCB (Little Cross Buildings) Agency, included enough venues to make it worthwhile for musicians to travel north. Albert Bonici was a musical impresario with connections to Tito Burns and Jack Fallon. He was determined that his home town of Elgin and the towns nearby – an almost forgotten region of the British Isles – would not be left behind in the race to deliver the new, modern music to the youth of the country. Thanks to Albert Bonici, young bands that were destined to be big names, performed on a regular basis in places like Nairn, Forres, Buckie and Elgin, and as far east as the Beach Ballroom in Aberdeen.

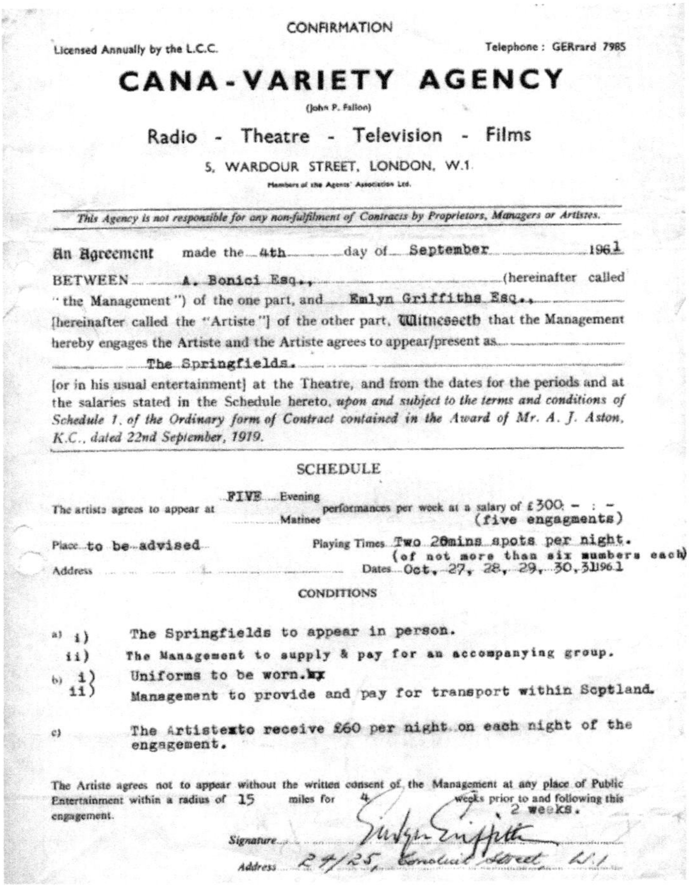

CONFIRMATION

Licensed Annually by the L.C.C.   Telephone : GERrard 7985

CANA - VARIETY AGENCY

(John P. Fallon)

Radio - Theatre - Television - Films

5, WARDOUR STREET, LONDON, W.1

Members of the Agents' Association Ltd.

This Agency is not responsible for any non-fulfilment of Contracts by Proprietors, Managers or Artistes.

An Agreement made the 4th day of September 1961

BETWEEN A. Bonici Esq., (hereinafter called " the Management ") of the one part, and Emlyn Griffiths Esq., [hereinafter called the "Artiste"] of the other part, Witnesseth that the Management hereby engages the Artiste and the Artiste agrees to appear/present as The Springfields.

[or in his usual entertainment] at the Theatre, and from the dates for the periods and at the salaries stated in the Schedule hereto, *upon and subject to the terms and conditions of Schedule 1. of the Ordinary form of Contract contained in the Award of Mr. A. J. Aston, K.C., dated 22nd September, 1919.*

SCHEDULE

The artiste agrees to appear at FIVE Evening performances per week at a salary of £300. - : - Matinee (five engagements)

Place to be advised   Playing Times Two 20mins spots per night.
Address   (of not more than six numbers each)
                                             Dates Oct. 27, 28, 29, 30, 31 1961

CONDITIONS

a) i)   The Springfields to appear in person.
   ii) The Management to supply & pay for an accompanying group.
b) i)   Uniforms to be worn.by
   ii) Management to provide and pay for transport within Scotland.

c)   The Artiste to receive £60 per night on each night of the engagement.

The Artiste agrees not to appear without the written consent of the Management at any place of Public Entertainment within a radius of 15 miles for 4 weeks prior to and following this engagement. 2 weeks.

Signature ....

Address 2 4/25, Conduit Street W.1

FIGURE 5.6 – CANA VARIETY AGENCY CONTRACT SEPTEMBER 1961 (COURTESY OF SCOTBEAT)

This particular tour took the Springfields to the Stewarts Hall, Huntly; St Ninian's Hall, Nairn; St Andrew's Hall, Buckie; the Palis Ballroom, Dundee; and the Two Red Shoes in Elgin. The contract stated that while Bonici's management company would pay for the accompanying group and transport within Scotland, the Springfields were responsible for providing their own uniforms. They were paid £300 for the five evening performances.[170]

---

170 https://scotbeat.wordpress.com/

'Bambino'

The Springfields recorded their third single, 'Bambino' in August, with 'Star of Hope' on the flip side, although the release was held until the end of October, with the aim of appealing to the Christmas market. This single was based on a delicate Neapolitan carol, 'Tu Scendi Dalle Stelle' (You Come Down from the Stars). With a history going back 250 years, and possibly longer, the song had been a favourite with Italian children for generations.[171] A story has emerged that during the Second World War, Italian prisoners of war in Orkney taught the song to their guards, who in turn, taught it to their children. It was discovered by the Springfields during a holiday in the sun-drenched Italian Riviera, when their Italian friend played the song to them, they loved it instantly. Ivor Raymonde made some changes to the melody and developed an arrangement, with English lyrics written by Tom.

The B-side, 'Star of Hope', was another song that conjured thoughts of Christmas, and the Springfields gave it a slightly folky quality for commercial appeal. Jo Stafford, with the Lee Brothers, had released a version of 'Star of Hope' in 1951, and Dusty, with her love and knowledge of the Jo Stafford catalogue, is likely to have suggested the song as the flip side of their latest release. *Record Mirror* described it as 'definitely a record to prove popular for this, and several Christmases to come'.

Critics were unanimous in praise of this recent single. Keith Fordyce in *NME* spoke about 'a delightful presentation of a most appealing song', and Don Nicholl in *Disc* said 'the trio sing it with all the freshness and polish that has marked their work to date', predicting big sales. The *Record Mirror* reviewer said that Ivor Raymonde matched the excellence of the trio with his inspired arrangement. He made special mention of the use of horns in the backing, along with the strings and the interesting rhythm.' "Santa Natale, Bambino Mio', are the words of the refrain as the group present this delightful song of the Nativity, a mother singing to her child.' [172]

---

171 https://en.wikipedia.org/wiki/Tu_scendi_dalle_stelle#Variations_and_arrangements

172 Review of 'Bambino', *Record Mirror*, 4 November 1961.

The Springfields first two singles, along with their B sides, were combined into an EP – 'Dear John'/'I Done What They Told Me To', and 'Good News'/'Breakaway'. Reviews for this release appeared in both the *Record Mirror* and *Disc*, where Nigel Hunter expressed his approval: 'The group have a refreshing, straightforward approach to their songs which I find very agreeable. No pseudo-intellectual nonsense about 'social significance' and similar pretensions concerning their work – just simple lyrics set to familiar tunes, sung and accompanied in simple but effective style. They are certainly achieving their goal of a happy medium between folk and pop.' [173]

The *Record Mirror* reviewer had this to say: 'What about these Springfields then? Aren't they terrific? I could listen to them all day without getting tired. These four offerings have proved to be pretty popular with the customers, and in fact, 'Breakaway' looks like doing just that and entering the charts. A sort of folk and pop mixture which will bring a great deal of success to this young trio.' [174]

The group had a second appearance on *Thank Your Lucky Stars*, hosted by Brian Matthew and Keith Fordyce. They joined Shirley Douglas, Ronnie Hilton, Chas McDevitt, The Temperance Seven, the Vernons Girls, and Danny Williams, with Jimmy Young as the guest DJ. They also took part in the Overseas Service radio show, *Commonwealth of Song* with host Wilfrid Thomas.

The trio didn't expect to be noticed in the *NME* Popularity Poll for the year, so they were shocked to hear they had been voted top in the vocal group category. It was even more of a surprise given that they had only been together for just over a year, and only had one minor hit, 'Breakaway'. In the history of this poll the success of the Springfields was one of the big surprises. The previous year's winners, the King Brothers, were ousted and the Mudlarks and the Dallas Boys were pushed well down the rankings. Closest to the Springfields came the Brook Brothers, with several hundred fewer votes. In the Keith Goodwin interview with the trio published in the December issue of *NME*, Tom was quoted as saying, 'We're amazed! It's the surprise of a lifetime and we're thrilled

---

173 Nigel Hunter, Review of EP, *Disc*, 9 December 1961.

174 Review in 'EP Corner', *Record Mirror,* 7 October 1961.

about the whole thing. Since we heard the news, our feet haven't touched the ground.'[175]

1961 ended for the Springfields with a mix of radio and TV performances. Their popularity continued to grow with their many appearances in popular shows such as *Saturday Club* and *Easy Beat*. Their residency with Jimmy Young on *Younger Than Springtime* continued and they took part in *Workers' Playtime*. In one of their three appearances on *Easy Beat* Dusty stepped forward from the two boys to take her place as the personality on the panel of critics. The group also appeared on ABC's *Thank Your Lucky Stars*, where they were reunited with Brian Matthew, Lonnie Donegan, and the Beverley Sisters. The Springfields' one and only appearance on the BBC's *Benny Hill Show*, which regularly attracted over 15 million viewers, came at the start of November. The group appeared between the sketches, whose humour relied heavily on scantily clad nubile young women being chased around the set by Benny Hill.

The success of 'Breakaway' was the first notable milestone in the Springfield's promising career. Winning the vocal group division of the *NME* poll was the second. A third milestone may have come about with little fanfare. On 17 December 1961, an advert for the Springfields fan club appeared in *Disc* magazine, as shown in figure 5.7. This was a sign of their growing popularity as now their fanbase was properly established. Followers could contact the group by sending a stamped addressed envelope to Pat Barnett, their agent's personal assistant. They would receive a regular newsletter with details of the group's activities and future schedule, and could write asking for signed photos.

FIGURE 5.7 – ADVERT FOR FAN CLUB, (*DISC* 17 DECEMBER 1961)

---

175 Keith Goodwin, 'Springfields Amazed by Victory', *New Musical Express*, 1 December 1961.

In his review of the year in *Disc*, the Springfields received enthusiastic praise from Don Nicholl. He said they were a natural, likeable talent with folksy material, and commented: 'The Springfields deserve to stick around and to grow in stature. There is room for them to become bigger. I would like to see them go way out with a wild gospel number.'[176] It's quite possible Dusty felt the same way; no doubt she felt great frustration at not being able to express herself musically as she would have liked.

THE SPRINGFIELDS . . . they have a natural likeable talent. There is room for them to become even bigger.

FIGURE 5.8 THE SPRINGFIELDS 'ROOM TO BECOME BIGGER'
(*DISC*, 23 DECEMBER 1961)

---

176 Don Nicholl, 'Don Nicholl Looks Back at the Discs of 1961', Disc, 23 December 1961.

1962

If 1961 had been a hectic year for the Springfields, 1962 was to prove even more so. For the first four months of the year the group were on a high. Buoyed by their win in the *NME* poll, their third disc, 'Bambino', had now climbed to number 16 in the charts and would stay in the Top 40 for ten weeks.

Peter Jones, who wrote for *Record Mirror,* became an advocate, supporter, friend and great fan of the Springfields, and later of Dusty herself. In his first report of 1962, he made the group his 'Star of the Week', offering his praise and approval for their latest record release. The trio were also interviewed by Brian Gibson of *Disc.* In both of these articles they spoke about their aim to change musical direction in the New Year. They were going to introduce some more upbeat numbers, though they planned to stick with the folksy sound that had made them popular, but steer clear of rock because others could do it much better. They aimed to be known as a group performing in the crossover between folk and pop, and whilst never forgetting their theatre audiences they were planning to do more TV to help to promote their new records. Along with the tours they already had lined up, they were working on an album and they still had regular bookings on the *Saturday Club* and *Easy Beat* radio programmes. By this time, the three had built a strong relationship with Brian Matthew, who hosted both of these programmes, and they had formed a bond with Bert Weedon, the resident performer.

FIGURE 5.9 WITH RECORDING MANAGER JOHNNY FRANZ
(*NEW RECORD MIRROR*, 3 FEBRUARY 1962)

As time passed, Dusty's image was slowly changing. In this photograph (Figure 5.9) with Johnny Franz, she looks super cool, out of her stage clothes and sporting short, bouffant blonde hair.

~

At the beginning of February, the Springfields had an appearance in the *Charlie Chester Music Hall* on the BBC. Known as 'Cheerful Charlie Chester' to millions at the height of his fame, he had started his show business career as a stand-up comedian. He became a major radio star in the 1940's and moved to television in the 1950's. An endearing, Jewish Cockney comic, he was a returned soldier who had perfected his comedy art while serving at the front during the Second World War. His programme included Lena Martell, a young Glasgow singer, with the Ivor Raymonde Singers; Dutch jazz violinists Sem Nijveen and Benny Behr, who had formed a comical violin duo in 1959; Dickie Valentine, a 1950's pop singer; and the Irving Davies Dancers.

Bobby Vee

On 9 February the Springfields began a two-week tour with Bobby Vee, a young – very young – American rock star whose lucky break had come about as a result of tragedy. On 3 February 1959 Buddy Holly, the Big Bopper and Richie Valens were killed in an air crash on their way to a concert in Minnesota. Bobby Vee, born Robert Thomas Velline, was just 15. He volunteered, along with the band he had formed just two weeks before, to take part in the show. At short notice the boys came up with an act, organised stage costumes and decided on a name, the Shadows.

That was the beginning for Bobby Vee. Recording for Liberty in the early 60s, he became one of the biggest rock'n'roll stars on both sides of the Atlantic. 'Rubber Ball', written by Gene Pitney, made number six in the *Billboard* charts and was a breakthrough hit for him in the UK, where it reached number four. Goffin and King, the song-writing duo who were to have a huge impact on Dusty a few years later, wrote 'Take Good Care of my Baby', which was Vee's only number one hit in the US and also claimed the top spot in the UK. Bob Dylan started out with Vee's band in Fargo, and he later described Bobby's voice as having a metallic, edgy tone to it, 'as musical as a silver bell.'[183] Besides his clear, ringing voice, Vee was also a skilled rhythm guitarist and occasional songwriter.

Still only 19 by the time of his UK tour in 1962, Bobby Vee was already a big star. This was an exciting time for the Springfields, as it was their first proper rock package tour. They joined the 15-night tour and alongside Bobby Vee they shared the bill with Clarence 'Frogman' Henry, Tony Orlando, Suzy Cope, and Jimmy Crawford and The Ravens. It was compered with down to earth humour by Billy Burden.

Ray Nortrop in the *Record Mirror* heaped praise on the performances. He particularly appreciated local talent, Jimmy Crawford and the Ravens who delivered solid rock numbers. Next on, Clarence 'Frogman' Henry, with his trademark croak, sang the song that had earned him his nickname, 'Ain't Got No Home'. He performed two more numbers, played two searing saxophone solos for the middle sections and ended with, 'A Little Too Much', his most recent Pye release. Sixteen-year-old

---

183 Jeff Baenen, 'Bobby Vee, 1960s teen idol, dead at 73', *Associated Press*, 24 October 2016 .

Suzy Cope was given an overwhelming reception, while Tony Orlando sang his Stateside hit, 'Halfway to Paradise', and a showstopper, 'Bless You', which was so popular he was forced to sing it twice.

The Springfields were given the honour of closing the first half. The number that was most appreciated was their ingenious version of 'Goodnight Irene'. Overall they performed with their distinctive blend of harmony. The *Stage* reviewer said; 'they must rate as one of the best vocal groups in the country, praising their fabulous sense of rhythm and harmony. He predicted that they were heading for the top.' [184]

The reception for the star of the show, Bobby Vee, was muted at the start. His performance on *Sunday Night at the London Palladium* had not gone down well, so the kids weren't sure what to expect. But in his 25 minutes onstage he gave everything he had. His set list included, 'Take Good Care of my Baby', 'Will You Love Me Tomorrow', 'Remember Me', 'Huh', 'Walkin' With My Angel', 'Raining in My Heart', 'So, You're in Love', 'Hark, Is that a Cannon I Hear', 'Little Flame', 'Rubber Ball', 'Go On', 'More Than I Can Say', 'How Many Tears', and his current chart entry, 'Run to Him'. Bobby gave a performance that glowed – it bubbled and burst with life. He showed that he was more than capable with this versatile act and his success was assured for the rest of the tour, which travelled all over England for the next two weeks.

By the time of the Bobby Vee tour in 1962, Dusty was still wearing her hair short, and now, as in this photo (Figure 5.10) with the American stars, it was bleached blonde and very bouffant. She still wore a long-sleeved blouse, buttoned to the neck with a floppy bow.

---

184 'A Record Plugging Time is had by All in Vee Show', *The Stage*, 15 February 1962.

FIGURE 5.10 THE SPRINGFIELDS WITH TONY ORLANDO, BOBBY VEE AND
CLARENCE 'FROGMAN' HENRY *(DISC,* 24 FEBRUARY 1962)

~

'Goodnight Irene'

The fourth single released by the Springfields, 'Goodnight Irene', was recorded in late January 1962. The Weavers recording of this song, written by Huddie Ledbetter (Lead Belly) and transcribed by John Lomax, had reached the top of the US charts in 1950. There were rather mixed reviews for the Springfields release in mid-February. It was an interesting version of the song which the *NME* reviewer said sounded like a 'back-street market in Cairo'. The B side, 'Faraway Places', included Ivor Raymonde's flawless accompaniment and a first-class vocal arrangement. Don Nicholl, in his review for *Disc,* loved the speed and attack of the number and the way it rocked. He predicted it was heading straight to the top of the charts. Reader D. Leonard gave his view, in a letter to the magazine, that British backing musicians weren't usually as good as the so-called Nashville sound. But this time he said that the backing on the Springfields recording of 'Goodnight Irene' actually improved on the Nashville sound, with the best-ever backing for a British disc.

~

Russ Conway

After their two-week tour with Bobby Vee and the American rock stars, the Springfields appeared in Val Parnell's *Star Time* on ATV TV. Then, with scarcely a break to gather their thoughts and prepare themselves, the trio joined Russ Conway for one night at the Southampton Guildhall, before joining him for a six-week season at the Liverpool Empire. This was in the more traditional variety-style of entertainment.

Bill Maynard, one of television's top comedy stars, was compere. He introduced Janie Marden, who became known for her great recording of the Goffin/King composition 'Make the Night a Little Longer'; impressionist Paul Andrews, who joined Russ on several of his tours; and Reg Wale, the leading vibraphone player in the country, along with his top-rated instrumental group, the Reg Wale Four. Once again, the Springfields closed the first half of this show.

During this season the group made numerous excursions to appear on BBC radio, including their residency on *Younger Than Springtime*. Their records were played on *Roundabout* and they took part in *Workers' Playtime* in Middleton, Birmingham, and Hyde. They also had guest appearances on television, including *The Billy Cotton Band Show*, and *Thank Your Lucky Stars*. But their most important TV appearance was their appearance on ATV's *Sunday Night at the London Palladium*.

FIGURE 5.11 COVER OF 'KINDA FOLKSY' LP

'Kinda Folksy 1'

Early in January, the group started looking for songs for their first album. The tracks they chose, to use Dusty's favourite word, were eclectic. In February news of their LP began to filter out. Three EPs would make up the entire LP.

The first EP from their album 'Kinda Folksy' was released in May 1962 to little fanfare. It was reviewed by Nigel Hunter in Disc on the 12th.

The first track on this disc, 'Wimoweh Mambo', had been a hit for the Weavers in 1952. But there were other versions by the Kingston Trio, the Tokens and Karl Denver. The Springfields' recording was unlike that of the Weavers and a million miles from the overblown rendition by Karl Denver.

The origins of this song are interesting; its beginnings, where it came from and how it has developed over the decades, have been researched and written by Rian Malan and an article published in Rolling Stone.[185] Solomon Linda was a Zulu tribesman who moved to the slums of Johannesburg and found work as a factory hand. On weekends he performed songs a cappella with his homeboys. They became a very cool urban act known as Solomon Linda and the Evening Birds: they wore pinstriped suits, bowler hats and dandy two-tone shoes. Linda was the Elvis Presley of his time and place. The group recorded several songs, but the one that became 'Wimoweh' was called 'Mbube', Zulu for 'the lion', recorded in 1939. It was a hit in sub-Saharan Africa and by 1948 had sold 100,000 copies.

The famous musicologists John and Alan Lomax, who had brought Lead Belly and his music to the US audience, acquired the original and took it to the US, where they offered it to Pete Seeger. It was adapted by him and recorded by his group, the Weavers. It is hard to know how much the Springfields knew of the real origins of the song when they chose it, first for performance in their TV special, and later for release as the first track on their 'Kinda Folksy' LP. The Springfields' version of the song is interesting as they add an introductory phrase and give a Caribbean/West Indian flavour to the number, which doesn't much benefit either the song or the group.

Today this song has been immortalised by being featured in the Disney movie *The Lion King*, under its more famous title, 'The Lion Sleeps Tonight'. This tune from South Africa is now known the whole world over, and through the decades it has become so deeply embedded into our consciousness that its origins have become forgotten.

The second track, 'The Black Hills of Dakota', was originally sung by Doris Day in the 1953 movie *Calamity Jane*. With music by Sammy Fain and lyrics by Paul Francis Webster, the song speaks of the singer's longing to go back to the country that she loves. The Springfields injected more of a country and western feel into the song.

---

185 Rian Malan, 'In the Jungle: Inside the Long, Hidden Genealogy of "The Lion Sleeps Tonight"', *Rolling Stone*, 14 May 2000.

The third track, 'Row, Row, Row' from the Broadway show, *Ziegfeld Follies of 1912*, was written by William Jerome and James V. Monaco. Debbie Reynolds sang a much faster duet with Carleton Carpenter in the 1950 film, *Two Weeks with Love*. The music hall arrangement gave the Springfields' version a jolly and comical sound: very fast and lively.

The final track on this EP was 'The Green Leaves of Summer', written by Paul Francis Webster and Dimitri Tiomkin for the 1960 film *The Alamo*. It is heard on the last night before the Battle of the Alamo; when asked what he is thinking, Davy Crockett, played by John Wayne, responds 'Not thinking, just remembering' as the song plays. The men of the Alamo reminisce on their lives and reflect on their own mistakes, faith, and morality. Dusty referred to the green leaves of Britain when it was featured in their TV special.

Don Nicholl in *Disc* reviewed 'Kinda Folksy', the trio's first LP, saying:

No inhibitions about this lively trio, that's for sure. They belt through a song with all the lusty enthusiasm and spirit necessary to hold the listener's attention and approval. The threesome's folky-pop policy has not yet paid off really substantial dividends in terms of the hit parade, which is a pity. This set is first class for their album debut, though, mixing the belters with quieter, more genuinely folky items like 'Green Leaves' and 'Two Brothers'. Ivor Raymonde backs up well throughout, and Tom and Dusty's liking for Latin is obviously responsible for the exciting sounds heard in the background of 'Wimoweh', 'Lonesome Traveller', 'Eso', 'Tzena' and others. [186]

~

Sunday Night at the London Palladium

Sunday Night at the London Palladium was a TV show that became a highlight for Britain's viewing millions, often reaching 20 million viewers. From the very start it had leapt to the top of the TV ratings and stayed there. This spectacular show featured the most celebrated homegrown and international stars, an extravaganza of music, dance and comedy that could be seen in the living rooms of Britain. It was a talking point for people when they went to work on Monday mornings.

---

186 Don Nicholl, Springfields really belt through debut LP, *Disc*, 12 May 1962

This appearance by the Springfields' came on 18 March 1962. By now the group could draw on a whole catalogue of songs, and it's likely they had little difficulty deciding which numbers to perform, with tracks from 'Kinda Folksy', as well as their recently released single 'Goodnight Irene'.

Bruce Forsyth had a seventy-year career in showbusiness, which included long periods as host of *Sunday Night at the London Palladium*s. But when the Springfields appeared on the show Norman Vaughan had taken over as host, while Forsyth recovered from exhaustion.

The host came onstage to applause from the audience; his microphone rose, as if by magic, from the floor. The opening overture was played and the curtains parted to reveal the Tiller Girls. Arms linked, they performed their high-kicking tap dance routine. Next, the London Palladium Girls and Boys appeared, followed by a fast-talking comedian. The American parlour Game 'Beat the Clock' was a mainstay of the show, when couples were plucked from the audience and invited to complete odd tasks, like catching table tennis balls in a butterfly net while being timed by a large clock at the back. Whenever a bell rang, the couple playing at that time would take part in a jackpot stunt for a cash bonus worth £100 for each week since the last jackpot was won.

One of the stars on this show was Larry Adler, the famous harmonica player, while star billing went to Eartha Kitt, who was once described by Orson Welles as 'the most exciting woman on earth'. She had been one of several American stars to headline at London's Talk of the Town in 1960 and she sang 'St Louis Blues' in the 1959 film of that name.

~

'Silver Threads and Golden Needles'

Sometime in March 1962 the group went into the recording studio again to lay down possibly their most country and western number to date. The song 'Silver Threads and Golden Needles' was co-written in the 1950's by Jack Rhodes and Dick Reynolds and first recorded as a B-side by Wanda Jackson. Jack Rhodes wrote or co-wrote some very popular 1950's rockabilly tracks, notably 'Woman Love', the B-side of 'Be-Bop-a-Lula', recorded by Gene Vincent.[187]

---

187 Dik de Heer, 'Jack Rhodes: This is My Story', accessed at https://tims.blackcat.nl/messages/jack_rhodes.htm April 2012.

It's not known how Tom Springfield had found the song, but all three members of the group had a keen interest in World music and throughout their careers would unearth some very unusual songs. Tom later said, 'I heard Silver Threads some months back but I wasn't too sure about its origins. I think it may be Scottish.'[188] That he made this claim about where the song came from seems strange, as it was credited correctly on the Springfields' record.

In the UK, reviews of 'Silver Threads and Golden Needles' were almost exclusively negative. *NME*'s reviewer, normally thrilled by the group's harmonising, wasn't on this occasion. Don Nicholl, in *Disc*, thought it might sell but said he had heard them do much better. The *Record Mirror* review was more positive, speaking of a simple and engaging tale of love and money. The B-side, 'Aunt Rhody', was one of many songs plucked from the Weavers' songbook. An old-time American song about a grey goose, it was a banjo and dulcimer favourite of the white pioneers.

The group followed up the release of 'Silver Threads and Golden Needles' with radio appearances on *Easy Beat*, *Ring a Ding Ding*, *Saturday Club* and *Workers' Playtime*. They had spots on *Thank Your Lucky Stars* and *All That Jazz*, on commercial TV, and on the BBC, they were guests on *Pops and Lenny*. April ended for the Springfields with a triumphant appearance at the Empire Pool Wembley, in the 1962 Poll-Winners Concert, where they collected the award for Top Vocal Group.

~

NME Poll Winners Concert

On a chilly April day in 1962, the Springfields appeared at the *NME* Poll-Winners Concert. The ten thousand noisy fans in Wembley stadium didn't feel the cold. They were there to watch the show and support their favourite acts. Two guests from America, singers Brenda Lee and Johnny Burnette, presented the cups, plaques and trophies to the winners.

Introduced by compere David Jacobs, Gordon Summers swung straight into 'Let's Twist Again', accompanied by Bob Miller and the Millermen. Teenager, Helen Shapiro, more assured now with each performance,

---

188 Alan Smith, 'The Springfields think the US Stunning', *New Musical Express*, 28 September 1962.

sang her hits, supported by the orchestra led by conductor Red Price. Next Billy Fury performed his best-known numbers for the fans, and celebrated his 21st birthday with the presentation of a huge, yellow, teddy bear by two girls from his Midlands fan club.

FIGURE 5.12 NME POLL WINNERS CONCERT (ALAMY)

The Springfields, sang 'Lonesome Traveller', 'Brazilian Love Song', 'Silver Threads' and 'Breakaway', and were described as a bubbling threesome. Adam Faith brought the crowd to fever pitch with a selection of numbers, some old and some new. It didn't matter, the audience loved him whatever he sang. Top of the bill was Cliff Richard, who backed by the Shadows, electrified the fans with his usual slick performance.

Part 6: Challenging Times

Dusty's Voice

By the beginning of May it is unlikely that the trio were feeling very positive. The poor reviews 'Silver Threads' received must have left them downhearted and questioning the direction of the group. But worse was to come; Dusty's voice was in trouble.

Dusty had problems with her voice throughout her career, and these are well documented. But by early 1962 she was plagued with throat and chest infections and her voice had begun to break down. It could be that her lack of voice training led her to use her voice the wrong way, but the permanent huskiness in Dusty's voice was a part of her unique sound. Now the problems she had producing any sound at all were getting worse. Doctors advised resting her voice, while further investigations showed she was suffering from tonsillitis. On 24 May Mollie Ellis reported in *The Stage*: 'Last week Dusty Springfield, the lady member of the vocal group the Springfields, had her tonsils removed in a London Nursing Home.'

During her hospital stay, Dusty was visited by John Leyton, a pop singer who was currently enjoying a very high profile. His single 'Johnny Remember Me', had reached the top of the charts, and a month earlier Leyton had performed, alongside the Springfields, in the *NME* Poll-Winners concert. Robert Stigwood, who was known in those days for his business partnership with Joe Meek, later of 'Telstar' fame, was his manager. With the networks that existed between artistes' managers in those days, it is easy to imagine Stigwood and Emlyn Griffiths dreaming up ways to ensure their charges stayed in the news. Dusty was indisposed and Leyton's record had dropped out of the charts by this time. The hospital was just off the Marylebone Road, and Robert Stigwood's offices were not far away in Edgware Road. Between them the managers came up with the idea of a photoshoot involving Dusty and John Leyton. One of them must have called the papers to tell them about the visit, as a *Record Mirror* photographer arrived to snap the two. Sitting in a hospital bed, Dusty's hair and make-up was perfect for the photoshoot.

NEW RECORD MIRROR. Week-ending May 12, 1962

DUSTY SPRINGFIELD at present under doctor's orders and in hospital—not with the **SPRINGFIELDS** vocal trio—likes visitors. When the NRM visited, we found **JOHN LEYTON** there. (NRM Picture.)

FIGURE 6.1 DUSTY IN HOSPITAL VISITED BY JOHN LEYTON
(*NEW RECORD MIRROR*, 12 MAY 1962)

In an interview years later, Leyton reminisced about Dusty: 'In the early days when I first met her, we talked about songs, because she was interested in who wrote 'Johnny Remember Me', and I told her about

224

Geoff Goddard and Joe Meek and everything. She was fascinated by the whole set-up, because the Joe Meek set-up was quite extraordinary ... it was all done in his flat in the Holloway Road, which was over a leather shop, she showed great interest in that side. '[189]

At the start of June, the Springfields heard that 'Silver Threads and Golden Needles' had been chosen for release in America. While Dusty was recovering from her tonsil operation, and the group were preparing to begin their summer season with Matt Monro, they learned that Philips' US branch were excited by their latest recording. A request was sent from the US for them to record an album of bluegrass songs for the American market. They took this as a sign that they must be doing something right. Unfortunately, this album was never recorded.

~

Matt Monro

On 8 June the group began their summer season with Matt Monro in, 'Wonderful Time'. They were going to spend three and a half months at the Weymouth Pavilion, winding up in mid-September. During this time the group also took part in *Parade of the Pops* and *Workers' Playtime* on the Light Programme.

---

189 Paul Howes, 'Breakfast in Bed?', John Leyton interview, in Dusty Springfield Bulletin No. 58, March 2006.

FIGURE 6.2 WITH MATT MUNRO, MIKE & BERNIE WINTERS AND THE MAYOR OF WEYMOUTH (*DORSET ECHO*, 8 JUNE 1962)

Matt Monro was a popular entertainer in the UK and internationally. Born Terence Edward Parsons, he had started performing during National Service. He entered a talent show on Hong Kong's Radio Rediffusion and won so often that he was offered his own one-off show, on the understanding he would not enter any further talent competitions.

The 'Wonderful Time' season at the Weymouth Pavilion was presented in two parts, with Matt Monro keeping his performance completely separate from the rest of the show. He ran through his usual repertoire, from the rhythmic opening number, 'Love is the Same Anywhere', to the closing, 'Softly as I Leave You', in his 20-minute final spot.

The Springfields had to work hard to make up for the imbalance this caused. They gave a bouncy performance, performing with Mike and Bernie Winters and Derek Dene, and joined in the 'Stage Door Johnnie' first-half finale with gusto. Their opening segment began with 'Ain't Gonna Travel No More', and then moved down to a lower gear with 'Playing a Cheating Game'. They sang a comedy number, 'The Man Who Never Returned. This was the absurd tale of a man named Charlie who was trapped on Boston's subway system (the MTA). They wound up their act with some evergreen numbers.

In his *NME* review of the show, Jack Fullford said: 'A great singer Matt, but he's definitely on his own in this show, and that may not go down well with the audience.' [190]

While they were in Weymouth, the trio debuted on *Day by Day*, Southern TV's weekday regional news programme, appearing again in late July. Southern TV covered an area along the south coast, from Weymouth to Southend.

'Silver Threads and Golden Needles' was released in the US and given a very positive review by *Billboard*: 'This British group has a powerful item for its debut disc. The country weeper is handled in the tradition of the Weavers. The flip is Aunt Rhody.'[191]

Now something interesting began to happen; *Billboard* started reporting on the trio. In late July 'Silver Threads' entered the US charts at number 117, bubbling under the Hot 100. This was nothing special, but it was good to know the US press was aware of them. A week later, *Disc* reported that the song had been chosen as Pick of the Week in the US, and was given equal billing with the Brook Brothers release 'Tell Tale'. Strangely, the release by the Springfields was listed by *Billboard* under the title 'Silver Threads Among the Gold', which was a completely different song.

~

'Swahili Papa'

The group's newest single, 'Swahili Papa', was released in mid-July, and the reviews that began to appear in August were much more positive than those for 'Silver Threads'. This number, written by Tom, was tipped for the charts; both the arrangement and the singing described as delightful, especially Dusty's. The *Record Mirror* review said: 'The African setting, with drums, etc., opens easily the most distinctive disc yet made by the ultra-distinctive Springfields, Dusty takes the lion's

---

190 Jack Fullford, 'Matt Monro Only in Act', *New Musical Express*, 15 June 1962.

191 Spotlight Singles of the Week, *Billboard*, 23 June 1962.

227

share of the lyrics [...] and you should listen very carefully, for there's a lot of humour floating about.' [192]

Peter Jones, always a great advocate for the Springfields, expounded on Tom's 'lucky touch' in his *Record Mirror* article. He felt that although only two of their discs had made it into the Top 20, the group had created more new sounds and ideas than any other vocal group in the country; he hoped this luck would hold out for their latest disc. Still, it was Tom's own songs that were most successful with the fans. Tom said, 'We think this new disc is vastly different from anything we have done before.' Dusty sang most of the main lyrics as well as catchy introductory and closing phrases, and the number showcased her husky voice. But she was always ready to admit that she produced her voice in the wrong way and constantly feared it would fail. She later said that one of her coaches had talked about the 'onslaught' she gave her voice and that it would surely cause problems.

The B-side of 'Swahili Papa' was 'Gotta Travel On', written by the Weavers. It demonstrated a polish by the Springfields that put the other tired old vocal groups to shame. They always sounded so *alive*!

~

The US Hot 100

One night in August, when they had just completed two gruelling shows at the Pavilion in Weymouth Richard Adam, from Record Mirror, called them with the news that 'Silver Threads and Golden Needles' had gone into the US Hot 100 at number 94. Tom was pleased to hear that their record had entered the US charts but his muted reaction surprised the journalist. Perhaps this cool reception resulted from weariness at the end of a long day. It may also have been because the group were wary of being labelled as country and western when they saw themselves as more of a folk group.

But because 'Silver Threads and Golden Needles' was a country and western number; Philips in America decided the Springfields should cut a country and western album. Discussions got underway between the trio, their manager Emlyn Griffiths, and Shelby Singleton, the recording

---

192 Record Mirror, 04 August 1962.

manager for Philips in the US, who was keen for them to record in Nashville. They weren't sure whether they had time for a trip to the US right then, and they also tried to push back on Singleton's wish for them to record purely country and western songs, they hoped to include some more folky numbers.

With spare time during their summer season in Weymouth they had been able to develop their act further. Once the season was over, they were booked solidly until December, and there would be little space for a trip to America.

Then, both *Record Mirror* and *Disc* reported that a promotional tour of the US was planned for early in 1963, it was to include two weeks of personal appearances, radio and TV shows and possibly night club dates. Three days would be set aside for recording in Nashville, with some of the town's top session singers booked to back the group, and it was expected that they would record a series of singles for US and British release. At the same time, Philips planned to issue the Springfields' LP, 'Kinda Folksy', to coincide with their trip.

Around this time Tim Feild was taken ill with stomach trouble, and *Record Mirror* reported that the group's stage shows in Weymouth were cancelled for a week. The break allowed them to relax for a few days and work with Griff on the detail of the artist biographies that had been requested for a feature in *Billboard*. [193]

As well as rising through the charts in America, 'Silver Threads' was slowly making its way up the charts in the UK, and by late August it was at number 41. But the group was amazed when they heard that it was still going up the charts in the US. It reached number 50 in the Hot 100, and then by the start of September it had climbed to number 37. They now had *Billboard* on regular order – each week they read it eagerly and found their record had jumped a little higher in the charts.

The group had regular excursions from Weymouth to take part in the Light Programme's *Saturday Club,* and ABC TV's *Big Night Out* with Mike and Bernie Winters. This time there was an added trip to the Norbreck Hydro in Blackpool for a pre-recording of BBC TV's *Saturday Show.*

---

193 *Billboard*, 25 August 1962

On 1 September *Billboard* featured 'Silver Threads and Golden Needles', and spoke of strong sales in the pop and country and western markets in Memphis and in Atlanta. The disc was now at 26 in the US country and western chart and 37 in the US Hot 100. A week later, *Disc* showed it at number 30 in the Hot 100 and *Billboard* listed it at number 28 in the country and western chart. Meanwhile, *Variety* had the disc at number 17 in the UK chart.

On 14 September the Springfields took part in *Winning Widows* with Peggy Mount. and *Melody and Rhythm*, both ATV productions. 'Ever popular threesome in happy harmony, sported quite the jazziest outfits seen on television for some time – a welcome change from the sober suiting of most of the artistes. Their harmonising, as usual, was smooth and a tonic at the end of the working week. In short, the programme was half an hour of cool music for jazz lovers.' [194]

The Springfields performed their last show at the Weymouth Pavilion on 15 September, by which time 'Silver Threads' had reached number 23 in the country and western chart and number 22 in the Hot 100. Their excitement built, as week by week the music magazines reported the steady rise of 'Silver Threads' in the US charts. It even achieved a place in *Billboard*'s Honor Roll of Hits, at number 25. Jim Lowe, a New York DJ, commented that British acts were taking over from Nashville as far as country and western discs were concerned, making particular mention of the Springfields' disc, 'Silver Threads', and Frank Ifield's 'I Remember You'.

The way 'Silver Threads' romped up the US charts prompted more negotiations between Emlyn Griffiths and Shelby Singleton. It made sense for the group to take advantage of the growing American interest in them – there were frantic transatlantic telephone calls, cables poured into Griffiths' office and a lightning trip was planned as a result. *Disc* magazine reported that the Springfields would probably make a flying visit to New York on Sunday 16 September, for a major TV show (most likely the Ed Sullivan show). There seemed no reason not to go, as their season in Weymouth had ended and their eight-day tour of Scotland

---

194 *The Stage,* 14 September 1962

wasn't due to start until the 24th; there would have been time to fit in a quick visit to the States.

Dusty had dreamed of America all her life. To her it was the ultimate place, where all her hopes lived. She knew a trip there would make all her dreams come true and she was thrilled at the prospect of flying to New York and appearing on TV in the States.

The Springfields were listed in *Billboard's* Top Record Talent and reached number 7 in the 'Most Promising Vocal Groups' category of the *Billboard* Annual Record Artist Popularity Poll. 'Silver Threads and Golden Needles' reached number 14 in the UK and hit the number 1 spot in Australia.

Then came a shock announcement: *Disc* reported that the group had said no to America because commitments in the UK left them no time to make the trip. In fact, only one booking might have clashed with the few days they would be away; there was the possibility their Scottish tour could have caused a problem. However, a letter from Jack Fallon of the Cana Variety Agency, dated 5 September, explained that it might be possible to release the Springfields from the contract for their tour in the north of Scotland. It is clear that this was not a barrier to the trio making the trip to America.

What seems more likely, given the news that emerged a few months later, is that Tim made it clear he had no intention of going to America. He had gone as far as he wanted to go with the group and a trip to America was too much.

The cancellation of the trip to America must have been a grinding disappointment for Dusty. To have her hopes raised up, with the anticipation of a trip to the land of her dreams and all the excitement that would entail, only to have them dashed, is likely to have left her feeling empty and desolate.

~

'Silver Threads' in the US Charts

In September in an interview with *NME*, the trio talked about how shocked they were when they discovered that 'Silver Threads' had gone into the US charts. UK interest had seemed slight and they had given up hope of getting anywhere with the disc; now they had to quickly adjust their thinking. The success the record was having in the States, filled then with energy. The disc was still in the *Billboard* top 20, and a flurry of offers had started to come in to appear in top shows in the US. But fearing that the American dates might clash with the start of their Scottish tour and with a recording session scheduled for the weekend they had decided against it.

In place of their trip to the States and with a few days to spare, Dusty, Tom and Tim went their separate ways for a short holiday. Tom went to the French Riviera then on to Italy, while Dusty stayed with friends in Rome, and Tim went to his cottage in Buckinghamshire. The day after their recording session for Philips on 23 September, the Springfields travelled to Ayr for the first date of their Scottish tour.

~

Second Scottish Tour

As the group set out on their latest tour of Scotland, we can only speculate as to how Dusty was feeling. Suffice to say that she must have been pretty down, and that probably wasn't helped as the week wore on and she realised the towns they had been booked into were at opposite ends of the country. During their first tour of the Highlands all of the venues they played in had been little more than an hour apart, with the exception of Dundee, which was a three-hour drive.

So it was, that instead of the much anticipated and exciting trip to America, the trio packed their bags, gathered themselves together and boarded the train for Scotland. Their schedule was crazy. On Monday 24 September they appeared in Ayr. The next day a four-hour journey north took them to Montrose, followed on Wednesday by three hours on the train heading south again to Gourock. Thursday saw them travel for almost six hours north to the Two Red Shoes in Elgin, and on Friday they endured a six-hour journey to the Scottish Borders, where they appeared in the Town Hall, Galashiels. Moving on they took three hours to reach Auchinleck, and their final destination on the Sunday was the Beach Ballroom in Aberdeen, which required another four to five-hour train journey.

Albert Bonici publicised the Springfields appearance at the Two Red Shoes Ballroom in Elgin with an advertisement in the local paper; he described them as 'The Famous Vocal Group'. On this, their second appearance at the venue, Albert Bonici was away on holiday and his youngest sister, Rosanna, was left to take care of the performers. She was the stage manager, responsible for ensuring the acts were in the right place at the right time. When Dusty arrived for that evening's show, Rosanna was downstairs and Dusty could hear her 10-month-old son crying in the flat next to the stage area. When Dusty got to the top of the stairs, she went straight into the flat to comfort the baby; she held his hand and sang him a lullaby. He stopped crying and looked curiously at her, but he didn't fall asleep.[195]

Rosanna remembers Dusty as very professional, and very demanding: she was the boss, and the two boys did as she said. She had to get her way, and when she said jump, they jumped. Rosanna said 'Some people you take to some you don't.' Rosanna took to Dusty.

John Rennie and the Apaches were the Springfields' backing group on their north-east tours. John played with several bands that found fame in the Scottish music business. He compared Dusty's personality with that of Sandy Shaw and Emile Ford. They were take-charge individuals who 'knew exactly what was to be done'. John Rennie, a teenager at the time, recognised that Dusty was the 'master of the situation'. He remembers chatting with the Springfields; Dusty was polite to him, but he found her to be quiet and a bit 'stand-offish'.[196]

The Springfields' fee for their second tour in Scotland was around £100 per night, and this had to pay for their travel and accommodation, as well as commission for their agent.

~

On 1 October, at the end of their Scottish tour, the group flew from Aberdeen to Liverpool where they appeared in cabaret for a week at the Royal Restaurant.

In the following days there was a great deal of activity; 'Silver Threads and Golden Needles' went to number 17 in the UK, and reached number 16 in the US country and western chart. A few days later, *Billboard* showed the record was still at number 1 in Australia, but by 6 October it had slipped to number 6 in Australia and 31 in the US Hot 100.

---

195 From Scotbeat, website with details of the Albert Bonici operation

196 From Scotbeat, website with details of the Albert Bonici operation

Variety reported that the Springfields were scheduled to take part in a new show, *Country Club*, on the BBC Light Programme, which was due to start on 25 October. The group were also booked for two recordings of *Linger a While*, a BBC Overseas Service programme, and the pre-recorded *Saturday Show*, from the Norbreck Hydro in Blackpool, was broadcast on 13 October.

Also on 13 October, *Disc* reported that a trip to New York and Nashville, for TV, radio and a recording session, had been arranged for the Springfields after all. Their manager's office was again swamped with telephone calls and cables, and the plan was for the trio to fly to New York on 6 December, spend three days there, then move onto Nashville to record material for albums and singles.

A guest appearance on the *Ed Sullivan Show* was scheduled for 16 December, and a month-long concert tour in the US was planned for January – it was even suggested they might visit Australia in the Spring. But, in the end, neither the January tour of America nor possible tour of Australia took place and the *Ed Sullivan Show* appearance didn't materialise.

The Springfields, Philips and their agent were determined to maintain momentum and US interest in the group. An album was released in America – 'Silver Threads and Golden Needles' was an almost exact reissue of their UK album 'Kinda Folksy'. *Billboard* gave this a warm response; the group had produced a rare and brilliant record for the American charts.[197] The tracks on the album were excellent and DJs were encouraged to play them for their listeners. A second single, 'Gotta Travel On', was taken from their newly released album, with 'Dear Hearts and Gentle People' on the B-side. However, US DJs turned the disc over and chose 'Dear Hearts and Gentle People' as the A side of the new single. Next the group recorded another single, 'Island of Dreams', with 'The Johnson Boys' on the B side, and they were also able to fit in an appearance on *Easy Beat*.

~

In the middle of October, the Springfields joined the Silver Jubilee Birthday Show at the Coventry Theatre – a seven-week season starring

---

197 *Billboard*, 29/09/1962

Arthur Haynes and Yana. Between 1946 and 1949, Arthur Haynes had worked with Charlie Chester in the BBC Radio series *Stand Easy*. He had his own shows on BBC Radio, first *The Arthur Haynes Show*, between 1962 and 1965, and later, *Arthur Again*. Joe 'Mr Piano' Henderson, complete with glass-topped piano and giant scenic candelabra, was in the line-up for this show. With his mix of old and new tunes he got the audience in the party mood, and his climax of 'Mack the Knife' and 'The Saints' had them cheering for more. Yana, dressed in a sparkling tight-fitting white gown sang her 'Climb Up the Wall' song. While she brought glamour to the show, she was a little too keen to please the audience and tended to overplay her act.

While the trio were busy with their season in Coventry, Griff monitored the progress of their records in the US and other parts of the world, putting *Billboard*, *Variety* and *Stage* on regular order alongside his usual order of *Disc*, *NME* and *Record Mirror*. The 'Silver Threads and Golden Needles' LP reached number 131 in the US, while 'Dear Hearts and Gentle People' entered the *Billboard* Hot 100 at 99. The album jumped from 131 to 95, but a week later it dropped to 113. 'Gotta Travel On' entered the US Hot 100 at 114 and climbed to 95. By early November the 'Silver Threads' single had reached number 20 in the country and western chart and *Billboard* confirmed that the Springfields recording in Nashville would be handled by Mercury Vice President Shelby Singleton. *Record Mirror* reported on their increasing worldwide fame: 'Silver Threads' had made the Swedish, Australian and New Zealand charts and reached number one in Fiji. Offers of tours in Sweden and France were now under consideration.

~

Changed Line Up

Suddenly, at the end of November, reports began to appear in newspapers and magazines. One of the Springfields was about to leave, and he was to be replaced. *NME*, *Record Mirror*, *Disc*, *Variety* and *the Stage* reported that an unknown, 21-year-old Mike Pickworth, was about to step in.

Tim Feild had come to the conclusion that he'd had enough. Writing in the Sunday People later, he revealed more of the reasons for his decision to leave the group. Being constantly on the road and living in digs was one. Lots of minor irritations had worn him down: he hated having to carry Dusty's voluminous petticoats in and out of theatres and he wasn't keen on eating steak and kidney pudding in a transport caff. His wealthy background meant he was used to eating in smarter restaurants. More crucially, newspapers reported that his wife was ill.

However, possibly the major reason for his decision was Dusty and Tom. Their lives were showbusiness, they had been consumed with a driving ambition since they were very small. They each had their own views about the direction the group should take and that meant they argued over every little detail of the act. Tim was different, he didn't share this drive for success. Now, faced with the prospect of a tour in America, he was forced to confront his priorities and what he wanted in the future. He had one overriding aim: to further his study of Sufism, the mystical branch of Islam.

Tim had enjoyed the whole adventure: being part of the Springfields had been fun, most of the time. The group were successful, but now it was getting too serious and he had other things he wanted to achieve. Basically, he was tired: tired of the constant travelling, of being away from home, of the bickering and backbiting. He decided to give it up and went into the antiques business. 'Finally,' he said, 'I decided to chuck it all in. I had gone into show business to prove I could be a success. That I had done. Now there was nothing left.'[198]

~

Mike Longhurst Pickworth

Tim was replaced by Mike Longhurst Pickworth, although there is confusion over exactly how he became a member of the Springfields. A quote from Tom Springfield in a Peter Jones article in *Record Mirror,* on 1 December 1962, said: 'Tim decided to pull out and go into antiques. Fortunately, we knew Mike Pickworth, his successor – and we'd fooled around on various numbers at parties with him. Though he was working in the city, he always hinted that he would like to make show business his career. Now he is with us.'

---

198 Tim Feild, 'Why the Springfields are Splitting Up', *Sunday People*, 29 September 1963.

In March of the following year, *NME* carried a report where Mike said: 'I had known Tom for some time and we moved in roughly the same circles. He played guitar, I played guitar. He went to parties and I went to parties. Of course, our paths crossed and we struck up a friendship. But he was a professional entertainer, and I worked in insurance. Then one day a few months ago, I got a cryptic phone call from Tom. What he said sent me haring up to Coventry, where the Springfields were appearing, and we had a session together to see if my voice fitted the harmony, and I was a Springfield before I knew it. [199]

FIGURE 6.3 WITH NEW BOY, MIKE PICKWORTH (ALAMY)

In Mike Longhurst Pickworth's later version of events, it was his mother who helped him land an audition with the Springfields. Without telling him, she had replied to an ad in *The Stage* for a guitarist and singer. He didn't know what it was about, but he knew his mother was on his side. Mike recalled: 'When I finally reached the small stage at Quaglino's, I asked the people I was unable to see behind the lights, what they

199 Mike Hellicar, Spring(field) Fever, *NME*, 29 March 1963

wanted me to do. A disembodied voice said, 'Anything you like.' I sang *Mess of Blues*, an Elvis number, and when I had finished, the same voice asked me if I could do a song in a foreign language. Having an Italian grandfather has some benefits so I did an old Neapolitan folk song. When I finished, the same voice said, 'We'll let you know.''[200]

A week later Mike received a letter from Tom Springfield inviting him to join the Springfields. 'I just went nuts, completely nuts!' he said. 'As far as I was concerned, I was going to go out and sing and make records. It was like a dream come true.'[201]

Mike Pickworth was born in Kilburn, north-west London, and first took to the boards at the Metropolitan Variety Theatre in London's Edgware Road. His mother, a former ballet dancer who trained at Italia Conti had run theatre schools for years. She encouraged her only child to sing 'Money Is the Root of All Evil' and 'California Here I Come'. The applause was rapturous. Mike also attended the Aida Foster Theatrical School in London.[202]

Tim stayed with the Springfields long enough to finalise their Birthday Show season in the Coventry Theatre. Meanwhile Mike went to Coventry to start rehearsals with the group. Now that the news about their new member was out, they confessed that they had kept this secret for two months. After several weeks of practice, Mike went into the studio to record their recent disc, 'Island of Dreams'.

The 24 November edition of *Thank Your Lucky Stars* was Mike's public debut with the Springfields; the group mimed to their new disc, 'Island of Dreams'. The following Tuesday the group were interviewed by Keith Fordyce on the BBC radio show *Pop Inn*.

'Island of Dreams' was a Tom Springfield composition, and he said of it: 'I don't say it's a particularly original sort of number. I just thought of all the country and western and Irish songs I could think of, and mixed them all together. But a lot of country music is based on Irish or Scots songs – and I must say I'm pleased with the commercial appeal of it.'[203]

---

200 'In My Time: The Mike Hurst Story', accessed at http://wrinkledweasel.blogspot.com/p/wavelengths-2.html

201 Nick Dent-Robinson (2006) Mike Hurst interview, accessed at pennyblackmusic.co.uk

202 Nick Dent-Robinson (2006) Mike Hurst interview, accessed at pennyblackmusic.co.uk

203 Peter Jones, 'Nashville', *Record Mirror*, 2 February 1963.

The track was a hymn of longing to a lost love; the singer dreams of the time she had spent with her lover and wished they could be together again.

Reviews of the disc were positive and predicted it would sell well, with the *Record Mirror* reviewer tipping it for the Top 20. He was right; after a faltering start it climbed to number five and stayed in the charts for an impressive six months. The harmonica, along with Dusty's breakout solo, and the boys harmonising gave the song an unforgettable charm. The country and western feel ensured it would be a hit.

~

In September, *Stage* had reported on Milton Subotsky's preparations for his new musical *Just for Fun*. The Springfields were among a plethora of British recording stars signed up to take part. With their new member, they were about to embark on a tour and recording session in America. Shooting of the film started at Columbia Pictures' Twickenham studios on 12 November. This was was a sequel to *It's Trad Dad* and designed to appeal to teenagers. The Springfields, with Mike Pickworth, joined the filming on 4 December. just before they left on their trip to the States.

While there were fears over how their fans would accept the change of line-up, these were settled by the realisation that there was little difference in the way the group sounded. In the main, the addition of Mike to the group caused very little reaction. Now their fortunes were changing, people began to ask, 'Was Mike the group's lucky omen?'.

239

Part 7: New Ventures

America

Going to America meant that Dusty would finally realise her dream! On 7 December the trio and their agent boarded a plane bound for New York. The night before they left, Emlyn Griffiths had invited Patrick Newman, the Entertainments Manager at the BBC, for a drink. Griffiths had an agenda; this wasn't just going to be a friendly chat about New York, he thought that this was a good time to talk about the fees the BBC paid the group; he had decided they should be offered an increase. After all the pleasantries and sharing some thoughts about New York, he introduced the subject of money. At this point the group was earning over £1,000 for a week's work and Griffiths asked Newman whether the BBC were paying the proper fee. How did they compare with the fees offered to acts such as the Mudlarks and the Raindrops? Newman was enraged by what he saw as an underhanded tactic. He recorded his response in a note to a member of his staff:

I poured out the usual torrent, culminating in a request that he should please discuss things with the booking assistant who proffered the engagement, adding that, as and when that assistant needed to discuss the matter with me, she would do so.[204]

~

New York

Arriving in New York at the start of their 12-day tour of the US, the group were greeted by the heavy wet snow and intense rain of a major winter storm. They landed at four in the morning after a very long flight, but excitement wiped out any exhaustion they should have felt; sleep was the last thing on their minds.

---

204 BBC WAC, The Springfields, Note from Patrick Newman, 6 December 1962

241

FIGURE 7.1 THE SPRINGFIELDS ARRIVING IN NEW YORK

America was the land of all-night television and Dusty switched on the TV immediately; the programmes were exciting and mostly in colour. When the trio went out onto Broadway they were dazzled by the sights and sounds of the city. Dusty fell in love with New York at first sight, it was a love affair that lasted for the rest of her life. The city was magical, clean, lively and filled with iconic buildings. The people were friendly and helpful, and the voices she heard a symphony of languages from around the world. As she wandered down Fifth Avenue she was amazed by the buildings, so many of them, so tall, soaring up like great fingers probing the sky and reaching for the moon. Times Square was filled with humanity, in spite of the hour, and the sound of music came pumping out of the record stores. Eventually, they found somewhere to buy strawberry shortcake and fell into bed at about seven. When Dusty looked out of her window the next day, she gasped at the sight of the hotel across the street. She reminisced:

It was one of the highest in the States. It was 50 floors high. I called Tom on the phone. 'Hey, have you seen the hotel opposite?' 'Yeah,' Tom replied. 'What about it?' 'Let's move in,' I said excitedly. 'Let's get rooms on the top floor.' So that morning, much to our agent's annoyance, we packed our bags and moved across. We didn't get on the fiftieth floor but we got on the forty-ninth. It cost the earth but it was worth it just to see the view. [205]

By a happy chance, the Springfields' arrival in New York coincided with the day the famous bluegrass musicians Lester Flatt and Earl Scruggs were scheduled to perform a concert in Carnegie Hall. Bluegrass music was better known in America than the bossa nova. Dusty, Tom and Mike went to the performance. This concert was legendary in the history of bluegrass. While the folk boom was in full swing, serious music critics still regarded bluegrass as lowbrow. A fact not lost on the bluegrass boys as they prepared to take the stage that December evening.

~

Nashville

The Springfields flew out of New York two days later, headed for Nashville. When they arrived, the snow was thick and the temperature had dropped to minus 22 degrees. To keep from freezing and stay warm, they had to stay indoors. Tom described the experience: 'It was so cold that when you went out for a stroll it felt as if your clothes were being frozen to your body.'[206]

---

205 Dusty Springfield, 'Fame has a Flipside too', *Woman's Own* 1965, in Dusty Springfield Bulletin No. 66, September 2008.

206 Peter Jones, 'Nashville', *Record Mirror*, 2 February 1963.

FIGURE 7.2 THE SPRINGFIELDS AND EMLYN GRIFFITHS ARRIVING IN NASHVILLE

Shelby Singleton

Shelby Singleton, the vice president of Mercury Records, produced the tracks cut in Nashville by the group. Singleton was a giant of the recording industry and he made a fortune from it; it was as if the man was born to produce hit singles. But he may never have gone into the music business if it hadn't been for his wife, Margie. Margie's ambition was to be a songwriter and singer, and Shelby gave her all the help she needed to achieve that aim. He used his influence to get Margie on the Louisiana Hayride, the nearest country music show, in Shreveport.

Singleton wasn't a musician himself, but he knew a hit record when he heard it. He discovered Jerry Kennedy who had played guitar for Faron Young, Johnny Horton and the house band at the Louisiana Hayride – he liked the way he played and they got along well. In time he came to rely on him, as Jerry could tell other musicians what Singleton wanted to do on a song, and their partnership began churning out hits. Jerry Kennedy said of Singleton's commercial instincts, 'He had the ears of a record buyer.'[207]

When they met Singleton the Springfields were deeply impressed. They were used to eccentricity; their own agent presented an idiosyncratic figure, but to them, Shelby Singleton was a more magnificent Nashville version. Clad in giant suits, with his black hair oiled back in a quiff, he was a vision of sartorial splendour. With his little brown cigarette clamped between his teeth, he told them how much he loved their music, and that he had already picked out the set of songs they were going to record.

This album was cut very quickly, with everything being worked out before anyone set foot in the studio. They had time for just a couple of rehearsals, and with such costly and sought-after musicians there was no time to talk about the finer points in the arrangements. Speaking to the *NME* about recording in Nashville, Tom said that the people in the studios gave them a lot of help and they were able to finish their last session ahead of time. So, they wrote two numbers and recorded them straight away. Everyone in the studio helped with these numbers. He said: 'it was strange to see some genteel lady violinists who weren't being used on that session were really with the beat, handclapping furiously!'[208]

207 https://cocaineandrhinestones.com/tap/shelby-singleton

208 Mike Hellicar, 'Springfields now international stars', *New Musical Express*, 4 January 1963.

FIGURE 7.3 IN THE RECORDING STUDIO WITH SHELBY SINGLETON
(UNIVERSAL MUSIC)

By the time the group arrived in Nashville, Dusty's look had undergone a major change. She was still dressed modestly, but now wore a tartan dress with a roll collar, which she is seen wearing on the album cover, and her beehive was furiously backcombed and huge.

Nashville tracks

In their three and a half days in Nashville the group recorded 17 tracks. These were a curious mix of country and western, bluegrass, and hillbilly, as well as some traditional railroad songs and a couple of ultra-sentimental numbers.

In the studio the Springfields met a roster of top country and western performers. There was Leroy Van Dyke, whose most successful single, 'Walk on By', went to number one on the US Hot Country chart and number five on the US *Billboard* Hot Singles chart, as well as reaching number five in the UK singles chart. Ray Stevens, who recorded several novelty singles and had a smash hit with 'Ahab the Arab', in early 1962. Webb Pierce was famous for his flamboyant rhinestone suits and twin silver-dollar-lined convertibles. Margie Singleton was there too. She had

246

signed with Starday Records and wrote both of the songs on her first single, 'One Step (Nearer to You)' with 'Not What He's Got' on the B-side, released in 1957. Neal Matthews, a member of the Jordanaires – the backing vocalists who spent 15 years with Elvis Presley – was also there.

Margie Singleton and Neal Matthews added their voices to some of the tracks recorded by the trio, which made them sound a little like the Weavers. The banjo-picking backing was supplied by Bill Justis, and Dusty sang lead on most of the numbers.

Among the songs recorded by the trio was 'Greenback Dollar', with Dusty leading and Neal Matthews one of the backing singers. This is a traditional bluegrass number that was also recorded as a skiffle number by Chas McDevitt and Nancy Whiskey. Mike had three solos on the album, one of which was 'Darling Allalee', a bluegrass song with a bouncy banjo-plucking arrangement that tells the story of a runaway Tennessee slave who realises his freedom has cost him the loss of his one true love.

'Midnight Special' was a traditional song about a steam locomotive train that passed the Louisiana state prison. The light from the train would shine into the prison cells, and over time a superstition developed among the mostly Affrican American prisoners that if you were in the light of that train, you would gain freedom and be blessed with good fortune. Lead Belly recorded a version of the song at Angola Prison for John and Alan Lomax, who mistakenly believed he was the author. Mike leads on 'Wabash Cannonball', another American train song recorded for the album. In 1944, Woody Guthrie sang this number on the BBC on *Children's Hour*.

'Maggie' was a poem written by George W Johnson for his sick wife. The words were set to music by James Butterfield and since then it has become a popular standard across the world. A beautiful song of love and longing, it was also recorded in 1925 by Count John McCormack. The Springfields rendition is perhaps a little too energetic. Possibly the most appealing song on the album was 'Cottonfields', written by Huddie Ledbetter (Lead Belly) and based on his experience as a cotton picker when he was young.

247

In the main, the trio enjoyed their time in Nashville, but they quickly discovered that recording techniques there varied wildly from what they were used to, especially how quickly recordings were produced.

~

Touring in the US

Once recording was over, the Springfields went on an eight-day promotional tour for Philips. They were accompanied on their travels around Cincinnati by Emlyn Griffiths and a team of record executives: Sheldon Tirk, regional manager for Philips from Cleveland; Joe Nathan, Philips' sales manager; and Hal Mills of A&I Record Distributing Company. They spent 16 and 17 December in Cincinnati, where they made the rounds of DJs and filmed a segment for Bob Braun's *Sunday Afternoon Hop* on WLW-T's coloured TV.

Ralph Emery was a famous local DJ at WSM, the station that produces the Grand Ole Opry. The Springfields were invited onto his show and spent 15 minutes talking to him on his nationwide radio programme. They knew that the show was being broadcast to millions of people all over the States and were amazed at how informal the experience was.

Mike Pickworth had officially been a member of the Springfields for just a few weeks when he set off on this American adventure, and in a call from Nashville he told Mike Hellicar of the *NME* that he could scarcely believe where he found himself now. The group had a hectic programme but they still had time to enjoy it; they were in great form.

This was an amazing trip that Dusty must have found stunning in every way, but later her main focus was on just two memorable events. The first took place in New York's Times Square very early one morning, when she heard the sounds blasting out from a record store. In an interview with *Mojo*, Dusty recalled:

> It was 'Tell Him', by The Exciters. 'I was standing outside the Colony Record Store on Broadway about two in the morning, hearing that voice, 'I know – something – about love' and going 'Wow! How do I do this?'. I knew it could work if I could adapt them in some way.'[209]

---

209 Paul du Noyer, 'The Dusty Springfield Interview', *Mojo*, July 1995.

This Bert Russell song was released in October 1962. Originally written for a man and recorded as 'Tell Her', it was unsuccessful. The Exciters then recorded 'Tell Him', arranged by George 'Teacho' Wiltshire and produced by Leiber and Stoller, under their new United Artists Records contract. This intense and powerful sound had a strength that Dusty had never heard on the radio in Britain. For her it was pivotal, it changed the view she had of herself as a performer and it changed the way women were perceived and presented in pop music. Dusty, who had been deeply influenced by African American singers since she was a child, said, 'I really wanted to be Mavis Staples!'

'Tell Him', was a hit – by the start of 1963 it had reached number 4 in the US Hot 100. Reviewed in *Disc* on its UK release, the reviewer said, 'This could be a minor surprise in the sales stakes, with its girl lead chanting the Bert Russell lyrics in a contagious beat frame'. The single peaked at 46 in the UK, while a cover version by Billie Davis got to number 10. Another cover version by Alma Cogan didn't make it to the UK charts but reached number 10 in Sweden.

The second memorable event, which Dusty recalled in a 1990 interview, happened in the Capital Motel in Nashville: 'I remember the Capital Motel with its red carpets. It was really glamorous; I'd never seen a really flashy American motel before. With all the right buttons to push, room service, the works. A really upmarket motel.'[210] Dusty had to sit down very quickly on the bed when she heard the sound coming from the radio. 'Don't Make Me Over', was a brand-new song, written by Burt Bacharach and Hal David, and released by Dionne Warwick in November 1962. Afterwards she would always associate that hotel with hearing Dionne Warwick for the first time, singing that particular number and thinking, 'My God, this is different!'

After his time in the US Army, Burt Bacharach had spent three years as pianist and conductor for popular singer Vic Damone and other performers. He next took on the role of arranger and conductor for Marlene Dietrich, the international film star, in her nightclub shows in Las Vegas. Later he became musical director on her concert tours, and travelled worldwide off and on with her until the early 1960's. 'Don't

---

210 Chris Bourke (1990) 'Dusty in Private', *Rip it Up* (New Zealand).

Make Me Over', was one of the songs he wrote with his writing partner Hal David while not on tour with Dietrich.

Dusty's Memories of Nashville

Thirty years later, when Dusty spoke about the Springfields' time in Nashville, she described it as disastrous for them, and despite its ground-breaking effect on her life she always had a tendency to downplay its importance. She said that although everyone was really helpful, the fact was that the Springfields needed time to rehearse. In Nashville the speed was breath-taking: songs were written in the morning and recorded in the afternoon. Dusty found the stress hard to bear. She recalled in a 1993 interview that it didn't work for them in Nashville because they weren't country singers. They were determined to try, but they didn't know how to work that quickly and stylistically. And as a perfectionist Dusty had to just block it out. All she could remember was going to people's houses, to their dens covered in flock wallpaper and curlicues.[211]

---

211 Dusty Springfield, The *Ultimate Interview 1993*, in Dusty Springfield Bulletin No.50 November 2003.

Part 8: The Final Chapter

1963

On the morning of 22 December 1962, the Big Freeze began in the UK. After the Springfields flew back from the States, on Christmas Eve, they separated to spend Christmas Day with their families, but on Boxing Day, when the first snowfall of 1962 was recorded, they met up again at the Bournemouth Winter Gardens where they were to appear with Norman Vaughan. The Big Freeze lasted for 67 days and was so severe that whole villages were isolated, and even the river Thames froze solid.

FIGURE 8.1 READING ABOUT THEIR SUCCESS IN AMERICA
(*NME*, 3 JANUARY 1963)

After an appearance on Southern TV's *Day by Day* on 27 December, they started packing for their trip to Holland.

Christmas the previous year had been just about the happiest the group had known. This was when they had found their way into the best sellers list with their single, 'Bambino'. The knowledge that they were in the charts had been the nicest present they could have wished for.

Looking forward to 1963, the Springfields wanted to be better known internationally. Their success with 'Silver Threads' would help with this, and their plan was to record in foreign languages and tour abroad extensively – offers had come in from Australasia, Sweden, France, Portugal, and America. But their main energies would be reserved for the UK. More than anything else, they aimed to re-establish themselves in the British charts – maybe they could even complete a hattrick of *NME* Poll successes.

1963 was effectively the gateway to the 1960's, and one that was filled with seminal events. The coldest winter for nearly 300 years in the UK, this was the year the Beeching cuts decimated the UK's rail network, and in the States Martin Luther King delivered his 'I have a dream' speech, in pursuit of his campaign for civil rights. President John F Kennedy was assassinated in Dallas and the war in Vietnam was escalated.

In Britain, the Secretary of State for War, John Profumo, was at the centre of a scandal that scapegoated Christine Keeler, Mandy Rice-Davies and Stephen Ward and resulted in the resignation of the Prime Minister, Harold MacMillan. The Great Train Robbery took place, and the Moors murderers began their reign of terror. The Beatles burst onto the scene, and Tamla Motown arrived in Britain.

After Dusty's visit to the States everything changed. This was the year that properly kicked off her drive towards stardom, singing her kind of music, it ended when she became a solo artist, and ultimately, a star. 1963 marked some the most important and iconic events in her musical career.

Dusty was already a regular at record import shops; she had started listening to Radio Luxembourg when she was very young, and now Motown music began to have an impact on her. Around the same time, Dave Godin started his fan club – the Tamla Motown Appreciation Society – and Dusty was one of the first to join.

~

Motown

Motown was the brainchild of Berry Gordy, songwriter and producer extraordinaire. Together with his siblings Anna, Gwen, and Robert, and various other collaborators, he wrote or produced over a hundred songs for various artists. He met a local seventeen-year-old kid, Smokey Robinson, in 1957, when Robinson fronted a vocal harmony group. His doo-wop style interested Gordy, who released 'Got a Job', for Robinson's group, the Miracles, and then went on to produce a number of other records under an arrangement with United Artists. In 1959, he decided to set up his own base, and bought a studio at 2648 West Grand Boulevard, which he converted into a recording studio and office (Hitsville USA). Now he would use the Tamla and Motown labels to release the songs he wrote and produced. He incorporated Motown Records in 1960, and Tamla Motown was the brand used outside the States.

By 1963, Motown acts had started climbing up the US charts in the wake of Smokey Robinson's hit, 'Shop Around'. In the UK, pop music didn't have the same bite as US songs, and even in 1963, when there was a passionate underground group of British fans, it was almost impossible to hear the Motown sound. Luxembourg played African American music for British fans, who met in the middle of the night to listen to the sounds that would change their lives. Rock'n'roll was grabbing all the attention, which meant a virtual media blackout on soul music. BBC radio concentrated on British artists and wouldn't touch Motown, and although Oriole released plenty of product, they couldn't get any support from the radio stations. Even the Beatles early hits were cover versions of records released by Motown – they all loved Motown – and because no one knew the songs weren't original, British bands could record the numbers as if they were their own. But, in reality, why would you want to listen to the Rolling Stones sing 'Can I get a Witness', if you could hear Marvin Gaye sing it? By 1964, Motown acts were making massive pop breakthroughs in the States, when the Supremes had three number one hits in that year. It wasn't until November 1964, that a major breakthrough happened and Motown finally reached number one in the UK pop charts, with 'Baby Love' by the Supremes.

Dave Godin had started the Tamla Motown Appreciation Society (TMAS) around 1961 or 1962, assisted by Clive Stone. At the beginning the numbers were small, but that was more than made up for in enthusiasm and fervour. Godin contacted Motown's Berry Gordy, and even went to Detroit for talks. Gordy believed the fan base was a lot bigger than it turned out to be, and organised the first Motown tour of the UK in 1965. With the aid of EMI, he started the Tamla Motown label. Godin publicised the tour, and kept UK fans up to date with all the Motown news, and he also arranged informal meet-and-greets with the label's stars for the TMAS members; however, other than a few devoted Mods, the tour had very poor turnouts and was considered a flop. The *Ready Steady Go Motown Special* on Associated-Rediffusion, hosted by Dusty was broadcast after the artists had left Britain. This was responsible for igniting interest in the Motown singers and songs.

~

British Music Scene

In the 1950's the UK charts had been dominated by American artists such as Bing Crosby, Al Martino, Doris Day, Mantovani, Frankie Laine, Guy Mitchell, Mario Lanza, Kay Starr and Johnnie Ray. Very few British performers were featured – those such as Max Bygraves, Lord Rockingham's XI, Vic Damone, Ted Heath and Russ Conway – and none of these could be described as representing modern trends in pop music.

1963 was the year when the British pop music scene began taking big strides into the modern world. The US no longer dominated, and the previously overwhelming presence of American stars at the top of the British charts had already been challenged. The Springfields were in the vanguard of British pop stars leading this challenge, which included Cliff Richard and the Shadows, Lonnie Donegan, Marty Wilde, Tommy Steele, Emile Ford and Adam Faith. At the same time, entertainers such as Russ Conway, The Beverley Sisters and Max Bygraves, who appealed to an older audience, were still popular.

~

The Beatles

But then something incredible happened. A convulsion ripped through pop music in Britain with the appearance of the Beatles. The Cavern Club in Liverpool was already firmly established as the Beatles home, where they had been the star attraction for several years. Crowds flocked in, brought by their name, and once there, were knocked flat by their performance. These boys won the love and devotion of their fans and were the backbone of the booking schedule; no other group created such excitement. Their lunchtime shows were awesome, and they became central to the lives of their audience.

By March 1962, the Beatles had appeared at the Liverpool Jazz Society with Gerry and the Pacemakers, and a month later at the Tower Ballroom, New Brighton, with Emile Ford and the Checkmates. On 21 September, they were mentioned for the first time in *NME*, then 'Love Me Do' was released on 5 October, reaching number 17 in the charts. On 28 October, they played the Liverpool Empire, followed by the Embassy Cinema, Peterborough, on 2 December. Christmas 1962 saw them sending best wishes to their fans from the Star Club in Hamburg. Their new single, 'Please Please Me', was released on 11 January 1963.

The Beatles' first proper solo tour of the UK began on 3 January 1963, in Scotland. They were following the well-worn path trodden by the Springfields, John Leyton, Eden Kane, Van Morrison, and a host of top pop stars of the 1960's. On that cold winter's night, four boys from Liverpool battled their way through the blizzards that had brought chaos to the roads in Moray. They were on their way north to the Two Red Shoes in Elgin to play the first gig of their tour. Albert Bonici, the impresario who brought them there, advertised them as the 'Love Me Do' boys, and paid them £42.00 for their evening's work. A little over a year later they were four of the most famous people in the world.

~

Black Nativity

The news of a Gospel musical that was creating a great tumult in New York, travelled across the Atlantic. The articles and adverts filled the pages of newspapers in the UK. There is no doubt that Dusty will have seen them, and been excited by the prospect of going to see this new musical. 'Black Nativity', a Gospel Song Play, had opened off-Broadway on 11 December 1961, to a response that was nothing short of phenomenal. This show, produced by Langston Hughes, was coming to London.

An all-Black cast had never depicted one of the most sacred dramas in Christian history before this production of 'Black Nativity'. This cast of professional actors and singers performed the Nativity story with gospel music. Marion Williams and her Stars of Faith, and Alex Bradford and the Bradford singers, were contracted to perform the music. Professor Alex Bradford was one of gospel's most well-loved and versatile figures. He put together his group, the Bradford Singers, composed of Kenneth Washington, Calvin White, Bernie Durant and Madeline Bell, the group's only female member. The blind soloist, Princess Stewart, was also recruited to take part.

After 57 performances in New York, Gian Carlo Menotti offered to present 'Black Nativity' at the Festival dei Due Mondi in Spoleto, Italy. The singers spent four weeks in Spoleto, and after an extremely successful run, the company moved on to London for the initial leg of a European tour. Michael Dorfman, an English theatre impresario, saw them when they were in London to record 'Black Nativity' for Associated-Rediffusion, and decided to put the show on at his theatre. In August 1962, 'Black Nativity' completed a spectacular four-week run in the Criterion and Coventry Theatres in London. It played before thousands, including British royalty, and received some of its strongest reviews.

Although Dusty must have seen the reviews, she probably had little opportunity to see the musical, first time around. The troupe left for a tour of Europe, then came back to London for a short season from 26 February to 16 March at the Piccadilly in London. Could this be when Dusty saw the show?

~

Madeline Bell

Madeline Bell was the only girl with the Alex Bradford Singers. She grew up in Newark, New Jersey, and was raised by her Gram, who had been a dancer in the Cotton Club in New York City. Their house was constantly filled with music and entertainer friends of her Gram, who would drop in to visit and talk about the old days. Madeline was fascinated by the stories she heard; they penetrated her soul and made her want that kind of life. At 16 she was in a group, the Glovertones, with her cousin Joanne. They still went to school during the week, but then at weekends they might travel 500 miles to sing at a church. They were paid very little for their performances.

Madeline sang with Alex Bradford's group in the late 1950's and early 1960's. She had been with them for a year and a half when he decided to spread his wings and joined the Black Nativity company, along with Marion Williams and the Stars of Faith, who had been part of the Clara Ward Singers. After Spoleto, they went to London to record the show for Associated-Rediffusion, where Michael Dorfman originally saw them. Madeline recalls the events of that time: 'I was 19 or 20 then and the show just snowballed. It got bigger and bigger. We were supposed to be in Europe for six weeks, but we came in June 1962, and eventually went home at the end of August 1963. We played all over Europe and we played London four times and when everyone went back, I stayed.'[212]

One year later at the *Ready Steady Go!* New Year party, Madeline was surprised when she met Dusty, to be asked: 'You are that Gospel singer, aren't you? Do you do sessions?' It was the start of a lifelong friendship.

~

Dusty's Sexuality

The entire time Dusty was with the Lana Sisters, they had no indication from her that she was attracted to women rather than men. In fact, the three members of the group focused so much on the act and their performances that there was no time to think about romantic attachments. Dusty's sexuality simply wasn't an issue. In a later interview, Lynne Essex recalled that Dusty had said to her 'Lynne, I wish I could do what you've done, leave the act and settle down and be happy with that.' At that time Dusty was a pious Catholic and said, 'I could never divorce. If I got married, I could never divorce.' This made Lynne believe that being gay wasn't in her mind then.

---

212 Spencer Leigh (2004) 'Madeline Bell: Wrap it up in Black Skin', accessed at
www.spencerleigh.co.uk/2013/05/madeline-bell/

Once Dusty joined her brother in the Springfields, there was a sense she could be more relaxed. A top London DJ, Norman Scott, recalled the time he was waiting outside the stage door after a performance, and Tom and Tim were shouting from their dressing room, 'Dusty's a lesbian! Dusty's a lesbian!' [213] It did seem an odd way for them to behave.

In an interview years later, Mike Pickworth talked about his time in the Springfields with Dusty and Tom. He said he could never work out why he never really got to know them. it could have been because they had no shared interests. He talked about Dusty always searching for the nearest Catholic Church wherever they went. That seemed at odds with their pop star lifestyle. Also, as an innocent 20-year-old, he found it strange that the visitors to Dusty's dressing room were mostly female, it was till much later that he realised that she was a lesbian.

Dusty lived the life she wanted to live. All of her committed long-term relationships were with women. Her sexuality was always a kind of open secret, everyone knew, even fans living in the north of Scotland. But the fear was always that her career would be destroyed if it was widely known she was a lesbian. So, in interviews she would prevaricate, neither fully denying nor confirming the truth. In fact, the reality is that so many female artists (ones that Dusty revered) were also gay: Bessie Smith, Ma Rainey, Sister Rosetta Tharpe, Billie Holiday.

In 1970, Dusty gave an interview to Ray Connolly of the Evening Standard in which she confronted the dragon head on:

A lot of people say I'm bent, and I've heard it so many times that I've almost learned to accept it. 'I don't go leaping around to all the gay clubs, but I can be very flattered. Girls run after me a lot and it doesn't upset me. It upsets me when people insinuate things that aren't true. I couldn't stand to be thought of as a big butch lady. But I know that I'm as perfectly capable of being swayed by a girl as by a boy. More and more people feel that way and I don't see why I shouldn't. [214]

~

---

213 Sharon Davis (2008) *A Girl Called Dusty*, London: Andre Deutsch Ltd, p. 27.

214 Dusty Springfield, Ray Connolly, *Evening* Standard, September 1970

After America

At the end of 1962, for the second year in a row, the Springfields had topped the British Vocal Group category of the *NME* Poll, and were voted third in the World Vocal Group category. Interviewed by Mike Hellicar for *NME,* they told him about their time in America. They had arrived back in London to find their single, 'Island of Dreams' climbing up the *NME* chart. They were disappointed when it dropped out again, but early in January it began to go back up the charts, and on 5 January *Billboard* reported it at number 25.

Returning from their trip to Amsterdam, the group arrived in the early hours of the morning to be met by blizzards, ice and snow that caused travel chaos for them. The car that was to take them to Birmingham for the telerecording of ABC TV's *Thank Your Lucky Stars* didn't arrive, and they were forced to take the train, arriving several hours late. The Springfields, Jet Harris, and Tony Meehan were among the few stars who did make it to the studio that day, and as soon as the recording was over, they had to go back to London for a BBC overseas programme the same evening.

The Springfields' Nashville single, 'Waf-Woof', was given a four-star review by *Billboard* when it was released in the US. On 14 January 1963, the group recorded two singles in French, specifically for the French market. 'Petit Enfant tu Dors' ('Bambino') and 'Leve Toi' ('Breakaway') were recorded in Stanhope Place. Ultimately, they were not released in the 1960's, and only appeared many years later, on a CD of continental recordings by Dusty and the Springfields.

Next came appearances on the BBC Light Programme in, *On the Scene* with Craig Douglas, *The Billy Cotton Band Show* and *The Beat Show*, introduced by Gay Byrne. They also joined Arthur Haynes in his television show, and filmed a TV commercial for Fairy Liquid.

The Springfields spent one night at the De Montford Hall, Leicester, with Frank Ifield. This handsome, yodelling, Aussie was a top-line entertainer in Australia, where his career was already established. Looking for another challenge, he was driven to leave Australia to seek out and conquer a new audience in Britain. His single, 'I Remember You' had topped the charts for seven weeks in May 1962. The Lana Sisters were on the same bill, with two new members, as Lynne had left the group some time before. Dusty realised they were about to sing 'Scarlet Ribbons', a standard in the Springfields repertoire, she was annoyed. As Iris introduced this song, Dusty was seen carrying a tray of crockery, and the next moment it smashed onto the stage behind them! It is said that Dusty pointed at Mike and declared, 'It was him, he dropped it!'

~

The Springfields' Hits

In February of 1963 the Springfields appeared on *Parade of the Pops, Easy Beat, On the Scene,* and *The Beat Show* with Gay Byrne. They also went to the BBC World Service to record a segment on *Linger Awhile.*

Along with their booking for a run of six Dick Emery shows starting in May, the Springfields were due to begin a series of alternate Sundays at Bournemouth Winter Gardens. Articles in *NME* and *Disc* talked about a future trip to the US, with a concert planned in Boston and a special St Patrick's Night concert with the Bachelors at Carnegie Hall. There was also talk of further visits to Nashville. It didn't work out that way, Tom, Mike, and Dusty never returned to the States as the Springfields.

'Island of Dreams' got to number 16 in the UK charts. They were thrilled with its success as it continued to climb up the charts all through February, and they began to pin all their hopes on it.

A report in *Billboard* said that, with the success of the Springfields' foreign language recordings, Philips had decided to take the group to Europe during the Spring, to make more records. Their recording manager, Johnny Franz, arranged for some of their biggest numbers to be recorded in Paris and Hamburg later in the year, while television work in Sweden was also planned.

Then it seemed clear that Dusty was emerging as a star in her own right. At the beginning of March she was chosen as a panellist on *Juke Box Jury*. A few days later she had a second solo appearance in a recording of *Here Come the Girls* on AR-TV. By now 'Island of Dreams' was at number seven in the charts and in mid-March it reached number two in Ireland.

The group's latest single, 'Say I Won't be There', had been adapted, by Tom, from the French folk song, 'Au Claire de la Lune', and he had given it new lyrics. Tom had taken this number to a publisher before the group made their first record, but was turned down. This new version was slightly different as he had made some changes to the lyrics when he brought it out of storage.

Reviews of the record were all excellent. It was described as an easy-beat version of an old French children's song, taken at a fast pace. Trumpets and steel string picking introduced the trio's harmonies that broke to allow Dusty's solo voice through. The words of this upbeat version had echoes of those of 'Island of Dreams'. It was a lament to a lost love. With its first-class arrangement and voices, reviewers from *NME* and *Disc* now placed the group among the world's elite. 'Little Boat', on the flip side was the number they had recorded for the film, *'Just for Fun'*. It was a lively rhythmic number. The disc was predicted to be a hit for the trio. And so it came to pass.

Round about this time the group recorded four tracks in German – 'Das Kostet Keinen Pfennig' (Settle Down), 'Ich Geh' Ohne Ruh' Durch die Strassen und Gassen' (Island of Dreams) 'Alles Gold und Alles Silber' (Silver Threads and Golden Needles); and 'Sag Mir, wo die Blumen Sind?' (Where Have All the Flowers Gone?). While two of these were German versions of their most successful singles, 'Settle Down' came from their LP, 'Kinda Folksy', and 'Sag Mir, wo die Blumen Sind?' was the German version of Pete Seeger's 'Where Have all the Flowers Gone?', which was currently enjoying a revival as a centrepiece in the phenomenally successful concert tours being undertaken by Marlene Dietrich.

'Kinda Folksy 2'

In March 1963, Philips released the second of the three EPs that formed the LP 'Kinda Folksy', almost a year after the release of the first EP.

'Silver Dollar', was written by Jack Palmer and Clarke Van-Ness in 1939. It was recorded by Eve Young and the Homesteaders in 1950 and was number one on the sheet music charts for six weeks.

The next track, 'Allentown Jail', is a folk-style song written by Irving Gordon. A man is caught stealing a diamond for his girlfriend and is imprisoned in Allentown jail. His girlfriend sings about how she is upset at his confinement, and that she wants to find a lawyer to release him. The Springfields recorded an up-tempo version with Dusty's voice as the focal point of the song. It romped along with great harmonies and orchestration. Jo Stafford had also released the song on Columbia Records in 1951.

'Lonesome Traveller', the third track, is a skiffle song written by Lee Hays and recorded by Pete Seeger and The Weavers in 1950. It was also recorded by Lonnie Donegan in 1958. The Springfields produced a fast, upbeat and high-energy version.

The final track, 'Dear Hearts and Gentle People', is a popular song first published in 1949, with music by Sammy Fain and lyrics by Bob Hilliard. The title comes from the words 'Dear friends and gentle hearts' written on a scrap of paper. This was discovered on the body of a man found dying in a New York hotel room in January 1864. Fain and Hilliard were inspired to write the song when they heard about it. Dusty sang solo on this track, with just backing vocals from the two boys. It is a beautiful version, with a country and western feel and excellent guitar work.

Next the Springfields spent five days in Lisbon making TV and cabaret appearances, then back in the UK, took part in *'Music Hall'* with Alfred Marks and Jill Day, followed by an appearance on Southern TV's *Day by Day*. On 11 March they provided the cabaret at the Lords' Taverners' Annual Charity Ball at London's Empire Rooms. The Lord's Taverners was a charity whose membership consisted of famous actors and well-known BBC commentators who loved cricket. They would sit in the Lord's Tavern pub in St. John's Wood Road, near to Lord's cricket ground, to watch the cricket. Money raised by the charity went to cricket projects, mostly for the installation of artificial pitches. In 1963 the president of the Lord's Taverners was Richard Hearne (Mr Pastry – one of the original television stars). Just a few months later, Dusty and Tom were guests at Mike's wedding, when he married Richard Hearne's daughter, Sarah.

On 16 March, the group heard the news that sales of 'Island of Dreams' had passed the quarter million mark, making it their biggest ever hit, and winning them their first silver disc. On the same day, they flew to Berlin to star in a TV spectacular called *Heute in Berlin* (Today in Berlin); it was to be televised in most European countries on 17 August. Later they joined Brian Matthew on ABC TV's *Thank Your Lucky Stars*.

Their album, 'Folk Songs from the Hills', recorded in Nashville, was released in the States, with an encouraging review in *Billboard*:

The British folk trio has clicked here with at least one single, 'Silver Threads and Golden Needles', and has other album offerings. This set, however, marks their debut US recording, and it was done in Nashville to the sparkling, banjo-filled arrangements of Bill Justis (the trumpet and saxophone player who worked with Sam Phillips at Sun Records before moving to Nashville where he became a successful record producer). The group has a tremendously infectious sound on such ditties as Greenback Dollar, Settle Down, Midnight Special and Cotton Fields. [217]

With their profile growing, the trio were being pursued for interviews by the various music magazines. *NME, Record Mirror* and *Disc* all wrote articles about them, and now there was almost a sense that these three could do no wrong. Could it be time for them to relax a little and enjoy their success? March ended with a visit to the BBC radio programme, *Pop Inn* and an interview with Wilfred De'Ath.

In these interviews the Springfields described their visit to the States, spoke about what was current in their lives and their hopes and fears for the future. Tom said they were older and wiser, and Dusty worried that their visit to Nashville meant they were being seen as a country and western act, although that wasn't their aim. Mike said the Springfields success came from a fresh and individual approach and an original style. But what was their style? In one interview Tom recalled the group's BBC audition. 'The producer said you must make up your minds to be a folk or a pop group, if you are going to be any success at all. Dusty said: 'one of the problems is that there is a lot of material we would like to sing, but we must be careful not to steer into any arty or poppy category. You see we haven't enough class for a folk group and not enough pop background for a rock concert.' [218]

Now life was good, and very busy. The group, possibly at the peak of their fame, were bubbling with excitement. This was as much for the holidays they had planned, as for the success of their records. Their next single, 'Say I Won't be There', quickly climbed the charts and went to number five, and it too stayed in the UK charts for many weeks. 'Island of Dreams' didn't enjoy the same success in the States as 'Silver Threads' had done, only skirting the lower reaches of the Cash Box Hot 100. The

---

217 Album Review – Spotlight, *Billboard*, 23 March 1963

218 Mike Hellicar, 'Spring(field) Fever', *New Musical Express*, 29 March 1963.

three of them, though, were just as thrilled by their new cars – Tom's very snazzy two-seater continental sports model, Dusty's MG 1100 and Mike's Triumph TR3 – as they were by the hits.

When the trio weren't working, they preferred their own space – they found they got on better that way – and each of them had their own home and set of friends. Tom's apartment was in a fashionable block in Chelsea, and Dusty had a flat in Baker Street. Holidays were separate too, Dusty loved the beaches of the Costa Brava and Mike went touring in France with Kenny Lynch, or shark fishing in Cornwall. Tom's love of Latin American music and Carmen Miranda meant he yearned to visit Rio for the Carnival, an ambition he would finally realise in 1965. As a diversion from constant touring, Dusty and Tom had started dabbling in photography. Tom enjoyed watching his Polaroid camera spit out its photos and develop them in less than a minute. Dusty, on the other hand, was thrilled with the new Balda she had been given, after years of making do with a Baby Brownie.

Other than these few days of downtime, the Springfields' schedule was filled with appearances on TV and radio: they headlined on Southern TV's *Day by Day*, and were featured in *Parade of the Pops*, *Side by Side*, and *Saturday Club*. After one night with Andy Stewart and Mark Wynter at Blackpool Opera House, they spent the next at Bournemouth Majestic Hotel with the Malcolm Mitchell Trio and Mike and Bernie Winters. Then, on April 18, they joined Ken Dodd when he presented *Star Parade* on the Light Programme. Performing on that show alongside the Springfields, were John Laurie, Judith Chalmers, Harold Berens and Cardew Robinson.

Norman Joplin's article for *Record Mirror* about the group was headlined 'The White Negress'.[219] This was the title, conferred on Dusty by Cliff Richard and the Shadows. She found it a pleasing compliment and was grateful for it. In many ways it wasn't surprising as some of her favourite singers were African American artists in groups like the Shirelles and the Crystals and she wanted to sing like them. Later Dusty spoke about the onslaught she gave her voice, and the problems it caused for her. She said, 'I don't have any vocal expertise; I just suck throat sweets and hope for the best.' But for now, in her drive to copy

219 Norman Jopling, 'The White Negress', *Record Mirror,* 6 April 1963

the sounds of her idols, her voice problems of the previous year were forgotten. Dusty had always loved rhythm and blues and gospel. Dusty later told Andy Beach from Beat Magazine about touring the record shops in America and making some real finds – Bo Diddley and Chuck Berry, as well as a whole lot of R&B records that hadn't been released in the UK yet. It's true the Springfields were normally associated with country and western numbers, but they also loved good pop and R&B. Was 'Island of Dreams' an ideal pub song? The group decided it became a hit because even drunks could sing it.

The trio had heard very little since their recording in Nashville, and weren't too sure about their level of success in the States. No one had asked them which singles should be released there, and they didn't even know their LP was available until someone told them they had seen it in Cashbox. In the article in *Record Mirror*, Dusty said, 'We've only just heard the finished product. Some of it is good, some of it is … well, you know.' She wasn't the only modest one. Tom said he didn't like any of the team's discs to date, preferring 'Silver Threads' and their latest to 'Island of Dreams', which all three agreed was a load of corn. 'That's the Springfields then, the candid yet modest group who have taken coals to Newcastle'.[220] The group had a down-to-earth attitude to their music; it wasn't authentic country and western, and they meant to keep it that way, as country music didn't appeal to their fans in the UK.

Nashville Recording

On 27 April, *Record Mirror* printed the UK review of 'Folk Songs from the Hills', the group's Nashville LP. 'Outstanding as their previous efforts have been, I feel that I can safely claim this to be their greatest yet. It's a lively set, but Nashville couldn't do much if the basic talent wasn't there first. If this one doesn't enter the best sellers, then there ain't no justice in the pop world.'[221] This collaboration between the Springfields and Nashville musicians was seen as a successful pop combination.

---

220 Norman Jopling, 'The White Negress', *Record Mirror*, 6 April 1963.

221 The Springfields, review of 'Folk Songs from the Hills', *Record Mirror*, 27 April 1963.

FIGURE 8.2 'FOLK SONGS FROM THE HILLS' LP COVER (UNIVERSAL MUSIC)

In the almost three years since the Springfields had formed, the way Dusty presented herself had undergone a gradual change. In this photo on the front cover of their Nashville album, Dusty's hair is a full blonde bouffant, and while her tartan dress seems not at all like her previous style of dress, it is equally chaste.

Now the rest of the world began to notice the Springfields. One Australian paper referred to them as, 'that first-class British group', and a South African writer suggested they should be known as the 'International Springfields'. German and Canadian articles said their origin was hard to tell, and once the group had climbed the US Hot 100, DJs and recording men struggled to believe that they hadn't just stepped down from the Nashville hills. Their future looked bright – they could tour almost any country in the world and be sure of a firm following.

Radio appearances in May included *Side by Side, Star Parade* with Bob Monkhouse and *Go Man Go* with the Rabin Band. On TV the trio starred with comedian Stanley Baxter in four fortnightly BBC TV shows, that began on 18 May. these were a replacement for the original Dick Emery series of the same name, *A Touch of the Sun*. Reviewers said Baxter's support was way above average for this kind of comedy show, including as it did, Joan Sims, one of the sharpest local revue talents, singer Gary Miller, and the Springfields, chart toppers who gave a lively performance of their single 'Say I Won't be There'.

Europe wanted the Springfields too. Offers were coming in from the continent, they had TV dates in Oslo on June 22 and 23, and in July, they were booked to go to Belgium for radio work and a British Forces Network concert in Ostend.

In the Spring of 1963, two big concerts took place within a few days of each other, and the Springfields were key to the success of both.

~

Royal Albert Hall Concert

At ten past nine on Thursday 18 April 1963, the BBC presented a massive showcase concert from the Royal Albert Hall. The first half of the concert was neither broadcast nor recorded, and only the second half of *'Swinging Sounds of '63'* was broadcast live. Sadly, no recording was made of the concert. It is lost to posterity.

Del Shannon topped the bill in this concert, and the Springfields had a starring role. Other stars included Matt Monro, Chris Barber and his Band, and a host of top-class entertainers, including BBC *Jazz Club* All Stars, and not forgetting the Beatles. The Springfields showed they had earned the distinction as one of Britain's best singing trios. It was a joy to see and hear their sense of rhythm, style, and harmony and they made a massive impact.

At the end of the concert The Springfields took part in an instrumental performance of 'Mack the Knife', with all the other acts.

From today's perspective, it might be hard to believe that Britain was host to a huge roster of stars and top pop acts in 1963. Contemporary searches report only on the Beatles; history has been swamped by them and it can be difficult to find reports on other performers. Any search for information about this concert focuses on the Beatles and their performance. While they were a phenomenon, it is unfortunate that they have been allowed to eclipse the many other amazing artists in the UK at the time. The Beatles were not the stars of this show, and their arrival on the British music scene had been very recent, although their fame was spreading rapidly. This was their first appearance at the Royal Albert Hall and was probably their earliest major concert.

~

NME Poll-Winners' Concert

On 21 April 1963, *NME* held their Annual Poll-Winners' Concert. Cliff Richard and the Shadows were the stars, and as always, the Empire Pool, Wembley, was packed to capacity with a whooping crowd of ten thousand for this all-star concert.

Readers of the *NME* had voted the Springfields winners in the Vocal Group category for 1962, and Roger Moore presented them with their trophy. The group performed their usual lively and folksy material, and Dusty was the only girl performer, as was usual in those days.

Gerry and the Pacemakers performed the number one record, 'How do You Do It', that had launched them onto the UK charts. The Shadows played their well-rehearsed routine and Joe Brown and the Bruvvers brought the house down with their fresh, bouncy performance.

FIGURE 8.3 Backstage at the NME Poll-Winners Concert with two members of the Kingston Trio (*NME*, 21 April 1963)

The Kingston Trio were big fans of the Springfields. When they arrived in the UK that April, their first question was, 'Where are the Springfields? I bet they're even better in person than they are on their records.'[222] Since this was one of the groups the trio had modelled themselves on, it was a gratifying endorsement. The Kingston Trio attended the *NME* Poll-Winners Concert, and watched as the Springfields were presented with their award. In this photo, Dusty is seen sporting her iconic bouffant wig. It is not clear whether she had worn this wig in public before. The wig is reputed to have been created for Dusty by Vidal Sassoon, although the style is very different from his geometric bobs, crops, and Greek Goddess styles. Her choice of dress was also changing; here the blouse is different, open at the neck and

---

222 *Disc,* 27 April 1963

more relaxed, and her wide skirts and hooped petticoats have been cast off, in favour of a slimline skirt and decorative braces.

The *NME* poll had taken place in 1962, before the Beatles hit the music scene. Although they hadn't actually won any awards, they were included in the concert because of their two recent number one singles. They played 'Please Please Me', 'From Me to You', 'Twist and Shout' and 'Long Tall Sally' for the screaming fans, and media observers declared they had stolen the show from the headliners.

Cliff Richard in black dinner jacket, and the Shadows neat in grey, performed with their usual polish and included songs from their film *Summer Holiday*. They closed the show to thunderous applause.

~

Del Shannon and Johnny Tillotson tour

After the poll-winners' concert, the Springfields joined the Del Shannon and Johnny Tillotson tour which kicked off in the Taunton Gaumont then moved on to Bournemouth. Headliners Shannon and Tillotson presented a polished show. Powerhouse performer Shannon, sang his current chart numbers and the crowd loved hearing Tillotson sing his hits live.

The Springfields were real show-stoppers on this bill. They closed the first act and in spite of the strong competition from the American acts, were given a fantastic reception for their performance. They romped through a lively set of numbers, clearly enjoying themselves as much as the screaming fans. Starting with 'Lonesome Traveller', they included 'Island of Dreams' and 'Say I won't be There', then threw in a Goonish version of the Lizzie Borden saga, 'You Can't Chop Your Granny Up in Massachusetts', before the barnstorming 'Cotton Fields'. Dusty stepped into the purple light onstage, dressed in sparkly pink she launched into her solo, 'End of the World,' and was met with a deafening foot stamp. [223]

It was on this package tour that Tom and Dusty met a young dancer who would become a close friend of both of them. Peppi Borza was well known for his version of 'The Twist' and he introduced a new dance with

---

223 Paul Adams, Shannon Storms Back, but the Springfields Steal the Show, *Disc,* 27 April 1963

'Can You Waddle', which he demonstrated as he sang, as well as a torrid 'I Never Danced Before'. He did several clever impressions of performers, including Frankie Vaughan, Elvis Presley, Billy Fury, Jet Harris and Joe Brown, singing 'Pop Goes the Weasel'.

They travelled on through the rest of April to Leicester, Norwich, Birmingham, York, Manchester, Newcastle, Bradford, Liverpool, Stoke and Hammersmith.

Andy Beach from *Beat* magazine caught up with the group in Bradford. The tour had hit the country town, and he described the crowds coming out of the cinema, chatting about the show they had just seen. He said: 'It proved again that the Springfields are three of the best entertainers we have got. Backstage the lone figure of Dusty was standing on the empty stage clad in knee length boots, sheepskin coat and dark glasses. That night she had had her stage clothes stolen from the tour coach, so she went on in jeans and denim shirt. Mike Hurst said, 'She looked terrific, the audience thought so too – she brought the house down!'' [224] The tour wrapped on 13 May in East Grinstead.

Just for Fun, the pop musical the trio had filmed in December, was released in the middle of their tour with Del Shannon. The *Disc* review praised the film, saying it was little more than a vehicle to present a swift-moving parade of star pop names. In the film, the country's teenagers are given the vote, and they form a Teenage Party, led by Mark Wynter and Cherry Roland. As part of their campaign the teenagers produce a political broadcast on TV that takes the form of a non-stop pop concert from London and New York. The established parties make hilarious attempts to sabotage the teenage party since they can't win the youngsters' votes.

Dick Emery presented a send-up of *Juke Box Jury*, taking the parts of all four guests. With a big cast of pop musicians providing the music, there was little time for anything but the sketchiest of story lines.

High spots of the film were: Ketty Lester's beautiful performance of 'Warm Summer Day', the top ballad of the film; Jet Harris and Tony Meehan's 'Hully Gully'; and the Springfields' bossa nova, 'Little Boat', which was the B side of their current hit, 'Say I Won't be There'. It also

---

224 Andy Beach, The Springfields on Tour, *Beat Magazine*, July 1963

featured Bobby Vee's 'The Night Has a Thousand Eyes', which was performing well in the charts; and Johnny Tillotson's catchy little ballad 'Judy'. The *Disc* reviewer reported that there really wasn't a bad number in the whole picture.

However, reviews of the film from the US weren't so complimentary. *Variety* was scathing when it was released there in June 1963. The reviewer described it as the picture that caused the 'we want our money back' commotion when it was previewed by Columbia at the Rivoli in New York, and said it should come with a health warning. He liked the comedy routines by well-known British comedy actors, Irene Handl, Hugh Lloyd, Dick Emery and many more. But he dismissed the music presented by all the performers in the film and said there was nothing very special about them. This review was published at a time when British entertainment was still regarded as second rate compared to music coming from America. The British Invasion was yet to happen, but it was soon going to bring about a sea change in attitudes.

NME and *Disc* reported that the Springfields, along with a band of buskers, had been added to *It's All Over Town*, the film Frankie Vaughan was scheduled to shoot in June. The trio were lined up to record two numbers for the film at MGM's Boreham Wood Studios on 13–15 June. Vaughan's next single, 'Hey Mama', was written by Tom Springfield, with Ivor Raymonde as the musical director.

~

'Kinda Folksy 3'

During their holiday the final four tracks on the third EP that made up the Springfields 'Kinda Folksy' LP were released to brilliant reviews.

'A bouquet to Ivor Raymonde musical director on the trio's discs. The powerful full-blooded instrumental sounds set off the Springfields style and character to perfection.'[225]

'They Took John Away', was a folk-style tune made famous by Buddy Greco, telling the saga of John's unfaithful wife, and 'Eso es el Amor' was a number one hit in 1958 by the Chakachas. Tom showed off his facility for languages by choosing this Spanish language piece of frippery, which

---

225 *Disc*, 18 May 1963

they had performed on their TV special. Dusty's interjections are notable, but this is very much an ensemble song. 'Two Brothers' was a song by Irving Gordon, who also wrote 'Allentown Jail'. This folk song of the Civil War continues to raise passions today. 'Tzena, Tzena, Tzena' was written in 1941 in Hebrew by Issachar Miron and was recorded by the Weavers in 1950, when they took it to number two in the Hit Parade.

~

At the start of June, after their holiday, the group appeared at the Dreamland Ballroom in Margate and their second outing on *The Stanley Baxter Show* was televised. On 3 June, the Springfields took part in a Teenage Pop Festival at Botwell House, Hayes, in Middlesex, sharing the bill with Del Shannon and Johnny Tillotson: compered by Pat Campbell.

BBC TV bookings were with Lenny the Lion and Terry Hall in *Pops and Lenny*, and on radio Brian Matthew introduced them on *Easy Beat,* while George Melly was their host on *Pop Along*. They had more appearances on *Side by Side*, introduced by John Dunn, and *The Beat Show*, introduced by Gay Byrne. Then they joined the line-up on *Saturday Club*, which was pre-recorded. Later in June they performed in *Parade of the Pops*.

Later that month, *Disc's* reporter, Tony Noakes, went to MGM (Metro Goldwyn Mayer)'s Boreham Wood Studios where the group were recording two numbers for the new Frankie Vaughan picture, *It's All Over Town*: 'If I was Down and Out' and 'Maracabamba'. He found Dusty looking gorgeously bronzed after her holiday in Spain. She launched into a conversation about the Liverpool boys, saying she felt sorry for them. She thought the beat associated with the city didn't come from there at all; it gave a false impression of that talent pool. Her farsighted view was that 'the Beatles will live on, but I believe the Liverpool myth will die a natural death'.[226]

The Springfields appeared in the third episode of *The Stanley Baxter Show*, broadcast on 29 June, and Marjorie Norris in *The Stage* thought it was a pity that there were only three because of Stanley Baxter's commitments. It had had a shaky start but picked up nicely after its sudden inclusion in the schedules.

---

226 Tony Noakes, 'Dusty feels sorry for some of these Liverpool Groups', *Disc,* 15 June 1963.

In this photo (figure 8.4) taken during *The Stanley Baxter Show*, Dusty's hair is blonde and bouffant, but now it is caught at the back with a black velvet bow. She is wearing a scooped neck blouse showing more of her neck and throat than ever before.

FIGURE 8.4 IN THE STANLEY BAXTER SHOW (*THE STAGE*, 29 JUNE 1963)

'Come On Home'

On 29 June, the Springfields released their next single for Philips. The A-side, 'Come on Home', was another Tom Springfield composition. By now Tom was making as much of a name for himself as a songwriter as he was as leader of the group.

This disc was given fantastic reviews by all the major music magazines. They predicted it was certain to be a hit. It had elements of R&B and gospel and a fast-moving and punchy sound. Dusty had sections of solo lyrics, and the drumming was described as brilliant. 'This trio whip up a veritable storm and produce more excitement than you get on a dozen usual discs. Beautifully arranged too.'[227]

---

227 Peter Jones, 'Long Wait is Over', *Record Mirror*, 13 July 1963.

On the B-side was 'Pit-a-Pat', an olde-worlde-style number with a slow folk charm, given just the right mood by Ivor Raymonde's accompaniment.

Royal Variety Show

Although at times Emlyn Griffiths might have given the impression that he did little to promote his charges – sipping pink gins in Quaglino's with his lunch and sleeping them off in his office afterwards – in fact, a great deal of his time was spent networking with agents, promoters and impresarios to ensure booking a multitude of engagements for the Springfields. While their appearances on TV and radio were now well established, others took more work to arrange. In February of 1963, a front-page article in *The Stage* announced the Royal Variety show, which was due to take place that July. The trio may have missed this, but Griffiths had not. He made use of his contacts to make sure his charges joined the cast at the Alhambra Theatre, Glasgow, for a Scottish Special Royal Performance. They would join a stable of national and international stars invited to entertain Queen Elizabeth and Prince Philip. As well as the Springfields, this show was to include the entire cast of the Five Past Eight show, plus international stars.

The director, Dick Hurran, had a new policy of using mainly London-based headliners, such as Max Bygraves, Bob Monkhouse and Bruce Forsyth, which upset many Scottish acts who saw the Alhambra as their natural home. Some of the Glasgow comedians were offended at what they saw as a slight, saying he valued acts from down south above anything the Scots could do and that they were being pushed out of the show. This disagreement meant that they may have missed out on the chance to take part. Hoping to pacify the Scottish artists, Hurran decided to allocate 30 minutes for a 'Stars of Scotland' scene. The Alhambra Theatre was only going to close for the night of the performance, so there would be no time to rehearse a special show.

The Springfields appeared at Blackpool Opera House on 30 June, and the following night at Brighton Town Hall, performing with Winifred Atwell, Yana, Eddie Calvert, and Bob Miller and his Millermen. Then they had to hot foot it to Glasgow to take part in rehearsals for their appearance in the Royal Variety Show.

On 3 July 1963, the car carrying the Queen and Prince Philip swept through the Glasgow streets and pulled up outside the Glasgow Alhambra. There the royal couple were met by Peter Meldrum, the Lord Provost, and greeted by crowds of loyal subjects. Stewart Cruikshank, the managing director of Howard and Wyndham, the company which owned the Alhambra, escorted them to their seats in the sumptuously decorated royal box. Earlier that day the Queen had opened the recently completed Clyde Tunnel, which ran under the river Clyde linking the north and south of Glasgow. It was a huge technical achievement that had been under construction for six years and cost the lives of two men.

The much-anticipated gala performance of the 'Five Past Eight at the Starlight Room Revue' had arrived at last and was introduced by its resident star, Max Bygraves. The cast of American stars included Connie Francis, who brought her own pianist and musical director, and comic Alan King. As well as the Springfields, British artists included singer Yana, in white top hat and tails, Acker Bilk with his Jazzmen, and comedian Bob Monkhouse. Numerous other top British and American acts made up the cast of the show.

The Springfields, representing Top of the Pops, appeared in a *Juke Box Jury* segment introduced by David Jacobs. They sang 'Why Don't You Help Me?' and their good-luck song, 'Island of Dreams'. They were followed by David Hughes singing the flower song from 'Carmen Jones'.

The 'Stars of Scotland' scene, lasting 35 minutes, took place before the final curtain. It featured Jimmy Shand and his Band, Johnny Beattie, Jack Radcliff and Larry Marshall, who sang of the beauties of Scotland with a backdrop that showed slides of its slums and less beautiful aspects of the city. Then came the kilted Kenneth McKellar to sing 'The Song of the Clyde' and introduce a cheerful Harry Lauder medley with the four comics. McKellar finished by singing 'Keep Right on to the End of the Road'. [228]

Once the show was over Dusty, Tom, and Mike stood in line with Max Bygraves, Connie Francis, and the many other stars waiting to be presented to the Queen and Prince Philip.

~

---

228 'Queen Graces Glasgow Gala', *The Stage*, 11 July 1963.

After their appearance in the Royal Variety Performance, the Springfields flew to Ostend to pre-record two radio shows and star in a British Forces Network concert. On Saturday 6 July the group performed alongside pop artists Sacha Distel and Duo Ofarim at the Kursaal Casino, Ostend. The group also featured alongside Ella Fitzgerald on the Light Programme's record show, *Roundabout*, introduced by Bob Wilcox, and they took part in BBC's *Pop Along,* presented by George Melly. Pete Murray introduced them on ABC TV's *Thank Your Lucky Stars,* along with Acker Bilk, Sam Costa, Craig Douglas, Rolf Harris and Johnny Kidd.

Next the Springfields topped the bill at the Sandown Pavilion and Shanklin Theatre, on the Isle of Wight, playing to near-capacity audiences and supported by Ann Romaine, Ronnie Brewster and comedian Norman Caley. From 14 July, they were the headliners in a weekly series of one-night tour dates at Scarborough Floral Hall, Bridlington Royal Hall, Bournemouth Pavilion and Belfast Plaza Ballroom, finishing at the Bognor Esplanade on 4 August.

In mid-July the trio joined Dick Emery in the first episode of his BBC TV show, which had been postponed from earlier in the year when Emery had fallen out with the BBC over his availability for rehearsals. Stanley Baxter had filled the slot with the same supporting cast, acting as a precursor to this show. The Springfields gave a lusty rendition of their latest record, 'Come on Home', and appeared on the next three fortnightly episodes.

~

Ready Steady Go!

Disc reported that Associated-Rediffusion was about to launch a modern fast-moving pop magazine programme, *Ready Steady Go!* (RSG). Brian Poole and the Tremeloes were guests when the show was scheduled for live transmission on 9 August.

Ready Steady Go! became an iconic pop music show, with its unforgettable slogan 'The Weekend Starts Here',. It was shown on Friday evenings from August 1963 to Christmas 1966. This thirty minutes of live music took hold of the UK boom in pop music. Following the model of the successful pop music show, *Six-Five Special*, where fans danced around on the studio floor in amongst the artists and the cameras. Disc Jockeys Keith Fordyce and David Gell were hosts on the series, and Cathy McGowan supplied additional presentation. Each week they would talk to young people in the audience about current trends in pop music and new records. Later Dusty would co-host the show, before her solo career properly began. RSG was particularly noted at the time for allowing the artists to perform the full version of their songs. The Springfields featured in the pilot show where various ideas were mooted for inclusion. Ultimately, most of these were dropped and the production concentrated on the artists and the dancing inside the studio itself. Elkan Allen, the show's producer, came up with the slogan, and several theme tunes were tried out before Manfred Mann's '5-4-3-2-1' was settled on.

When *Disc* reporter Nigel Hunter found the Springfields at the recording of the pilot show, in early August, he wanted to talk to them about their recent record 'Come on Home'. All three were modest about their chart success. Dusty claimed they were flat all the way through 'Island of Dreams', but that she was fairly happy about 'Say I Won't be There'. Speaking about their Nashville LP she thought they could do it much better now! She said: 'Things like the Isley Brothers' 'Twist and Shout', were exciting to listen to. A great noise and plenty of beat is the formula, and that is where we come in'. Tom said that 'Come on Home' was less country than their earlier singles and that they were being influenced by current trends in music. Dusty was sure they were going to be accused of copying the Beatles.[229]

In an interview with *Disc*, on July 6, speaking about their record, 'Come on Home', Tom described it as different from the Springfields' usual recordings. He had decided it was time for a new direction; he wanted this single to be R&B but to keep a commercial edge. On the track, Tom played a 12-string guitar for the introduction, while Mike had a guitar solo. Dusty featured throughout the track instead of just getting the middle eight, and backing was provided by a group of girl singers. The sound on the new disc didn't differ too much though, and in fact, none of the three had got their way completely. Tom's preference was for Latin American, Dusty went for out and out gospel and Mike liked country and western: the disc was a compromise of all three. Sadly, it

---

229 Nigel Hunter, 'Springfields Are Such a Modest Trio', *Disc*, 03 August 1963.

didn't have the same success as their two previous recordings, only managing to reach number 30 in the UK charts.

~

Ann Wallace

One day in early August, two young girls were at a loose end and looking for adventure. They went to the train station in Eastbourne, where they lived, and found there was a train going to Bognor Regis. Although they had little idea of where Bognor was, the station posters made it look like a lovely seaside town so they bought tickets without any plan of what they were going to do when they got there.

Strolling along the front in Bognor Regis, a red sports car pulled up beside them and a young woman with a shock of blonde hair stuck her head out. Seeming harassed, she asked, 'Do you know where I can park?' Ann and her friend shook their heads and told the woman they didn't live there. As the car drove off, they looked at one another. 'Wait a minute! Do you know who that was? It was Dusty Springfield!'

With that sudden realisation, no more words were needed. The girls ran after the car and caught up when it stopped in a side street not too far away. By the time they reached her, Dusty was already unloading her stage clothes, instruments, vanity cases and all the other paraphernalia she needed for her performance. She simply started handing items to them saying, 'Here, help me with all of this.' Ann and her friend were drawn into Dusty's orbit and helped her carry everything into the theatre on the Bognor Esplanade. With everything in place, Dusty took a good look at the girls and began to ask questions: Who were they? Where did they come from? She was shocked to realise they had had such a long journey with its change at Brighton. She invited them to stay and see the show, and they later met Tom and Mike. Recalling that time years afterwards, Ann said, 'Tom was a lovely bloke, very caring. He was worried about us, and said we shouldn't have come all that way on our own.' It was an auspicious meeting. When Dusty learned that Ann's mother had recently died, she introduced her to Kay O'Brien. Recognising a lost soul, Kay took Ann under her wing, invited her to their home and generally gave her the love and support she so greatly needed. After that Ann spent a lot of time with Kay, and they went to many Springfields performances together.

World Stars

The Springfields were winning praise from all over the world; disc reviewers from New Jersey to New Zealand raved about them. At the same time Americans had trouble accepting that the group had not just come from Nashville. Peter Jones of *Record Mirror* marked the Springfields out as the best vocal group in the business and had supported and promoted them from their very beginning. Now he was glad to see they were being recognised in British showbusiness. They had had a major hit in the States, and now they had made it in the UK too. Peter admired the way they had stuck to their guns and produced first-rate discs one after another, even though their failure to make an impression on the UK charts had left the feeling despondent at times.

In the *NRM* survey of discs from January to June of 1963, the Springfields' hit, 'Island of Dreams' took the number one spot. It was a comfortable winner, having stayed in the charts for six months, and their disc 'Say I Won't be There' was sitting at number 22 in the chart. In addition, the group were number four in the list of stars of the UK chart during this 26 weeks of the year, ahead of such stalwarts as the Shadows, Jet and Tony, Billy Fury, and even Buddy Holly and Elvis Presley. The Beatles though, were already at number two in the chart.

The Springfields released an EP which reprised their recordings, 'Silver Threads and Golden Needles', 'Island of Dreams', 'Little Boat', and 'Say I Won't be There'. *NME* were full of praise for the disc, saying it was 'laden with pop impact, and proving once more that this trio are world beaters of their kind – with Ivor Raymonde accompaniment', and *Disc* gave the group five stars, saying:

You won't need any description from me about this! I've heard no one else on record who can hold a candle to the Springs for sound and attack. They tackle their material with a zest and a vigour which is only rivalled here by the Liverpudlians. Dusty's voice soars out with a forceful spirit you seldom hear from a girl, and Ivor Raymonde's accompaniments are full of the same lusty qualities. These three country and western inspired items and the bossa nova Little Boat are triumphs in every respect.[230]

---

230 Nigel Hunter, 'Springfields Show Just How Good They Are', *Disc*, 20 July 1963.

While the Springfields' EP was promoted in *Disc*, Nigel Hunter also reviewed the Exciters' LP: 'These three coloured girls and a boy had the original American hit with the title tune, by which Billy Davis scored chart success here.'

Three TV spots were lined up at the end of August and beginning of September. They were first joined by Matt Monro and the Dallas Boys in the Rolf Harris programme *A Swingin' Time*, on 29 August. *The Stage* review described it as a cheerful, unpretentious show for children, although it wasn't clear what age group it was really aimed at, it seemed to swing quite violently from a 'jolly Uncle Rolf and the kiddiewinkies' attitude one moment to the sophistication of a love-sick ditty from Matt Monro the next. It was a professional production and all performers, including the Springfields, gave a slick presentation, but the children stole the show.

Next, on 30 August, the Springfields had their first official appearance on AR-TVs *Ready Steady Go!*, along with Johnny Kidd and the Pirates and the Fourmost, followed by an appearance on 'Discs a Go-Go' on 2 September. On 5 September, Everton Football Club held a ball to celebrate winning the English League Championship having missed the top spot in the previous 24 years; the Springfields provided the cabaret for their private party in Liverpool. The Springfields were also guest artists on *The Beat Show*, introduced by Gay Byrne.

The group topped the bill at Manchester Domino and Princess clubs on 12 September, before moving on to ABC TV's *Big Night Out*, broadcast from Manchester on the 14th. As well as the Springfields, Mike and Bernie Winters introduced Joan Regan, Bill Maynard, Freddie Frinton and Lionel Blair. Video has since emerged of the Springfields' on the show, singing 'Come on Home' and 'Foggy Mountain Top'.

~

Tour of Ireland

Now, the trio began preparations for their tour of Ireland. This was going to be a departure for the group: it was a pilgrimage for Dusty and Tom. The tour opened on 14 September, with performances at the Bray International Ballroom and the Dublin Palm Beach Ballroom. After a quick hop back to Blackpool for a date at the Opera House on 15

September, they picked up their Irish tour and this time Kay and OB went with them. Many years later, Dusty said the Springfields' ballroom tours were always in the middle of a field somewhere, and they started very late, which suited her. No matter what time the performance ended, the shops would be opened for them, or the hotel kitchen provided them with steak and mash or bacon and eggs at four in the morning. Dusty thought that the best thing about Ireland was the way it seemed unstructured, but there was a lot of laughter. The trio started at the Ballymena Flamingo Ballroom, but the following day several hundred fans were left disappointed when the group missed a train connection and couldn't appear at the opening of a Belfast record shop. Luckily, they made it to their engagement at the Agricultural Hall in Limavady that night. The next night they appeared on Ulster TVs *Show Band Show*, singing 'Come on Home'. This was a live show compered by Paul Russell, the impresario who booked Irish tours for many overseas acts. There was a studio audience who got up on their feet to dance, and the trio were supported by the resident group, Irish showband the Caravelles. Brian Lynch, a member of the Caravelles, said they played several live numbers on the show and also provided the backing for visiting acts from Britain and America. A few days before transmission, the producer would give them copies of the 45s of the upcoming acts and they rehearsed the songs to death, until they could reproduce the sounds needed.

In those days, travelling down Irish country roads was a challenge for Dusty. She still sometimes wore her big, hooped skirts and she found she was constantly sitting on these hoops in a small car on the way to the next venue, that was only down the road but took four hours to get there.

The final destination on this tour was Tralee, Kay O'Brien's hometown, which she had last visited in 1935 to attend the funeral of her father, Maurice P Ryle. The Springfields were greeted with a grand welcome party in Tralee, organised by the Ryle family. This reunion followed the Springfields' performance at the Catholic Young Men's Society (CYMS) Hall. Many members of the extended family were looking forward to their visit and planned to greet them in fine style. The *Kerryman* announced their impending visit in an article that described how the committee of the CYMS had arranged a 'This is Your Life'-style gathering of the Ryle clan to meet their sister, Kay, and their famous Springfield cousins. Kay's two brothers, Jack and Colm, were well-known printers in Tralee and her relatives included Tom Ryle, manager of the Eire Savings Bank. Miss Honor Kennedy, one member of the group of Irish teachers who had been received by President Kennedy at the White House a few weeks before, was also present. The spectacular welcome given to the Springfields in Tralee gave Dusty a sense of coming home!

FIGURE 8.5 THE SPRINGFIELDS WITH LIAM O'REILLY AND JIM CONLON
(IRISH-SHOWBANDS.COM)

Speaking about her roots, Dusty often said she was happy that she was Irish, and glad her mother came from Kerry and her name was Mary Isabel Catherine Bernadette O'Brien. She watched as Ireland came alive, felt the vibrancy in the music and recognised the strength of the Irish culture.

After their Irish tour, the group arrived home on 22 September. Dusty was the featured artist in a solo spot on 'Non-Stop Pop' with Tony Calder on the 27th, and on 28 September the Springfields appeared at the Northwich Victory Memorial Hall with the Wall City Jazzmen, Bruce Harris and the Cavaliers.

The Springfields Breakup

And then came the shock announcement. Reports began to appear in the music press that the fabulous Springfields, voted top vocal group in the UK for two years in a row and with a worldwide reputation, were going to break up and launch separate careers. They were at the peak of their popularity, commanding fees of more than £1,000 a week and had reached the top 20 in the US charts with 'Silver Threads and Golden Needles'. So why disband and why now? It was reported that the decision to split had been kept a closely guarded secret for several months beforehand.

In truth, Dusty had been restless since their trip to the States the year before. Differences between the members had grown wider over the months since, and musically their ideas were miles apart. Dusty's heart was with R&B, while Tom loved Latin American music. Dusty was aiming for a solo career and it was predicted that she could become the UK's top girl singer. She had already begun to rehearse a new stage act, and was in talks to select and record her first singles with Philips; she also said she hoped to write some songs for herself. It had been quite some time since Cliff Richard had dubbed her as 'The White Negress' because of the soulful edge in her voice.

Tom had always known that he wanted to devote his energy to writing and arranging. In an interview with Peter Jones in *Record Mirror*, he explained that they had been working towards solo careers for quite a while. It had been hard for them to make the decision to break up. but he believed this was the right time. While the Springfields were at the height of their popularity, it could be a stepping stone to further success as solo artists. The creative and imaginative founder and leader of the group, Tom had written all their hits, as well as top numbers like 'Hey Mama' for Frankie Vaughan, and 'Angie' for the Swinging Blue Jeans. Tom launched his publishing company and signed to the Philips label, and he later formed his own orchestra which produced singles and LPs.

Mike Pickworth wasn't as certain. He had joined the group less than a year before, and as very much the junior member he didn't have a great deal of say in what was to happen. When Tom and Dusty announced that the group was to fold, Mike could only accept it. The fact is, joining the Springfields had opened doors for him in a way he could never have imagined. In an interview earlier in 1963, he said 'I think I'm the luckiest person alive. Joining the group and all this happening.'[231]

Mike also signed a recording contract with Philips and debuted soon after. He wanted to broaden his scope as an actor in films and television. 'I never dreamed of joining a vocal group until the chance to take Tim's place came along,' he said. 'I've had ten wonderful months with Tom and Dusty, and I'm immensely grateful for the experience which should do my future prospects a world of good.'[232]

None of them knew for sure whether they about to give up on fame or this would propel them to even more success as solo acts? They didn't know what was likely to happen; nor whether they could be successful on their own.

Tim Feild, part of the original line-up, was able to give some insight into their reason for going their separate ways; he believed that they were splitting up because they were getting on each other's nerves. It wasn't so much that they hated each other, but that the three of them living and working together, constantly just didn't work. 'They couldn't live like this, closer than love-struck honeymooners. Even though they had had lots of fun times together, he had made the decision to leave when he reached that point.'[233]

The Springfields performed onstage as a group for the last time at Blackpool Opera House on 29 September. Two days before that, in their last appearance on *Ready Steady Go!*, they were interviewed about their career and sang some of their hits. Dusty said:

We'll have mixed feelings on Sunday. When we started, we gave ourselves three years to see what would happen, and we've been extremely lucky. I hope to build myself up into a solo singer on the Pet Clark international pattern, although I don't particularly want to leave this country for too long a time.[234]

~

231 Nigel Hunter, 'Springfields Are Such a Modest Trio', *Disc,* 03 August 1963.

232 Springfields Split Up', *Disc*, 28 September 1963.

233 Tim Feild, 'Why the Springfields are Splitting Up', *Sunday People*, 29 September 1963.

234 Springfields Split Up', *Disc*, 28 September 1963.

Last TV Appearance

On 6 October the Springfields appeared on *Sunday Night at the London Palladium*. The host, Bruce Forsyth, introduced the regular Palladium acts in the first half. The second part of the show was reserved for the stars. Acerbic comedian, Jackie Mason, a Jewish American with a caustic sense of humour who wrote most of his own material, came on straight after the break, and the audience gave him a great reception.

FIGURE 8.6 THE SPRINGFIELDS ONSTAGE AT THE PALLADIUM (SHUTTERSTOCK)

Although this was the Springfields' final appearance on live television, they weren't the stars of this show. Top billing had been given to Giuseppe di Stefano, but he wasn't able to perform because of a throat problem.[235] His place was taken by a young Luciano Pavarotti, who was making his debut with the Covent Garden Opera Company as Rodolfo in *La Bohème*. His appearance on UK TV, in front of an audience of many millions, allowed Pavarotti to demonstrate his potential and his ease in this television showcase. Signed by Decca, his performance of 'Che Gelida Manina' (Your Tiny Hand Is Frozen) was his first ever recording. The Springfields gave their usual lusty performance. The Palladium management had asked them to say goodbye at this Sunday night show. Later Dusty said, 'We decided – or rather I did – that our last number would be 'So Long, it's Been Good to Know You'. Tom, who is rather more cynical than me, thought it was just too corny for words, but heck, what's wrong with corn?'[236] Mike recalled they had done everything they wanted to do as a group and now there was just one last gig.

'There we were at the Palladium and there were about 20 million people watching the show. We got paid £375 between the three of us. Bruce Forsyth presented us with a silver cigarette box each and Dusty said to Bruce, 'What's in it? Money?' We got paid zilch for that, our final gig.' [237]

235 'Pop Music on British Television 1955–1999', *TV Pop Diaries*, 6 October 1963.

236 Dusty Springfield, 'Fame has a Flipside too', *Woman's Own* 1965, in Dusty Springfield Bulletin No. 66, Sept 2008.

237 'In My Time: The Mike Hurst Story', accessed at http://wrinkledweasel.blogspot.com/p/wavelengths-2.html

FIGURE 8.7 THE SPRINGFIELDS WITH THEIR SILVER CIGARETTE BOXES
(SHUTTERSTOCK)

This final performance of the Springfields was overshadowed the following week by the Beatles first appearance on *Sunday Night at the London Palladium*. Dusty had often warned that their group would be eclipsed by these new kids on the block, and she may well have been right. It was another of the reasons they had decided to split.

~

The Future

All three kept Emlyn Griffiths on as their agent – he had nurtured them from the start, when Tom and Tim formed their duo in 1960. Johnny Franz continued as their recording manager and Keith Goodwin took care of their individual publicity.

And then it was over. The Springfields had performed together for the last time.

A week after the group's final appearance on *Ready Steady Go!*, and two days before their swansong on *Sunday Night at the London Palladium*, Dusty had her first proper solo engagement when she shared hosting duties with Keith Fordyce and introduced some of the acts on *Ready Steady Go!*. It was a memorable Friday night; Dusty interviewed the Beatles on their first-ever appearance on the show. Footage of this interview can be found on YouTube.

Pete Goodman, writing in *Disc,* said that there were predictions that they would be just as successful as solo performers as they had been as a group. Tom was calm and confident when he spoke to Pete after the hubbub had died down. Tom was already established as one of the most imaginative songwriters in the business; within a week of writing 'Hey Mama' for Frankie Vaughan he was inundated with requests for specially written material.

Reflecting on her time with the group Dusty said:

I really grew up when I was with the Springfields. Or perhaps I mean toughened up. I had to. But it's only outward toughness. Show business hasn't toughened my mind or my sensitivities, but it's toughened my exterior. One just cannot remain a shy little girl when one gets into the rat race that is the pop world today.[238]

When Dusty spoke about 'Silver Threads', she said she loved the song! She thought it was a really good record. The Springfields weren't country singers but Nashville thought that they were.

Between 1963 and 1969 Mary O'Brien, as Dusty Springfield, went on to score 12 top twenty records, and one number 1. She performed and recorded songs written by many famous British and American songwriters. In the process she became an international star.

The early part of Mary O'Brien's life story ends here.

Many biographies have been written which present details of Dusty Springfield's career after she became famous.

---

238 Dusty Springfield, 'Fame has a Flipside too', *Woman's Own* 1965 in Dusty Springfield Bulletin No. 66, Sept 2008.

Post Script – After the Split

In January 1964 the Springfields released their last single, including the two numbers they had recorded for the film *It's all Over Town*. 'If I was Down and Out' began with Dusty's vocal introduction – a few bars without any accompaniment - it's pure blues - and then the tempo picks up with the typical Springfield sounds. This intro shows she was bursting to get out of the group and do her own thing. 'Maracamba' on the B-side is a great Latin song sung in Spanish.

One song, 'No Sad Songs for Me', was written by Tom and recorded by the group in June 1963. Later it was covered by a number of artists, including the Walker Brothers and Hildegard Knef. 'The Springfields' Story', an LP released in 1964 includes the song, it had not had a previous release by the group. This LP also included an alternative take of 'Allentown Jail'.

Dusty as Musician

Later, when Dusty launched her solo career, she asked The Echoes, a top 60s group, to be her backing musicians. Leader, Douggie Reece, has shared his memories of their time working together. He spent a lot of time with Dusty working on the songs and treatments she wanted. He said, 'A lot of thought went into what and how we played. Our performance was even better with Dusty singing out in front.'

Douggie talked about how Dusty's drive for a soulful sound caused conflicts with the supporting musicians in the recording studio. These were professional session musicians, mostly from the Big Band era who were skilled at reading music and played it as it was written. But Dusty was influenced by American soul and R&B coming from the States. She wanted to inject the same soul and feel into her music and needed people around her who could help her achieve that. He described how Dusty was different because she knew exactly what she wanted both musically and orchestrally. She knew a really good song; she could pick great material and was really fussy on vocals.

Derek Wadsworth played trombone in a three-piece brass section that became part of her group. Derek worked with Dusty for 15 years as musician and arranger. We are indebted to him for his description of Dusty's dedication to the study of music. In a 2007 interview he said, it was immediately clear that the founder Echoes loved her to death and were in awe of her musical judgement.' He saw how she approached the work of singing and music and said that:

She was born with talent and enthusiasm for music, but she had craft. She worked and worked and studied and listened and analysed and tried to put these things into practice. Yes, Dusty really knew her business. [239]

Derek's assessment gives us important clues towards understanding how Dusty's profound knowledge and skill with music developed. He

---

239 Derek Wadsworth, 'The Dusty I Knew', BBC Northamptonshire, 2007.

spoke about how she would adjust musical keys to create the maximum emotional impact. She asked him to bring the rhythm section to the front supported by the brass section, rather than leaving it round the back playing a backup role, thus demonstrating her knowledge of unusual arrangements. Derek hadn't come across this before. It was unusual, really interesting and different. It was a big change. He recognised how she understood the bigger musical picture: 'It was like putting a jigsaw together. Dusty would have made a great scientist, because she analysed every detail.' [240]

It is clear to see how Dusty's musical ability was recognised from the many accolades given to her by people she worked with later in her career. Simon Bell, Dusty's friend and backing singer, talked about her great taste and her instinct to pick the right songs. He said she was influenced by people like Baby Washington, Maxine Brown, and Mitty Collier who did quality material – she heard their amazing sound; the richness in their voices and she recognised the great songs they sang. He said that, 'in comparing the original versions on 'Oh No Not My Baby', or 'I had a Talk with My Man' with Dusty's recordings, it is evident that her musicians are more capable while her vocals are more sophisticated and have more thought behind them'. [241]

Ted Scott was a sound engineer who worked with Dusty at the height of her fame. He said:

> *Her avid interest in the audio aspect of the show was evident from the number of hand-written notes that she used to send imploring me to dip the strings at bar 12, enhance the choir over her voice level during the coda etc etc. Called to her dressing room once, while she was being made up, and with eyes closed, she went through the entire show virtually sound mixing it herself. A free singer in every sense, like Cleo Laine, Dusty was not happy miming a track. On the rare occasion when she did, and was uncertain of the exact start point to sing, her out-stretched hand would momentarily come between her mouth and the camera lens, covering any discrepancy.*

---

240 Adam Sweeting, 'The Invention of Dusty Springfield', *Independent*, 26 March 2006.

241 Simon Bell, Dusty's friend and backing singer: email to author

She often reminded me that the vocal didn't always have to be out front. Certain orchestration points were equally important and backing voices should be considered as equal in many cases. I had never been given such an opinion before. Singers, to my mind, wanted to be out front. Dusty considered the arrangement, the meaning of the words, the blending of voice and orchestra. The number of times I remembered her words while mixing other artists, if only they knew. Clever girl was Dusty and a great performer. [242]

Simon Bell also recalls the time during recording of the Royal Albert Hall concert, Dusty spent time at the sound desk, while he sang 'I Close My Eyes and Count to Ten'.

---

242 Ted Scott, Cue Tape Please Ted, 2009

Dusty's Ancestors

Dusty's parents both came from middle class families, but their upbringing and early lives could not have been more different. Mum, Kathleen Ryle, was born in Dublin and lived in Tralee until she was sixteen. While her dad, Gerard Anthony Joseph O'Brien, was born and lived in India in the days of the British Raj. He was enrolled in boarding school in England at the age of eleven, and I haven't been able to find any evidence that shows he ever returned to India

Dusty's Mother

Dusty's mother was known as Kay O'Brien. Though her baptism certificate shows her name as Catherine Anne Ryle, she is listed in the 1911 census as Kathleen Ryle, and that is how she was known by her family.[243] When Kathleen was born, in 1900, her father, Maurice P Ryle, was acting editor of the *Irish Daily Independent,* and she was the newest member of the family.

Maurice P Ryle - Grandfather

Maurice Patrick Ryle was born in Tralee in 1868, the son of Thomas Ryle and Mary Lawlor. He was baptised in 1868, by Mary Lawlor's brother, Father Tom Lawlor, who was Parish Priest in Valentia and Killorglin. Father Lawlor had trained for the priesthood in Paris, and had a significant influence in their lives. He was prominent in the Irish National Land League, formed in 1879 to demand land reform.

Mary Lawlor and Thomas Ryle (Great Grandparents)

Maurice's mother, Mary Lawlor, was born in Kerry in 1831. Her family emigrated to Halifax in Nova Scotia in the 1850s. They were just one family, among the millions, to escape from the Great Hunger in Ireland. On 20 August 1854, she married Patrick Donoghue, in Lowell, Massachusetts, USA. Her son, John Francis O'Donoghue, was born there

---

243 1911 Census

in 1857. Mary, Patrick and their son John, moved back to Tralee in 1860. Patrick O'Donoghue died in 1861, leaving Mary a widow. Mary Lawlor married Thomas Ryle in 1862; the couple had five sons: Denis, Patrick, Maurice Patrick (Dusty's grandfather), William, and Patrick Michael.

Both Thomas and Mary came from farming backgrounds, but shortly after their marriage they acquired a business in Bridge Street, Tralee; essentially this was a public house. The income from this business meant that Maurice and his brothers were well educated; they were given opportunities denied to earlier generations of their family.

Bridget Myles (Ryle) - Grandmother

Kathleen's mother, Bridget Myles, was born in Tralee in 1870, the daughter of Mary Brosnan and William Myles. Bridget had a brother, William, who was one year older, and a sister, Dorothy, two years younger. Family tradition suggests that Bridget and her sister, Dorothy, were well educated.

Bridget Myles, involved herself in the community, and was kept busy caring for her expanding Irish Catholic family.

While it is possible to gain a good understanding of Maurice Ryle, his passions and beliefs, it is much harder to find out about Bridget's life. Her experience was very different from that of her husband. In all 13 babies were born to the family. Bridget suffered the tragedy of watching two of her babies die in infancy. Later she had to endure the illness and subsequent death of her eldest son Denis, at only 28 years of age.

Bridget was a very kind and talented person. She was an accomplished pianist and was played the organ at St John's Church on Sundays.

Maurice P Ryle and Bridget Myles were married in Tralee in 1895.

Mary Brosnan and William Myles (Great Grandparents)

William Myles was a plumber to trade. His parents ran a public house and off licence in Nelson Street, Tralee. When her husband, William, died at just forty years of age, Mary took on the running of the public house. Before they were married Mary was recorded as a shopkeeper, but she was originally from farming stock.

William was Methodist, so when they were married in Tralee, in 1868, two ceremonies were recorded. One in the Church of Ireland and the other in St John's Catholic Church. Mixed marriages were not typical at the time – Mary was a courageous, independent lady.

Ryle Family

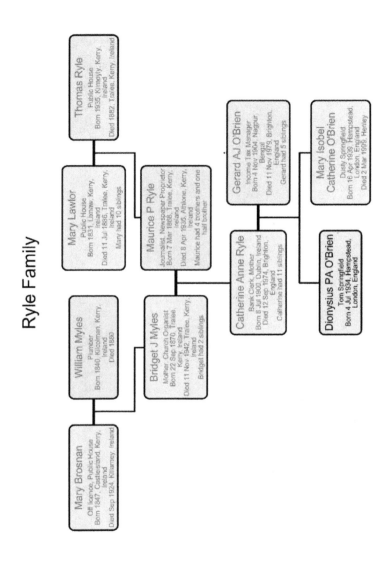

Thomas Ryle
Public House
Born 1835, Kilmoyly, Kerry, Ireland
Died 1882, Tralee, Kerry, Ireland

Mary Lawlor
Public House
Born 1831, Lixnaw, Kerry, Ireland
Died 11 Jul 1886, Tralee, Kerry, Ireland
Mary had 10 siblings

Maurice P Ryle
Journalist, Newspaper Proprietor
Born 7 Mar 1866, Tralee, Kerry, Ireland
Died 8 Apr 1935, Athlone, Kerry, Ireland
Maurice had 4 brothers and one half brother

William Myles
Plumber
Born 1840, Kilcolman, Kerry, Ireland
Died 1880

Bridget J Myles
Mother Church Organist
Born 22 Sep 1870, Tralee, Kerry, Ireland
Died 11 Nov 1942, Tralee, Kerry, Ireland
Bridget had 2 siblings

Mary Brosnan
Off licence, Public House
Born 1847, Castleisland, Kerry, Ireland
Died Sep 1924, Killarney, Ireland

Gerard AJ O'Brien
Income Tax Manager
Born 4 Nov 1904, Nagpur, Bengal
Died 11 Nov 1979, Brighton, England
Gerard had 5 siblings

Catherine Anne Ryle
Bank Clerk, Mother
Born 8 Jul 1900, Dublin, Ireland
Died 12 Sep 1974, Brighton, England
Catherine had 11 siblings

Mary Isobel Catherine O'Brien
Dusty Springfield
Born 16 Apr 1939, Hampstead, London, England
Died 2 Mar 1999, Henley

Dionysius PA O'Brien
Tom Springfield
Born 4 Jul 1934, Hampstead, London, England

The Ryle Family

Maurice began his career as a journalist in Tralee and continued in Dublin when he moved there to take up a post as editor of the *Evening Herald* and as a staff reporter on the newly founded, Parnell supporting, *Irish Daily Independent*. Maurice was an ardent admirer of Charles Stewart Parnell, and was known to cry at any mention of his name. Charles Stewart Parnell was one of the most important politicians in 19th century Great Britain and Ireland. He fought for Irish Home Rule and founded and led the Irish Parliamentary Party. This highly charismatic figure was regarded by William Gladstone, the British Prime Minister of the day, as the most remarkable person he had ever met.

In 1902 Maurice left Dublin and went back to his birthplace, Tralee, the capital of County Kerry and its busiest market town. People flock there from the districts all around to buy food and other essentials from its shops and stores. In 1899 Maurice Ryle published a book called *The Kingdom of Kerry,* which extolled the virtues of his native county. Kerry is the most westerly county of Ireland; it draws visitors by the score to its rocky Atlantic coast and romantic scenery. They come to explore the bleak and mountainous landscape, the lakes spread with islands, the craggy peaks, old castles hidden among steep cliffs and ruined abbeys. This was where Kathleen did most of her growing up, and where she was educated at the Presentation School by the Presentation Order.

Returning to Tralee Maurice had a plan. It was to campaign for Home Rule and fight for the rights of his fellow Irishmen. He followed up this plan by publishing his own Catholic and Nationalist newspapers. The first edition of his weekly *Kerry People* was printed on Saturday 27th September 1902, its sister paper the twice weekly *Kerry Evening Star* came out a few days later. Maurice was very conscious that many of his fellow Irishmen; particularly if they were Catholic, did not have the same chances he had been given. He believed that the lack of national self-determination was holding his country back. His passion was social reform, and through the pages of his newspaper, he supported the common man in Ireland. He continued this fight and campaigned throughout his life for Home Rule for Ireland, and for the improvement of working and living conditions of the ordinary folk of the country.

Maurice moved his family into an eight bedroomed Victorian Terrace house at 19 Garryruth in Ballymullen. Which is, or was, a picturesque suburb of Tralee. The name is an anglicization of "Baile an Mhuillin" which means "The Town of the Mill". 19 Garryruth was in a row of what were attractive middle-class houses. It was big but could only just contain all the family. They numbered fourteen in total, Mother Bridget; father Maurice; Denis, the first born; Jack, then Agnes and Kathleen; Colm and Bridie; Josephine Francis was born in 1906 but did not survive her childhood. The younger ones were Patrick and Roma and there were two little ones Thomas and Norman. As well as all the family there were two nannies, Josephine and Ellen.

In front of the house in the open landscape the river Lee leads out towards Tralee Bay where the ships used to sit in the Ship Canal. Not far away there was a military barracks, from which the "Munsters" regiment marched off to the Great War. Beyond the barracks the ruins of an old castle were central to the character of the area, and further down the road was a prison. The military presence, as anywhere in the world, created its own set of problems especially, in Tralee, which suffered from great poverty.

Maurice had a somewhat Victorian outlook, he kept himself aloof from the rest of the family in the sense, for example, that he liked to eat his meals alone. Kay's brother Colm told his son Muiris about the many dinner parties that were held in the house, with crates of wine being delivered. He said that on one occasion he mischievously pulled his mother's chair from under her as she was about to sit down at one of these parties. She fell, grabbing the table cloth and all hell broke loose. He said she stood up for him despite what he did.

Maurice Ryle was a passionate and committed man with a dynamic approach to life. Some people would have said that he was obsessive in pursuit of his goals. Many members of his family are equally passionate in striving for perfection. And the crusading spirit that came from him has passed down to his descendants. Several of them have continued his love of the print media: his granddaughter Barbara Nugent became a Managing Director of *The Sunday Business Post* in Dublin, and her sister Judith wrote for the now defunct *Sunday Press*. One great grandson, Gerard Ryle, became the director of the *International*

Consortium of Investigative Journalists, a body of journalists which investigates the most important stories in the world. Barbara's son Ryle Nugent, became a sports journalist/broadcaster and head of sport in the national broadcasting authority RTE. Four of Maurice's sons were also printers. A distant relative is historical author and journalist T. Ryle Dwyer. His great grandfather was Maurice Ryle's brother. One grandson was County Librarian of Dún Laoghaire-Rathdown and also worked at European level on cultural and literary issues. There are many more members of the extended family who are involved with none of these things. And, of course, his granddaughter, Mary O'Brien, became the international singing star, Dusty Springfield.

Mary (Dusty) also personified Maurice's spirit of perfectionism and his high-octane approach to life.

Maurice and Bridget had a volatile relationship with vociferous disagreements mostly over politics. Bridget had a fierce belief in Irish independence; that Ireland should be completely independent of Britain and in control of her own destiny. In contrast Maurice believed Ireland should remain under the umbrella of Great Britain whilst having much greater control of her affairs. It was a source of many arguments between them and it meant they had difficult a relationship. But Maurice was, by all accounts a very good and gentle man.

The Ulster Volunteers was a unionist militia, formed with the intention to block Home Rule for Ireland. They were based in the northern province of Ulster, the part of Ireland where Unionists and Protestants were in the majority. In 1913, the militias were organised into the Ulster Volunteer Force (UVF) and were determined to resist any attempts to 'impose' Home Rule on Ulster. In April 1914, the UVF smuggled 25000 rifles into Ulster.

As a response, late on 25 November 1913, Irish nationalists established the Irish Volunteers at the Rotunda in Dublin, with the declared aim "to secure and maintain the rights and liberties common to the whole people of Ireland". Maurice Ryle, along with John Redmond, presided over a well-attended public meeting held in the County Hall Tralee on 10 December 1913. The purpose of the meeting was to set up a company of the Irish Volunteers in the town. John Redmond [244] was leader of the Irish Parliamentary Party and a good friend of Maurice Ryle. After that, Ryle spoke at the principal Nationalist rallies throughout County Kerry.

Volunteers spread rapidly throughout the county. John Redmond gave his enthusiastic support to the organisation. A mass parade of some 2000 Volunteers from the region was held in Tralee on 14th June 1914. Local MP Thomas O'Donnell declared that 'training and arming are the essentials of the movement'.

In July 1914, Maurice Ryle and local MP Thomas O'Donnell co-founded the *Kerry Advocate*, edited by Ryle, which supported Redmond's recruiting policy in support of the British war effort at the outbreak of WWI. Later Maurice Ryle's views were to change, he worked with O'Donnell on the 1918 anti-conscription campaign.

Once the War for Independence was over, in 1921, a further battle arose between two opposing groups, the pro-treaty Provisional Government and the anti-treaty Irish Republican Army (IRA), over the Anglo-Irish Treaty. This is known as the Irish Civil War. During this conflict Maurice was compelled to print official notices for the Irish Free State Army and, as a result, his printing office was wrecked by their adversaries in the Irish Civil War. Kerry was one of the strongest Sinn Fein areas in Ireland. It subsequently became a Republican stronghold.

The *Kerry People* ceased publication in 1928. Later, when the family fell on hard times, they left the house in Ballymullen and went to live in Strand Street. After his newspapers folded, Maurice took up a post as editor of the Athlone based papers, the *Westmeath Independent* and *Offaly Independent*. He died in 1935, after a long illness and was buried in New Rath Cemetery, Tralee.

Bridget died in 1942, and was buried alongside her husband in New Rath Cemetery, Tralee.

---

[244] De facto leader of the Irish Nationalist Party in the House of Commons -

Dusty's Father

Dusty's father, Gerard Anthony Joseph O'Brien, was born in Nagpur, Bengal, in 1904, the only surviving son of Joseph Aloysius O'Brien and Isabella Frances MacLeod.

Joseph Aloysius O'Brien - Grandfather

Gerard's father, Joseph Aloysius, was born in Calcutta in 1860, the youngest of a family of seven with three brothers and three sisters.

Edmund O'Meara O'Brien and Anna Malvina Cornelius – (Great Grandparents)

Joseph's father, Edmund O'Meara O'Brien, was born in County Kerry in Ireland, and most likely first travelled to India as an NCO in the army.

Joseph's mother, Anna Malvina Cornelius, could trace her family back to the 18th Century. Her great grandfather was Captain Jan Cornelius, a Dutch Sea Captain whose wife, Maria, was killed during the 'Black Hole of Calcutta' uprising in 1757. Maria's five-year-old son, Charles Cornelius, survived. He later married Roza Urage. Anna Malvina's father, Charles Cornelius, was born in 1790.

Isabella Frances McLeod – Grandmother

Gerard's mother Isabella Frances McLeod, was born in Allahabad in 1868, the first-child of Alexander MacLeod and Catherine Flood.

Catherine Flood and Alexander McLeod (Great Grandparents)

Isabella's father, Alexander McLeod, was a Printer for the Indian Government; the son of a Scottish family of six.

Isabella's mother, Catherine Flood, was just 13 years of age when she was married, and 14 when she gave birth to Isabella one year later. After that, Catherine gave birth to seven more babies, and died at the age of 26, two days after the birth of her last child, William Goodfellow. Cause of death is recorded as anaemia, probably caused by loss of blood.

Catherine's father, Michael Flood, had arrived in India as Staff Sergeant to the Royal Artillery in Jalandhar where he married her mother, Frances McCartney, in 1847

.

O'Brien Family

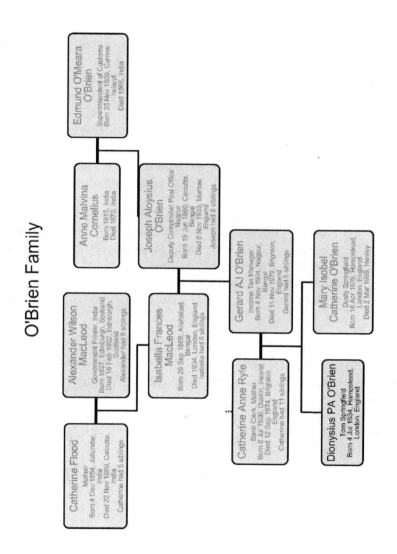

Edmund O'Meara O'Brien
Superintendent of Customs
Born 25 Nov 1809, Curnow,
Treland
Died 1866, India

Anne Malvina Cornelius
Born 1815, India
Died 1870, India

Joseph Aloysius O'Brien
Deputy Comptroller Post Office
Nagpur
Born 19 Jun 1860, Calcutta,
Bengal
Died 6 Nov 1933, Marlow,
England
Joseph had 8 siblings

Alexander Wilson MacLeod
Government Printer, India
Born 1837, Edinburgh, Scotland
Died 16 Feb 1902, Edinburgh,
Scotland
Alexander had 6 siblings

Isabella Frances MacLeod
Born 29 Sep 1868, Alahabad,
Bengal
Died 1934, London, England
Isabella had 6 siblings

Gerard AJ O'Brien
Income Tax Manager
Born 4 Nov 1904, Nagpur,
Bengal
Died 11 Nov 1979, Brighton,
England
Gerard had 5 siblings

Mary Isobel Catherine O'Brien
Dusty Springfield
Born 16 Apr 1939, Hampstead,
London, England
Died 2 Mar 1999, Henley

Catherine Flood
Mother
Born 4 Dec 1854, Jullundar,
India
Died 22 Nov 1880, Calcutta,
India
Catherine had 5 siblings

Catherine Anne Ryle
Bank Clerk Mother
Born 8 Jul 1900, Dublin, Ireland
Died 12 Sep 1974, Brighton,
England
Catherine had 11 siblings

Dionysius PA O'Brien
Tom Springfield
Born 4 Jul 1934, Hampstead,
London, England

The O'Brien Family

In 1841 Edmund O'Meara O'Brien, Gerard's grandfather, joined the Customs Service in Calcutta with the rank of Inspector. Edmund married Anna Malvina Cornelius in 1846. By 1849 Edmund had been promoted to Inspector of Preventive Services and became a member of the Board of Trustees of the Roman Catholic Cathedral of Calcutta. Five years later he became Head Inspector of Customs in Calcutta, on a salary of 500Rs per annum. He rose through the ranks, finally reaching the post of Superintendent of Customs Services in 1856. On a salary of 800Rs, he was one of the most highly paid uncovenanted civil servants in the city.

One of the myths spread by the British is that they governed India, a country of many millions, with a few thousand people who made up the Indian Civil Service. They did, but they also had an army of uncovenanted civil servants who did thousands of other jobs such as, Customs, Post, Prison Service, etc. They were largely retired Army and Navy officers and NCOs who chose to stay in India rather than return to poverty in the UK.

Edmund was recorded as being on leave in England in 1862, after which there is no further record of him. In 1868 Mrs A O'Brien was reported as being in receipt of an uncovenanted widow's pension of 32.00 per annum.

Gerard's father, Joseph Aloysius O'Brien, made his career with the Indian Finance Service.

Joseph Aloysius O'Brien and Isabella Francis McLeod were married in Bandel, Bengal on 16th July 1889.

In 1898, Isabella Frances O'Brien, as she was now known, travelled to the UK with her very young daughter, Maude Mary. She visited Elgin where she spent some time as a guest of her aunt and cousin. Her second daughter, Isabel Mary, was born there in 1899. She is recorded in the 1901 census in Pokesdown, Hampshire, with her two daughters and her father, who was now retired from the Indian Government Printing Service and resident in Ailsa Lodge, Stourwood, a suburb of Bournemouth.

When Gerard was born, in 1904, his father Joseph was Deputy Comptroller of the Post Office in Nagpur, his early years were passed there. Nagpur was developed during and by the British Raj, the area is majorly dominated by grand and beautiful buildings in the colonial style.

Gerard spent his early years living amid the heat, and the smells, and the noise, and the dust of India, with his parents and two sisters, Maude and Isabel. A typical colonial family home of the time was an Indian Bungalow; a simple structure with primitive bathrooms, whitewashed walls, and muslin cloth ceilings. Bamboo furniture, with lots of cushions, filled the big rooms, the beds were draped with mosquito nets, to protect from mosquito bites. But, 'just as British women in India wore British clothes, so they dressed their surroundings with as much as they could of Britain. They covered Indian made furniture with chintz and cretonne from Home'. The women put up pictures – reproductions, photographs of their families, their own watercolours. They allowed Indian touches, brass pots from Benares or tables whose legs were antelope horns'. [245] A cooling breeze in the living area was provided by the punkah (a great cloth sail on a frame suspended from the ceiling). This was operated by the punkah wallah who lay on the verandah, with the cord around his big toe, lazily pulling the punkah back and forth with his foot. Rows and rows of pots of chrysanthemums were lined up along the verandah.

His mother will have been responsible for the compound, enclosed with a wall, it contained the bungalow (a large, single storey building which was the usual dwelling for middle-class Europeans in India) and servants' quarters set in an expansive garden. The bungalow didn't have a kitchen because the cooking was all done by the servants in the cookhouse, which was part of their quarters. The garden was cared for by an army of servants. And another army of servants catered to the needs of the family. When he arrived home, his father's bearer would kneel at his feet to clean the dust from his shoes with a duster. This is the home that Gerard will have known as a young boy. It was a luxurious

---

[245] *Margaret MacMillan (1988) Women of the Raj p77*

life which he simply accepted as the norm. It was little different from growing up in the aristocracy of Great Britain.

Gerard will have had an ayah, someone who was a constant presence in his life from the time he was born. She was there to care for him and soothe him to sleep with stories and lullabies. By the time Gerard was five his sisters disappeared from his life; sent to boarding school in Belgium, where they were educated for the next five years. This left him as the only child at home, loved and cherished by his parents. Gerard was the sole surviving son: two boys and a girl, born in the first years of his parents' marriage, had died as infants; he never knew them.

When in 1914, Joseph took up the post of Secretary to the Council in Simla – the Viceroy's summer capital – the time had come for Gerard to continue his schooling in Britain. His parents truly believed that the best education for him was to be had in the home country. They duly arranged passage for him and his mother on a steam ship to England.

> *Any parents who could possibly manage it sent their children away to boarding schools by the time they were seven years old, partly after the example of the middle classes at Home, but also because the fears about the effects of India on the children took ever more elaborate forms. Children brought up in India were felt to be somehow of inferior quality, a belief that affected the marriage prospects of girls and the careers of boys.* [246]

Gerard boarded the ship with his mother. He was about to embark on an exciting adventure, with a thousand fascinating things to discover on the big Caledonian Line steamer. There was so much to see and to ask questions about that he almost forgot his life in India, and had trouble remembering a few words of the Hindustani that was once his second-language. The ship docked in London after a rough three-week sea crossing.

His arrival in Britain must have been a deep culture shock for Gerard, with a gradual realisation of how privileged his childhood had been. He

---

[246] *Margaret MacMillan (1988) Women of the Raj p139*

would see that his white skin, no longer set him apart nor allowed him to easily separate himself from the workers who were also white. Gerard and Isabella spent more than a year moving from place to place, visiting relatives, while he grew accustomed to life in Britain. His two sisters had now completed their schooling in Belgium, Gerard and his mother were reunited with them in England.

Then the day came when his mother began preparations for his start at school. Gerard was enrolled as a boarder at Mount St Mary's College, in Derbyshire. Isabella assembled the various items of his school uniform: a blue suit of Oxford mixture, with jacket, waistcoat and trousers, a blue cap and black stock, as well as a suit for everyday wear; six shirts, six handkerchiefs, six pairs of stockings, three pairs of shoes and two blouses of brown Holland, to wear over his dress during the hours of recreation.

On 29 September 1915, Gerard arrived with his mother at Eckington Station, one mile from the school.[247] A pony and trap was hired to complete their journey to this 70-acre site surrounded by mature trees, with the ancient school buildings encircling the lawn. His introduction to the school was a rude awakening for Gerard. No longer nestled in the bosom of his family, indulged by his father, loved by his mother, and spoiled by his ayah. Now he was to bed down in a huge, cold and draughty dormitory, with endless rows of beds, and surrounded by hordes of boys he knew nothing of. Pastoral care, health and well-being for all of the boys, was in the hands of Matron and the Headmaster's wife.

The parting from his mother must have caused him speechless anguish, that was almost too much for Isabella to bear. She had no way of knowing when she would see her son again. Later, Gerard would come to realise that it would be almost impossible for him to go home, even in the long summer holidays. A sea passage that used up six weeks of the holiday would be too difficult and very costly, so that it could not be

---

[247] Mount St Mary's School Archive

undertaken easily. The great distance to India meant he spent most of his time at the school until it was time to for him to leave.

The College prospectus listed the subjects taught: Reading, Writing, Arithmetic, Book keeping, Geography, History sacred and profane; Elocution and a sound grammatical knowledge of the English, French, Latin and Greek languages. Gerard's time at the school was undistinguished but it is clear that he learned to play the piano there, and developed his love for classical music.

The 1921 census lists 16-year-old Gerard at 15 St Andrew's Square, Surbiton. His mother Isabella, is shown as a visitor at the same address. It can only be assumed that she came to England in order to spend some time with Gerard during his holiday from school that summer. It is only by chance that they have both been recorded in the census, as it was originally planned for April 24 that year, but was delayed due to a threatened general strike.

When Joseph Aloysius retired from the Indian Civil Service in 1926, he and his wife Isabella Frances, set up home in Colville Terrace, an area of London known as Little India. Gerard went to live with them there, until their move to Marlow, where Joseph died in 1933. Isabella died in London a year later.

In 1927 Gerard passed the entrance exams for the Inland Revenue. He had to satisfy the Civil Service Commissioners that he was a natural born subject of his Majesty; that he was between the ages of 19 and 22 on the day of the examination; that he was unmarried and without family, and of good health and character. He was examined in Handwriting, Orthography, Arithmetic (to Vulgar and decimal fractions), English Composition. He then took up a post as Junior Assistant Inspector of Taxes and Ministry of Health Junior Assistant Auditor. [248]

---

[248] *London Gazette 1927. Civil Service Evidence of age*

Acknowledgements

In the very long gestation period of this book, I have come to rely on a number of people for support and encouragement. Not least among these are members of my family, my granddaughter Cal and her husband Magnus. My daughter-in-law Helen, my daughter Marcia, my son Lucien and my sister Tina. All have listened patiently and offered me advice while I discussed the finer points of the manuscript with them.

I am particularly grateful to Sam Gates who has been a ready source of suggestions for topics that I could investigate. He has found newspaper and magazine articles, suggested books and radio programmes and recommended alternative ways of approaching the task. I offer my heartfelt thanks to Sam for his support and inspiration and for all of the time and effort he has given me over the years.

Anne and Paul Matthews read my manuscript and greatly helped me by providing essential feedback on it. Stuart Cosgrove gave me advice on the publishing process. Janine Jackson, my B&B landlady during many visits to Ealing, became a friend and supporter.

I have to thank T Ryle Dwyer who helped me make contact with Dusty's cousin Sean Ryle. Through him I had meetings with Dusty's cousin's Gerard Ryle and Muiris O'Raghaill, who gave me copious amounts of information about the family and about Tralee.

I am thankful to Ian and Angela Hunter who supplied me with the O'Brien family tree and information about the family in India. I am also very grateful for the memories of meetings with Dusty and her family Angela Hunter has shared with me. I was pleased to talk to Marcia Newton, the archivist of Mount St Mary's College, who gave me details of Gerard O'Brien's time as a pupil at the boarding school in Derbyshire.

I also want to thank those people from Dusty's life who have offered me information and guidance: Pat Rhodes, Simon Bell, Douggie Reece, Jonathan Cohen, Tarra Thomas, John Harding, David Hay Gibson, Paul

Howes, Sharon Davis and Martha Reeves along with her manager Dundee Holt.

Through the *Let's Talk Dusty* forum and at Dusty fan gatherings I have met a great many dedicated Dusty fans. Important among these are Wendy Hampson and Jane Langley, who spent an afternoon helping me to proof read my website, also my long-time friends and collaborators, Cas Sutcliffe and Lynn McDonough. In addition, I want to thank Carole Robinson, Carole Gibson, Carole Roberts, Karen Jenkins, Valda Fisher, Lynda Brignall and Pat Dunham for their help and support over the years. Many thanks go to Darren Carstairs, Carina Bartleet, Linda Dunbar and all of the admins and experts on *Soul and Eyeliner: The Dusty Springfield Project*. Special mention of Michael Davenport, Corinna Müller, Kimberley Head and my many friends in this group.

I particularly want to thank Michael Muccino who took me on a tour of Staten Island during my visit to New York. He treated me to lunch and then took me to his alma mater, Wagner College, where we spent the afternoon.

In a search for information about High Wycombe I discovered an article by Sally Scagell. This led me to Mike Dewey, of the Bucks Free Press, who printed an article asking for memories of the O'Brien family while they lived in Sands. A number of people responded: Russell Chamberlen talked about his time as a friend and neighbour; Paul Davies; David Gardiner, Mary Dawson, Lavina Gee and Maureen Townsend all shared their memories. Ken Wakefield and his wife Rita opened their home to me and hosted a meeting of the members of this group. Richard Bond told me about his sister Doreen who was Dusty's childhood friend.

I learned about St Anne's Convent from Yvonne Messenger, Kate Davies, Sylvia Clayton, Patsy Batchelor (Eileen O'Leary), Angela Ralph, Anna Scott, Mary McGrath, Angela Patten, Jo Pilsworth and Kate Desmond. Tony Henderson and Tom Gibbon of GMS Estates gave me information about Kent Gardens. Leonard Gibbs told me about St Benedict's social Club and important information about Place House (which housed St Anne's Convent) was supplied by Duncan Cameron of Little Ealing History.

Peter Miles and Nick Bowyer gave me more detail about Dion O'Brien and the Pedini Brothers. Tony Hare provided background on the Royal Grammar School, High Wycombe and Tony Cash about the Joint Services School for Linguists.

I am grateful to Lynne Essex for the very detailed interview she granted me about the Lana Sisters and Nola York for giving me permission to use photographs of the Lana Sisters. Thanks to Ann Wallace for sharing her memories of the Springfields, Brian Lynch of the Caravelles Irish Show Band, David Dills of Scotbeat, John Lupton and Chalice Verlag on Tim Feild, Gerard Eastick and Nick Dent-Robinson on Mike Hurst.

Others for whose help I am grateful are Ted and Sue Scott, John Comer, Brian Higham, Christopher Low of Ealing Civic Society, Rose Collis, Steve Cann, Kathryn Allen, Mo Ferrington and Graeme Smith.

Thank you to my editor Denise Cowle and to Simon Dowling for reviewing the manuscript for me.

Finally, I offer my very great thanks to my niece Gwen Dunabie who, with care, attention to detail and patience, designed and produced the cover of this book for me.

Sources

Bibliography

1963: That Was the Year That Was, Andrew Cook, Stroud, The History Press, 2013

A Biography of Peggy Batchelor, Carole Hawkins, London, Authorhouse, 2012

A City called Heaven: Chicago and the Birth of Gospel Music, Robert Marovich, Chicago, University of Illinois Press, 2015

A Girl Called Dusty, Sharon Davis, London, Andre Deutsch, 2008

A Trouser Wearing Character: The Life and Times of Nancy Spain, Rose Collis, London, Cassell, 2007

Austerity Britain, David Kynaston, London, Bloomsbury, 2007

Big Time: The Life of Adam Faith, David, Caroline Stafford, London, Omnibus Press, 2015

Black Pearls, Daphne Harrison, Chicago, Rutgers University Press, 1988

Black Vinyl, White Powder, Simon Napier Bell, London, Ebury Press, 2001

Cue Tape Please, Ted Scott, London, Ted Scott, 2009

Dancing in the Streets: Confessions of a Motown Diva, Martha Reeves, New York, Hyperion, 1994

Dancing with Demons: The Authorised Biography of Dusty Springfield, Penny Valentine, Vicky Wickham, London, Hodder & Stoughton, 2001

Dusty Springfield, Edward Leeson, London, Robson Books, 2001

Dusty Springfield: In the Middle of Nowhere, Laurence Cole, London, Middlesex University Press, 2008

Dusty: A Biography of Dusty Springfield, Lucy O'Brien, London, Sidgwick & Jackson, 2000

Dusty: An Intimate Portrait of a Musical Legend, Karen Bartlett, London, The Robson Press, 2014

Dusty: Queen of the Postmods, Annie Randall, New York, Oxford University Press, Inc, 2009

Easy Lessons in Singing, Jo Stafford, New York, Carl Fischer, Inc., 1951

First Confessions, Patten, Christopher, London, Penguin, 2017

Langston's Salvation: American Religion and the Bard of Harlem, Wallace D. Best, New York, New York University Press, 2017

Life in London: 1950s, Mike Hutton, Stroud, Amberley Publishing, 2014

Little Ealing: A Walk Through History, Residents Association, Ealing Fields, London, EFRA, 2002

Looking Good isn't Always Easy, Paul Howes, London, Paul Howes, 2013

Luba Gurdjieff: A Menu with Recipes, Luba Gurdjieff, Marina C. Bear, USA, Ten Speed Press, 1993

Mother of the Blues: A Study of Ma Rainey, Sandra Lieb, USA, The University of Massachusetts Press, 1981

My Green Age, Terence Keough, Bloomington, Trafford Publishing, 2009

Owning Up, George Melly, London, Wiedenfield & Nicholson, 1965

Rock and Pop on British TV, Jeff Evans, London, Omnibus Press, 2017

Rock n' Roll Files, Vince Eager, Peterborough, VIPro, 2007

Scissors and Paste: A Collage Biography of Dusty Springfield, David Evans, London, Britannia Press Publishing, 1995

Secret Classrooms, Geoffrey Elliot, Harold Shukman, London, St Ermin's Press, 2003

Shout, Sister, Shout: The Untold Story of Rock-and-Roll Trailblazer Sister Rosetta Tharpe, Gayle Wald, Boston, Mass., Beacon Press, 2007

Skiffle, Chas McDevitt, London, Robson Books, 1988

Song of the Open Road, Jo Stafford. Paul Weston, Albany, GA, Bear Manor Media, 2012

The Coder Special Archive, Tony Cash, Mike Gerrard, London, Hodgson Press, 2012

The Complete Dusty Springfield, Howes Paul, Richmond, Reynolds & Hearn, 2007

The Fifties and Sixties: A Lifestyle Revolution, Miriam Akhtar, Steve Humphries, London, Boxtree, 2001

The Growth of High Wycombe, Roger Cole, Stroud, Ottakars, 2001

The History of British Rock and Roll: The Forgotten Years 1956 – 1962, Robin Bell, Sweden, Robin Bell Books, 2013

The Old Time, John Comer, Victoria, Canada, Trafford Publishing, 2009

The Restless Generation, Pete Frame, London, Rogan House, 2007

The Story of the Rosary in Prose and Verse, Alan Rye, Sussex, Ditchling Press, 1952

Women of the Raj, Margaret MacMillan, London, Thames and Hudson, 1988

Publications

Entertainment Industry Magazine Archive
Associated Press
Beat Magazine
Billboard
Bucks Free Press
County Times and Gazette
Daily Mirror
Daily Record
Disc Magazine
Dusty Springfield Bulletin
Evening Standard
Herald Sun (Australia)
Independent
Los Angeles Free Press
Melody Maker
Mojo
New Musical Express
New York Herald Tribune
Pop Weekly
Pop Weekly Annual
Radio Times
Record Mirror
Rip it Up
Rolling Stone
St Anne's School Magazine
Sunday People
The Guardian
The London Gazette
The Mirror
The Stage
The Village Voice
Variety

Websites

http://www.archieandrewsonline.com/page18.html

https://getoutside.ordnancesurvey.co.uk/local/birch-green-east-hertfordshire

https://www.chrisbarber.net/ottilie-2011/

https://www.bradfordtimeline.co.uk/music.htm

http://www.arthurlloyd.co.uk/HerMajestysTheatre.htm

https://www.allmusic.com/artist/jack-good-mn0001247084

http://ohboy.org.uk/jack-good

https://www.theguardian.com/music/2014/jul/03/johnnie-gray-obituary

http://www.arthurlloyd.co.uk/Liverpool/EmpireTheatreLiverpool.htm

http://www.arthurlloyd.co.uk/MossEmpires.htm

https://www.greenwich.co.uk/blogs/mary-mills/obituary-owen-bryce/

https://www.theguardian.com/news/1999/jun/07/guardianobituaries2

https://genome.ch.bbc.co.uk/

https://www.chrisbarber.net/tours4/tharpe-1957-home.htm

https://scotbeat.wordpress.com/2014/06/02/dusty-and-the-springfields/

http://www.sixtiescity.net/menupage.htm

www.mikepratt.com

http://www.turnipnet.com/whirligig/tv/adults/rocknroll/rocknroll.htm

https://www.theguardian.com/stage/2016/dec/13/west-side-story-musical-london-1958

http://www.teletronic.co.uk/herestv9.htm

Donella Campbell lives in Glasgow close to her family and friends. She has been a fan of Dusty Springfield ever since her teenage years. Remembering Dusty about ten years ago she became determined to investigate her life and music in more depth. What followed was a period of intensive research to discover Dusty's life as a child and young woman, before she was famous.

Printed in Great Britain
by Amazon

18415744R00193